ONE SMALL WILDERNESS

~~~~~~

ROSANNE ALEXANDER

By the same author

SELKIE

ONE SMALL WILDERNESS

ROSANNE ALEXANDER

ANDRE DEUTSCH

First published in Great Britain 1992
by André Deutsch Limited
105-106 Great Russell Street London WC1B 3LJ

Cataloguing-in-publication data for this title
is available from the British Library

ISBN: 0 233 98714 2

Typeset by Falcon Graphic Art Ltd
Wallington, Surrey
Printed in Great Britain by
WBC Print, Bridgend

So many people did so much for us during our ten years on Skomer that it was possible to mention only a few of them in this book. But I still remember with tremendous gratitude everyone who made that period in our lives special.

Skomer Island is owned by the Countryside Council for Wales and managed by the Dyfed Wildlife Trust (formerly the West Wales Naturalists' Trust). The role of such Trusts in protecting Britain's wildlife is of vital and growing importance, and it is public support for the conservation movement that will ensure the survival of places like Skomer.

Reproduced with the permission
of the Countryside Council for Wales

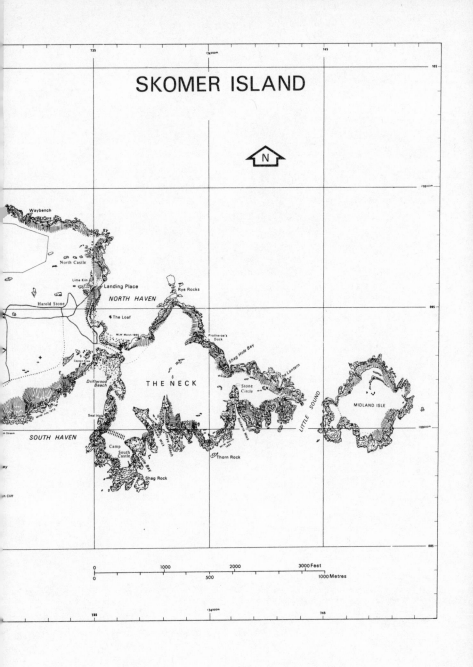

SKOMER ISLAND

N

Waybench

North Castle

Lime Kiln
Landing Place   Rye Rocks
Harold Stone   *NORTH HAVEN*

The Loaf

MLW March 1965
Protheroe's
Dock
Shag Hole Bay

Driftwood
Beach   *THE NECK*   The Lantern
Stone
Circle

Seal Hole   *MIDLAND ISLE*

SOUTH HAVEN   *LITTLE SOUND*

Camp
South
Castle
                    Thorn Rock
Shag Rock

| 0 | | 1000 | 2000 | 3000 Feet |
| 0 | 500 | | 1000 Metres | |

ONE

I DO NOT BELIEVE that I will ever see Skomer again. It is in the past now, and the memories are too precious to be disturbed. Skomer was my life for ten years and its windswept cliffs and blue-green seas are as real in my memory as they were when I still walked beside them. Returning now as a visitor it would be impossible to reach below the superficial beauty of the island and to become part of it once more. To see Skomer again would be inviting to the surface all the feelings of loss and desolation that have been so carefully hidden. So Skomer must remain a perfectly preserved decade in my mind. I did not expect to grow to love Skomer as I did. I cannot even remember now why I wanted so much to live there. I think it was no more than a youthful sense of adventure; a desire to do something different and exciting.

Although I may never see the island again, I am sure a day will never pass when I am not thinking of it. My feelings for Skomer were so immediate and overwhelming that I felt at once that I had known it forever, and I found it impossible after a week on the island to believe that I had ever lived anywhere else. I can still recall vividly those first days on Skomer. I remember above all the sheer sense of wonderment at how quickly everything had happened. It all felt so familiar I had to remind myself repeatedly that I had only just arrived. Strangest of all was the thought that a few weeks earlier nothing could have been further from my mind.

Less than a month before I had been a student, studying Wildlife Illustration and living in the small Welsh town of Carmarthen. My boyfriend, Mike, was a student at the same college studying Fine Art Sculpture.

One evening he asked me, 'How would you like to live on an island?'

I looked up expectantly, wondering what he was going to say.

'I met a friend today,' Mike continued, 'and he showed me an advertisement in the paper. They're looking for a new warden of Skomer.'

The island needed no introduction. I already knew that it was a nature reserve, famous for its seabirds, off the rocky coast of Pembrokeshire. My only personal experience had been a visit to the island on a wild, rain-drenched day, and so most of my knowledge of Skomer came from Mike. He had strong ties with the island, and had spent a great deal of time there in his teens. He was no stranger to islands, he had been assistant warden on nearby Skokholm and warden of the Calf of Man. But it was Skomer for which he had a real attachment, and he had talked to me about it so often that I felt I knew it well.

My thoughts were interrupted as Mike added hesitantly, 'Of course, you realise we will have to get married.'

This jolted me back to reality; it was no longer a fantasy, but something very serious. Marriage seemed so irrevocable, far more so than going to Skomer, and it was something I had never really considered.

We discussed it for about five minutes, then finally I asked, 'What do you think are your chances of getting the job?'

'About forty to one against,' Mike laughed.

'All right then,' I made up my mind instantly. 'We've got to try.'

My decisiveness stemmed partly from the fact that it seemed unlikely that my resolve would ever be put to the test and secretly I was hoping that Mike would not get the job. The upheaval of leaving college, getting married, and starting a new life on a strange island seemed too much to contemplate, but at the same time this was a once-in-a-lifetime opportunity, and something was telling me that I could not let it pass without at least giving it a try.

The job was for a married couple and Mike was so anxious not to jeopardise our chances that we stated clearly in our application that we would get married before taking up the appointment. Once the application had been made my feelings changed completely. Thoughts of Skomer dominated our lives, and more than anything

2

I had ever wanted before, I wanted to live there. I have never been an optimist, but from that time on I was unable to persuade myself that we might not be going to the island. We talked of nothing else, and heard ourselves saying, 'When we go to Skomer,' then quickly correcting 'when' to 'if'. The days that passed strained our optimism to the limits. We knew that a new warden would need to be on Skomer by early spring, and the end of February was fast approaching. Perhaps everything was already decided. Perhaps someone else was already in possession of what we were so desperately hoping for. We did not allow ourselves to dwell on these thoughts.

At last the letter arrived. It was brief and to the point: Mike was invited to an interview on 4th March, only days away. They were just a few lines typed on a piece of paper, but we read and re-read them as though they contained some profound meaning. Several times each day we took the letter from its envelope and carefully studied it again, afraid there might have been a mistake, afraid the words may have changed their meaning overnight.

The day of the interview was one we will never forget. We arrived in the quiet little town of Haverfordwest in plenty of time, and being early closing day it was quieter than ever, so we could do nothing but park the car and wait. We were too tense to speak, and so waited nervously as the interview approached until, with a final check of his watch, Mike forced a smile and left. I watched him, an unfamiliar sight in a jacket and tie, his hair cut short, until he disappeared out of sight. I cannot remember how long I waited, but with agonising slowness the minutes stretched into hours. I left the car in search of a newspaper – anything to take my mind off what was happening. Returning empty-handed I could only sit gazing across the River Cleddau at the back of a row of deserted shops. Even now, when I see that view the intervening years are forgotten, and I remember how I waited, sick with apprehension. When Mike returned carrying a single sheet of yellow paper, I thought I could detect a suppressed exuberance, but he was non-committal about the interview.

He was to return at four o'clock, so we faced yet another wait. We turned our attention to the sheet of paper headed 'Conditions of Employment', and read it together. It held no great surprises until we came to the section marked 'Salary'. We looked at each other in dismay. Could we really live on

3

£1200 a year? We did some quick calculations; it was less than our combined student grants. We felt uncertain and slightly subdued. Finally our longing for Skomer mixed with naive optimism overcame common sense, and we decided that if that was the pay being offered it must be possible to live on it. These discussions helped to pass the time, and as four o'clock approached Mike left again. When he returned for the second time his exuberance was no longer suppressed; he had got the job.

As we drove back to Carmarthen so many thoughts crowded into my mind that none of them made sense. The practicalities that had played no part in our fantasies now had to be considered. We were to make the crossing to Skomer on 14th March. We had just ten days to leave college, pack all our possessions, and prepare for our new life. Above all we had just ten days in which to get married. How would we tell our families? What was everyone going to say? We had hardly told anyone that we had even applied for the job since it had seemed at the time no more than a private dream. I rang my parents that night to tell them about Skomer, but I could not bring myself to tell them over the phone that we were getting married. That bombshell would have to wait until the next day when we could visit them. The enthusiasm of our friends at college was encouraging. Our story seemed to catch everyone's imagination, and we were swept along on a wave of excitement. We were much in demand for farewell drinks and dinners, but time was short and we had a lot of preparations to make. The day after the interview, a Friday, was spent in loading all the possessions we could live without into a hired van and taking them to my parents who had agreed to store them. All the way there I worried about the most tactful way of explaining that we needed to get married the following week. There is no doubt it came as a shock, but the need to make plans was so pressing that everything else was brushed aside, and my parents rose to the occasion wonderfully.

It was agreed that the wedding would take place in Carmarthen on the Wednesday of the following week. As the notice was so short we needed to get married by licence, and this was arranged on Monday. On Tuesday my mother and I went shopping for a wedding dress. She wisely dissuaded me from the garish red that caught my eye, and we settled instead for a simple blue dress. Late on Tuesday afternoon Mike and I hurried off in search of

4

a wedding ring. We looked in every jewellers until I had found the ring I wanted, and then went inside. The assistant solemnly placed a dark blue velvet-covered tray of rings on the counter and handed me the one I had chosen. I slipped it on to my finger. It was huge. I asked for a smaller one, but was told it *was* the smallest.

'Can it be altered?' I asked.

'Of course. It will only take a week.'

A week! We would be on Skomer in a week, and I needed it the next day. There was no wedding ring in my size in the shop, so we tried another jewellers. There was no point in being choosey. I held up the third finger of my left hand and asked if they had a wedding ring to fit. A cheerful woman brought all the trays of wedding rings and we began grabbing for the smallest, unable to suppress our nervous giggles as ring after ring failed to fit. Nearby a soberly-dressed man stood watching in silent disapproval. Finally he rolled his eyes to the ceiling, and without a word measured my ring finger. It seemed that madam's finger was not a standard size. We left the shop no longer amused. Closing time was fast approaching; there was only one tiny jewellers left to try. Without much hope we entered the last shop.

'Do you have a wedding ring in my size?'

'Yes. Which one would you like?'

'I just want one that fits. You see my finger's not a standard size.'

'That doesn't matter, we can alter it.'

'But I need it tomorrow.'

'You choose the ring you would like, and we'll alter it for you now.'

Outside we could not believe our luck. At last we had a ring, and when we went back to collect it, it was accompanied by a gift-wrapped wedding present.

Our wedding day was not the most romantic of occasions. Wednesday is market day in Carmarthen, and it was something we could not afford to miss. We spent the morning before the wedding wandering round the market together with the farmers, in their wellington boots, flat caps and coats tied with string, who were in town for the day. We left well satisfied with our morning's shopping; Mike clutching a sturdy axe for chopping firewood, with me trying to carry a large tray of cabbage plants.

'I hope you won't be disappointed one day that you didn't have a proper wedding,' my mother said as I changed into my new blue dress.

'Of course not,' I replied.

I had never given marriage much thought, and had certainly not dreamed of a white wedding, but I knew I might regret it forever if I gave up this chance to go to Skomer. Despite this, I could not help feeling sad for my parents that this was not to be a more conventional wedding. When we arrived at the registry office Mike could not be found, but he arrived shortly after, red-faced and breathless. The ceremony was over in a few minutes, and I was surprised that there was so little to it. The rest of the day passed quickly with lots of our friends gathering at a room in our favourite pub, and lots of embarrassing speeches. (It was strange how, now that we were leaving, we had suddenly become the best students the college had ever had!) This was followed by dinner at Carmarthen's smartest hotel, and when we finally escaped to our hotel room there was a bottle of champagne waiting for us.

The next morning I was delighting in the luxury of a relaxed hotel breakfast after all the chaos of the past few days. I stretched out my hand for another slice of toast and marmalade.

'You haven't got time for that,' said Mike, already making for the door.

He was right. The honeymoon was over, and today we were to have our introduction to the coastguard. We drove to the very tip of south west Wales where the land stretches out into the Irish Sea, finally reaching the village of Dale. The pastel-coloured houses huddled close together following the curve of the bay and nestling in the shelter of the trees which rose steeply behind them. All was quiet for the winter. Only the dozens of pink and orange mooring buoys, brilliant against the sea, and the boats lining the shore under their drab winter covers, foretold the bustle that the summer would bring. Leaving the shelter of the village the road climbed quickly and we were soon on the bleak, wind-lashed promontory of St Ann's Head. And there, way in the distance set in a steel-grey sea was Skomer, its imposing cliffs fringed with white as the waves pounded against them relentlessly. There it was, empty and isolated, waiting for us. I think we both felt our hearts miss a beat, and Mike squeezed my hand. This was the first time we had seen Skomer since we had known it was to be our home. Soon we had reached the end of the headland, watched over by St Ann's lighthouse, its white paint immaculate, and its light criss-crossed by diamond-shaped panes of glass. Nearby stood the coastguard station, where we were warmly welcomed by the chief coastguard. Seated in his office I fidgeted self-consciously with my brand-new wedding ring, feeling it must stand out like a beacon on my finger.

Our first task was radio practice, and we were instructed in the use of marine VHF radio, which would be our only link with the mainland. The scene was set; we were to imagine that a yacht was in distress off Skomer, and talk through the incident as though we were in radio contact with the coastguard station at St Ann's Head. We were handed our radios, and an obliging coastguard set off into the next room similarly equipped. The radios crackled but refused to pass any communication. Voices rose, while radios remained stubbornly mute, until calls of 'Can you hear me?' were passing directly through the walls without the assistance of modern technology. Mike and I studiously avoided each other's eyes, afraid that a glimpse of a smile on the other's face would trigger uncontrollable laughter.

Our next lesson was in the use of distress flares, in case we needed to attract help in an emergency. The procedure was explained to us and Mike put it into practice. We watched fascinated as the flare arced through the sky. Then it was my turn. I took the flare, released the trigger as instructed, and squeezed it gently. Nothing happened, so I pulled harder, gritting my teeth in anticipation of the explosion.

'Keep the flare away from your face,' said a voice at my side.

I squeezed harder and harder, all the while pointing the flare further from my face. By the time it went off I was holding it horizontally, and it shot with impressive speed through several fields, causing a group of sleepy horses to flee in terror. Everyone politely ignored this minor fault in my flare-firing technique, but Mike wasted no time in teasing me about it as soon as we were alone.

The days that followed were spent in shopping and packing, with Mike rushing off from time to time to be briefed on various aspects of managing Skomer as a nature reserve. Everything we were to take with us was carefully packed and made waterproof. The stack of boxes in their neat, black polythene covers grew by

7

the hour until it was hard to imagine how we could need so much. Shopping for Skomer was both fascinating and daunting. We had no idea how long it would be before we could get fresh supplies, and so decided to stock up with enough for about three months. But what should we buy? We would be entirely dependent on tinned and dried food, together with a few fresh items that would last for the first few weeks at least. We bought the sort of things we had never eaten before, such as lentils, dried peas and porridge, and very soon we wished that we would never have to eat them again. Our fresh supplies consisted of sacks of potatoes, carrots and hard, white cabbage. As we had little money we made the mistake of buying only functional food, and soon found ourselves craving the luxury of a biscuit or tin of fruit. Then there was the problem of bread. I had never made bread before, so we equipped ourselves with a comprehensive cookery book, and then made our way to a local mill where we bought two sacks of flour, one brown and one white. We were terrified of forgetting something vital, and so made endless lists. I visualised arriving in Skomer and thinking, 'Where's the soap?' only to realise that we had forgotten to buy any, and now faced weeks without a proper wash.

It was on 14th March, the fourth day after our wedding, that we were due to go to Skomer, and somehow we managed to get everything ready, only to discover that the weather was too bad to make the crossing. Our disappointment was tempered by the fact that the delay would give us time to make a few last minute preparations and, besides, we were quite enjoying the continuing round of farewell celebrations. Each day we expected to be gone, but the weather did not improve, and we found ourselves repeatedly saying goodbye to friends only to meet them the next day and have to tell them we were still around. By this time we were growing anxious to leave, and we were overjoyed when the wind finally dropped and the day of departure arrived. We were to cross from the tiny harbour of Lawrenny in the upper reaches of Milford Haven. This had the advantage of offering complete shelter for loading our supplies, but lengthened the outward journey by some twenty miles, taking the boat in a wide arc round St Ann's Head and past the island of Skokholm. Helped by some friends from college, we transported our supplies to its muddy shores. With a lot of slipping and sliding in the mud our huge pile of boxes was finally loaded into the boat. As the first port of call was Skokholm it was decided that we should join the boat at Martin's Haven, the nearest landing point on the mainland to Skomer. But it was not to be; in a couple of hours the boat was back at Lawrenny. We heard tales of mountainous waves and ten gallon drums of petrol rolling round the deck like ping-pong balls. Our black polythene covered boxes were returned to us intact, but wet and muddy.

And so came our introduction to Lockley Lodge. Mike decided that we had left Carmarthen once and for all, and were not going back. Lockley Lodge was a tiny, wooden house nestling on the slope overlooking Martin's Haven. It was owned by our employers, the West Wales Naturalists' Trust, and we reluctantly installed ourselves in this building. The lodge had not been lived in for many years, as the layer of mouse droppings covering every surface suggested. We arranged our boxes so that there were pathways between them leading from room to room. We quickly learned to keep all the boxes containing food in the bedroom, and to place our shoes carefully by the bed. Under cover of darkness the mice would set about finding their way into our food supplies. When the nibbling and scratching reached such a crescendo that we were sure the mice were about to make a breakthrough, we would flick on the light and hurl a shoe hard in the direction of the unsuspecting creatures. They soon learned that our aim was not very good, and began to pay less and less attention to these little interruptions.

The days that followed were increasingly frustrating, particularly when we discovered that we had no money left. We had spent every penny, including wedding presents, on supplies for Skomer, our first pay cheque was a month away and the bank manager did not look favourably on a loan. Finally we had no option but to break into the supplies we had intended to take with us. We watched the sea constantly for signs of improvement, and woke repeatedly every night to listen to the wind just in case it had stopped blowing. By climbing on to the Deer Park, the headland above Martin's Haven, we could see Skomer. The tiny island of Midland lies between Skomer and the mainland, and is flanked by Little Sound and Jack Sound. These rock-strewn stretches of water have wrecked many ships in the past, and the strong currents cause the sea to move like a fast-flowing river. As we waited, staring across the Sounds, Skomer seemed frustratingly inaccessible.

When at last the weather improved and we were due to

leave for the island we decided that we would not believe it until we had actually arrived. At least we were on the spot, and in a relatively short time we had moved our supplies to Martin's Haven beach. The boat had to be loaded using a small dinghy plying back and forth from the beach. This was a slow process, and the tide receded with alarming speed. As soon as everything had been piled at the water's edge the sea was gone, and our mountain of possessions had to be leapfrogged stage by stage down the beach chasing the retreating tide. After many hours the boat was loaded, and we headed for Skomer in a drizzly mist. We strained our eyes for a glimpse of the island, and did not have to wait long. It was beautiful, even in the rain. We reached North Haven, the main landing place on Skomer, and there saw our house perched precariously on the cliff top. I just wanted to sit and look, but there was no time; everything had to be taken ashore. Boxes were piled into the dinghy until it seemed dangerously top-heavy, then somehow Mike and I fitted in along-side them. Mike took the oars and rowed the dinghy smoothly towards the shore until it bumped gently against the beach. The tide was now right out, and the stones were thickly covered in slippery, green weed. I was just wondering how to negotiate my way across this when we were distracted by shouts from the boat. It seemed they wanted Mike to carry me ashore. Well, we were just married, and this was our new home. Mike lifted me from the dinghy and I clung to him expecting at any moment to find myself in the water, but he manoeuvred swiftly and skilfully across the slimy rocks and deposited me on the beach to cheers of approval from the boat. We had finally made it. I hardly dared believe it. I looked around trying to take it all in and wondered if the date, April 1st, had any significance. But it was true, we had arrived, even if we were over two weeks late.

The rest of the day was spent unloading the boat. The tide turned and was soon chasing us up the beach. Once everything was ashore Mike went in search of the tractor which was in the garage by the house on the cliff top directly above us. As it was so late in the afternoon the boat and our helpers had to return to the mainland leaving us with our mountain of possessions piled up at the edge of the sea. I was now forced to run with the boxes to keep one jump ahead of the incoming tide. I could only move in short stages as carrying everything to the top of the beach would take too long, and half the pile would be under water before I had time to move it. I lost count of how many times I picked up those boxes and put them down, but I came instinctively to recognise which were very heavy and which were less so, and my heart sank when I saw one that felt like lead waiting for me next in the pile. I was becoming exhausted, and every time I stopped to catch my breath I strained my ears for the sound of an engine, signalling that Mike was on his way with the tractor, and help was at hand.

We had eaten nothing all day, but I felt too tired to be hungry. In all this time I had not given a thought to my new house, but suddenly I realised that we had been on the island for hours, with the house on the cliff just above, and there had been no time for even a glimpse inside. Eventually Mike returned with the news that the tractor would not start. He was working on it, but in the meantime I would have to continue moving things by hand. By about seven o'clock, as the grey evening light was fading slightly, I had everything piled on the path above the beach, and safe from the sea. It was at this stage that the tractor finally put in an appearance, but I was filled with dismay when I saw the carrying box on the back. It was only about three feet square. It would take dozens of trips to carry everything to the top. Although the house was straight above us, the tractor route was long, steep and winding, and had to be taken very slowly. In another hour the light would have gone. I would have to carry as much as I could to the top of the cliff by hand, while Mike continued to snake back and forth on the tractor.

The footpath was a more direct route than the tractor track, but it ran perilously close to the cliff edge. Piling my arms with as much as I could carry, I set off up the path, but the weight seemed to double every twenty yards, and I was soon struggling. I had been told about the burrows on Skomer, but this did not prepare me for what I now saw. There was not a square yard that did not contain a burrow entrance, and walking through this obstacle course was an art that took me a long time to master, but at that stage I had to pick my way as best I could. Even placing my feet carefully on apparently solid turf did not guarantee that the ground would not open up, sending me crashing into a burrow dug dangerously close to the surface. This, along with the problem of being hardly able to see over the pile of packages in my arms, and the fact that I was very conscious of the ground dropping away vertically to my left, meant that I had to feel my way very carefully step by step. Every muscle was tense, and by the time I reached the top my legs were shaking from the exertion.

Mike arrived on the tractor as I approached from the opposite direction.

'Come and see the house,' he called.

We went inside together. I was very surprised to discover that it was clean and bright and modern. The outside was timber, and I had expected it to be a quaint old log cabin.

'Wait till you see the kitchen,' Mike said.

It was huge but, more importantly, the view was breathtaking. The house itself was only yards from the cliff edge, and the kitchen looked out across North Haven to take in the whole expanse of St Bride's Bay beyond. The light was failing now, but it still looked magnificent.

'There is still a door I can't find the key to,' Mike said.

We tried several keys until eventually the lock clicked undone. As the door swung open we stared in amazement; it was a bathroom. I certainly had not expected plumbing as well as everything else. It felt almost like cheating; this was very far from the rough existence I had imagined. I wanted to carry on looking round, but we could not spare the time, so it was back to carrying. As I made my way up the cliff path for the second time it was almost completely dark. I could just make out shapes in the greyness, and I felt my way more cautiously than ever. Suddenly I heard a thump at my feet. Something must have fallen from the pile I was trying to balance. I peered round in the darkness, but could see nothing. I rearranged my load trying to get a better grip, and then set off. I had not gone far when again something hit the ground beside me with a dull thud. Again I searched anxiously but saw nothing. These strange noises in the darkness were beginning to make me feel slightly uncomfortable and I moved on, hoping that the missing things would be found in daylight.

As I climbed the path with my third load not a glimmer of light remained. Once more I heard a thump at my feet, but before I could stop to investigate I heard another and another accompanied by a slight rustling in the undergrowth. The noise increased until I could hear things crashing to the earth all around me. Then I began to hear little, strangled cries. They were faint and intermittent at first. Just one close at hand, then another in the distance, but they grew louder and more frequent until the ground itself sounded alive. I wanted to get away, but I could not move any faster on the dark, precipitous path. Each step was slow and painstaking as I felt cautiously for solid ground, and my arms ached under the weight they were carrying. I could not see where I was going. The more I tried to hurry the slower I seemed to move, and all the time the spectre of the cliff edge at the side of the crumbling path was in my mind. I was beginning to think that my tiredness was making me less than rational. I was overwhelmed with relief when I reached the lights of the house and found Mike outside unloading the tractor. He was ecstatic, all tiredness forgotten.

'Have you seen the shearwaters?' he called, as I approached.

I realised immediately, and with some embarrassment, that I had been hearing shearwaters, those ungainly nocturnal seabirds that inhabited the thousands of burrows I had been so carefully avoiding.

'Shall we have a closer look?' Mike said.

Before I could ask what he meant he darted through the undergrowth, and gently took hold of a shearwater which sat impassively, making no attempt to escape. In the light from the house I could see it clearly. It surveyed us sadly with its large, dark eyes. I had never before come across a bird that would sit on the ground and allow itself to be picked up. It looked so gentle and trusting that I was immediately captivated by it.

The birds continued to return to the island in their thousands, crashing to the ground all around us. Their high, shrieking calls increased to fever pitch, and as I walked back to the beach for yet another load I wondered how it would ever be possible to sleep through such a noise. I was surrounded by shearwaters shuffling through the undergrowth. I had to walk with extreme care; every time I took a step the shearwaters were intent on placing themselves between my foot and the ground, and it was almost impossible not to tread on them. It seemed that the airborne shearwaters were not used to finding stray people in their way, and they continued undaunted, causing me to duck frequently. Wings whistled past my face, the noise swooping out of the darkness and then disappearing again almost before I had time to react. It was not until after midnight that we decided enough was enough, and left the rest of our belongings at the landing point to be collected the next day.

Our first meal on Skomer was sausages and wine. Sausages because they were all we could find, and wine because we felt the need to celebrate. I swallowed the food with great difficulty, almost too tired to chew it. We found the most comfortable room and, after unpacking a few personal things and placing them on the bedside table just to prove that this really was home, we quickly went to bed. As soon as I lay still the aching in my muscles stopped. There was only one cloud on the horizon; tomorrow we would have to start all over again. I closed my eyes and listened to the shearwaters, but within seconds everything was silent.

TWO

W E FOUND THAT ALL OUR careful packing had been worthwhile. Peeling away the wet and grimy plastic coverings we saw that everything had survived the two rough journeys dry and intact. Settling in had none of the problems I had expected. There was no sense of strangeness, only an overwhelming feeling that I had come home; that this was where I should have been all my life. I had imagined that it would be many months before I came to terms with some of the deprivations of living on an island, but in reality, even from those early days, there was nothing I missed. I was only made aware of the fact that we did not have any electricity by the way I found it impossible to enter a room in the dark without feeling automatically for a light switch.

At first we dutifully confined ourselves to the house, unpacking the heaps of boxes that seemed to fill every room, and generally making our home habitable, but as soon as we were free to escape the first place we made for was the old farmhouse. It stood tall and imposing on the highest point in the centre of the island, and even in the previous weeks when we had stared at Skomer from the mainland we could see it silhouetted on the skyline. Apart from our own, it was the only house on the island and it exerted a powerful dominance over its surroundings, but as we approached it was a sad sight that met our eyes.

The house had no roof or windows, and only the unusual slate-clad walls recalled its former grandeur. As we passed through the gateway of the high-walled farmyard I was not prepared for the sight that greeted me, and stopped in surprise. We seemed to be standing in a garden that someone was still lovingly tending, although I knew the island to have been uninhabited for many months before our arrival. A smooth, green lawn stretched before

15

us and in front of the house a neat border of daffodils grew. The whole farmyard was fringed with daffodils and in one corner, huddled in the shelter of the tall walls, stood a tree. It was a black poplar and, prevented from growing any taller by the vicious winds which howled overhead, it had stretched its branches into a shady arc above the lawn. The whole thing looked so incongruous in the middle of this windswept little island that I could only stare in amazement. In fact this farmyard had been untouched for very many years and it was only nature that now maintained it. The rabbits kept the grass close-cropped and, compared to the surrounding rough, bracken-strewn fields, it looked like a bowling green. The daffodils had bloomed in abundance since they were planted more than fifty years previously and now wanted no further attention, while the black poplar needed only the protection of the sturdy walls in order to thrive.

Standing in the farmyard it was impossible not to feel close to the people who had once lived on the island. Had they loved it as we did, or was it just a place of work? A little of both I imagine; their lives must certainly have been much harder than ours. As I came to feel more and more part of the island and almost to forget that there was any world outside, I would sometimes sit at the entrance to an old field and stretch out my hand to feel the rough, rotting wood of a gatepost, and wonder who had put it there. And if, on looking up, I had seen a man coming towards me following a horse-drawn plough, I think I would hardly have been surprised. The past was everywhere on Skomer, and farm implements from a more peaceful age still littered the fields. In time it was possible to free some of these from their prisons of bracken and bramble, and return them to their rightful place at the farm.

On our first visit we entered the farmhouse with great difficulty. The rooms were waist-high with rubble and some of the roof timbers still hung precariously above us. In the years that followed, the rooms were cleared and the walls made safe by capping with cement. We always dreamed of seeing the house restored and often walked through the silent rooms imagining how they would have looked, and how they could look again. I believe now that the house will always remain a shell, but at least it is preserved for future generations to exercise their imaginations on as we did.

16

It was on that first day as we wandered among the farm buildings that I encountered the Skomer vole, a creature unique to the island. As we walked over the tumbled stones of a half-collapsed wall I was amazed when Mike plunged his hand towards a glint of reddish fur and caught a vole. I was even more surprised when he carried the animal towards me and I saw it sitting contentedly on the palm of his hand. Mike explained that the Skomer vole was a sub-species of the bank vole, and that this exceptional tameness was one of its most unusual characteristics.

As he placed the vole into my hands it seemed at first intent on sleeping, and nestled down to take full benefit from the warmth of my hands. I watched it as it sat quietly. It was considerably larger than a bank vole, and its sleek, chestnut-brown fur shone red in the sunlight. Its tiny ears were flattened back against its head until they almost disappeared and this, together with a blunt, rounded face, gave it a much more benign appearance than that of a sharp-nosed, large-eared mouse. Sitting up, its short tail now uncurled and stretching across my palm, the animal decided that it was time for a wash. It moved its tiny paws swiftly and skilfully, so that they seemed as dextrous as any human hand. Not a hair on its head was left untouched, from the tips of its long whiskers to the back of its ears. Satisfied that it was now presentable, the vole set about exploring with the practised ease of a pet hamster. Running up my arm it perched briefly on my left shoulder before crossing my back to the other shoulder. This continued until, fearing that it might fall, I enclosed it again in my cupped hands. Much as we enjoyed this performance we decided that the time had come to replace this creature in its own environment. That endearing animal and the unexpected brilliance of the daffodils against the slate-grey house are forever imprinted in my memory of that first day exploring the island.

Skomer is not a large island, measuring only about two miles long by one-and-a-half miles wide and being only about 720 acres in size, but we never felt it too small, never felt confined by its shores and never felt that there was nothing new to discover. Ours was the only habitable house on Skomer, the only other accommodation being provided by the small research quarters for visiting scientists next to our house and the very limited facilities offered by the converted stables at the farm which were available to visitors in the summer months. The result was that for much of the year we had the island completely to ourselves.

The main part of the island is shaped like a diamond lying on its side, the longest axis running east to west. The Garland Stone lies offshore at the most northerly point, and at the base of this stone grey seals bask. Off the southern end is the Mew Stone, a nesting place for cormorants, which was so encrusted with golden lichen it almost glowed in the low evening sun, while the outlines of cormorants were silhouetted along its top. These rocks which border the northern and southern extremities of the island are tall and imposing, rising from the sea like great, carved monuments and forming an intrinsic part of the island's distinctive shape. At the eastern end of Skomer lies the Neck, a triangular piece of land, like the head of an arrow, with its tip pointing towards Little Sound and the tiny island of Midland. The Neck is joined to the main part of the island by a very narrow isthmus, and it was at the edge of this isthmus that our house was situated. The two large bays of North Haven and South Haven cut into the island at this point almost meeting back to back, with only the isthmus to keep them apart. From the low isthmus, only about sixty feet above sea level, the land rises steeply behind, sheltering the house from the west and south-west, but exposing it cruelly to the winds that howled in from the north and south-east.

The island is fringed by steep cliffs, the main beaches being at the heads of the relatively sheltered bays of North Haven and South Haven. The cliffs are scored by faults, and deep inlets and caves have been worn away by the relentless action of the sea. It is these that make the coastal scenery of Skomer so spectacular, and which provide perfect, sheltered nesting sites for the thousands of seabirds that flock to the welcoming cliffs.

Inland, the main part of Skomer is a flat plateau cut by two valleys which provide shelter and variety of habitat. The flatter parts in the centre of the island are united by a mosaic of fields, small by mainland standards, but large in the context of Skomer. There are no trees; only ridges and rock outcrops interrupt the view to the island's edge and the distant sea. The fields are now disused, and mostly overgrown; they have been reclaimed by the tangle of vegetation that invaded stealthily from all sides. Now the field boundaries are highlighted only by the walls, painstakingly built

18

from rounded boulders of grey rock. The walls varied greatly in their aesthetic appeal. Some were straight, regular and even; as perfect as the day they were built. Some were a sturdy tumble of mismatched rocks, large and small clustering together, while others, with earth at their core, had proved too much temptation for the burrowing rabbits and had fallen, unnoticed, into decay.

The larger fields centred around the farmhouse were the most recent, dating mostly from the same period as the farm buildings, the middle of the nineteenth century. Sadly, this was also the time that saw serious farming on the island drawing to a close. Modern methods and modern markets did not adapt easily to an environment as temperamental as an island, and farming drifted into decline. One final brave attempt was made to revive the island as a farm in the 1940s, but this proved disastrous and the fields were at last abandoned to the wilderness. It was the fields immediately behind the farm that had been most impervious to the onslaught of bracken and bramble. These still opened out in a broad sweep of close-cropped turf spreading away to the west.

Walking away from the relatively flat, smooth fields towards the rougher outlying areas was to step back through the centuries. Here the island had lain undisturbed for perhaps two thousand years. Among the smothering plants were stone hut circles, field systems and enclosures that traced out the history of a forgotten age. Subsequent farming had concentrated on clearing more accessible land, and so these fragments of the past had been preserved. At first we were aware only of the more prominent hut circles, obvious even to our untutored eyes. We were both fascinated by them, and were drawn regularly to visit their primitive stonework. I used to stand inside the circle of stone and wonder how many people had lived confined by such a tiny space. I wondered too who had passed between those large, upright blocks that formed the narrow doorway and who had stood exactly on the spot where I stood and called it home.

In time we learnt more about the history of these relics. In later years archaeologists from Cardiff University came to study the island, and we took pleasure in listening to their explanations of what they found. We discovered that hardly a stone was placed by chance; almost every cluster of rocks once had a purpose. It made us see our surroundings afresh. Our hut circle no longer stood in isolation; adjacent to it was an enclosure for animals and opposite, on the rise of a steep ridge facing south into the sun, a row of small, oblong walled fields. A way of life was preserved intact in this small corner of the island. Even the changing patterns of vegetation reflected the ancient land use. Whole villages of hut circles dating from the late bronze age or early iron age lay hidden beneath the undergrowth.

We particularly liked the walls that dated from this period. Unlike the walls around the farmhouse, carefully pieced together with small stones, the ancient ones were composed of huge, immovable boulders. These were not continuous walls, but had large, regular gaps between each boulder wide enough to walk through. It was not certain whether these had once been continuous walls and were subsequently robbed of stone, or if they remained intact and had been intended only as a ritual boundary, never forming a physical barrier. These walls were at their most spectacular in the evening light. As we walked the south coast towards Skomer Head the most westerly of the walls appeared on the skyline in silhouette, a regular procession with a dark, commanding presence. With the sun sinking rapidly into the sea the sky dimmed to a shot silk back-cloth of reds and purples. In such an atmosphere just to feel the roughness of the lichen-covered rock still warm from the sun, and to imagine with what effort and to what purpose they were placed there thousands of years ago, was to bring the past almost too uncomfortably close.

When we first came to the island I wanted to see everything, to discover all there was to know immediately, and for this I relied on Mike. I drew constantly on his knowledge of the island and questioned him about everything around us. Suddenly we were in a place where nothing was routine or predictable, where the sea and weather took precedence over everything, and yet I knew that I wanted to adapt to this dramatically different way of life. To me it was an overwhelmingly exciting place. Every rock and inlet had a strange, romantic name: Pigstone Bay, Tom's House, Kittiwake Cove, Protheroe's Dock, and yet one day they would all become familiar and friendly. I greeted each day with a sense of ecstatic disbelief that we were really there to stay, and for Mike there were all the pleasures of rediscovery.

His previous experience of Skomer had been in a more carefree voluntary capacity, but the job of warden brought with it responsibility for the island and everything on it. As well as the physical maintenance of paths, landing areas, buildings etc. there was also a great deal of survey and monitoring work to be done. This was not just study for the sake of study, but a way of detecting long-term trends and changes and identifying problems that may have affected the survival of certain species. I was surprised to realise that even in a situation as remote as Skomer one of the most important aspects of the job would be dealing with people. Since visitors would come to the island in the summer months it was essential that everyone should understand just how vulnerable the breeding birds were. Great emphasis would therefore be placed on the need to meet every visitor and give them a proper introduction to the island. True success in wardening would be achieved not just by protecting the birds from disturbance but by ensuring that visitors would leave with an even greater insight into the reasons for preserving such unspoilt places.

The sheer number of birds and the way we lived so completely surrounded by them was wonderful, and yet I felt a little overawed by the situation. Everything seemed to hang in such a fragile balance. In some places the shearwater and puffin burrows were so frail they would collapse if walked on, the cliff-nesting birds might panic and shower their eggs or young into the sea if I came too close, and even the ground nesting birds were at risk from predators if accidentally disturbed. At first it was only when I was with Mike that I dared to stray from the areas where I knew I could walk safely. I began to wonder if I might always be a prisoner of the footpaths and open places, but it was surprising how quickly I learnt to recognise the warning signs, when to back away, when to keep clear or tread carefully. Soon these things became instinctive, and I could walk freely about the island without fear for its inhabitants.

It was far more disturbing to learn how vulnerable the birds were even without any human interference. Mallard were among the earliest birds to breed on the island. Their eggs were hatching long before many of the other birds had even started nest-building. As soon as the ducklings hatched the female mallard was consumed with an overwhelming instinct to take her young to the mainland. The fluffy ducklings, deep brown and yellow, were active from

their first hours and were marched scrabbling, tumbling and cheep-
ing with alarm if they were left too far behind, on a tortuous route
through the undergrowth to the cliff edge. The first I saw of this
procession was a string of ducklings, with the mother at the head,
teetering precariously close to the cliff. Then suddenly, in a flurry
of downy, flightless wings, the chicks rained down, splashing into
the sea. They formed themselves into a confused and excited line
stretching out behind the female, and she attempted to lead them
out of North Haven towards the mainland. They progressed well,
the chicks babbling and splashing, and finally reached the open
sea beyond Rye Rocks. But they could not escape the notice of
predators forever, and eventually this little flotilla of food acted
as a magnet to the gulls who circled in the air above screaming
menacingly and swooping to pick off one of the train of chicks.
The mallard fought back, rearing out of the water and trying
to fend off the gulls. Amid thrashing wings and salt spray
she became separated from the chicks who, calling frantically
with loud, repeated cheeps, were sitting targets for the gulls.
Eventually the attack receded and the female mallard regrouped
her depleted family. One chick was left behind and was quickly
found by the gulls. The others went on their way, but the gulls
continued to look down from above, noisy and agitated, awaiting
their moment. I strained my eyes until I lost sight of the little group
of ducks, feeling depressingly certain that none of the ducklings
would reach the mainland.

As we were beginning to establish ourselves on the island one
of the first things we did was to prepare the old chicken shed at
the farm to receive its new occupants. Terry Davies, who ran the
boat out to the island, had promised us six point-of-lay pullets
and we expected their arrival at any time. When they did come
I was instantly captivated by their glossy, rainbow-black feathers
and golden-red heads. To everyone else they were all completely
identical, but I knew each one as an individual, and by name.
Henrietta was my favourite because she was so bossy, but she had
such an embarrassing habit of making a flying leap and snatching
food straight from an unsuspecting victim's hand that I often felt
like disowning her.

In my innocence I took 'point-of-lay' to mean that they
would start laying immediately – the day after their arrival. So
when, after they had had a night to settle in, and I walked the

half mile to the farm to inspect their carefully straw-lined laying boxes, I was quite disappointed to find them empty, but put it down to the disturbance of the boat journey. It was in fact a discouraging six weeks of daily searches through the ruffled straw before I found the first egg, smooth honey-brown and perfect (I refused to notice how small it was). But it was worth waiting for, and as the hens gained in experience they began to produce eggs so large they would not fit into an egg-cup, and with the darkest gold yolks I have ever seen.

Spring, with its display of flowers, followed very closely our arrival on the island. First came the sea campion; its white flowers and creeping green leaves topped almost every cliff. It was a pretty, if unspectacular, flower, but what it lacked in looks it made up for in its perfume. Sweet but not sickly, under the heat of the sun the smell was intoxicating. Then came the bluebells. The first flower was found in South Valley on its sheltered, sunny, south-facing slopes. Then more appeared until, looking into the distance, the island was just tinged with a blue haze. Finally, with unexpected suddenness, they all burst into life so that the whole island was bright blue. It was possible to stand looking over acres and acres of bluebells until at last the purple blue of the flowers met the green blue of the sea in a strangely unharmonious mix of colours. The lesser black-backed gulls which had long since chosen their nest sites among the rough grass and fronds of dead bracken now found themselves caught up in a sea of blue flowers. Surely gulls never looked more spectacular, their white breasts, steel grey backs and yellow beaks vibrant against the vivid blue?

The scent of the bluebells mixed with that of the sea campion so that the whole island exuded a rich, heady perfume. There were no car exhausts, factory chimneys or even farmyard animals to taint the smell of the flowers. In the hot sunshine the fragrance seemed trapped above the island in a pocket of warm air. Sometimes, returning by boat as the evening light faded, a warm, dry, scented wind flowed down from the island to meet us, contrasting sharply with the cold sea air. As the bluebells reached their peak, the pink flower heads of the red campion began to appear among them, and gradually the island turned to purple as the pink and blue flowers became completely mixed. We felt sad when the bluebells faded, as their flowering season was undoubtedly the most spectacular time on Skomer, but the loss was softened by the lingering red campion. Around the cliffs at this time the thrift was starting to come into its own. The heavy grazing pressure of the rabbits kept many cliff-top plants at bay, leaving the way clear for the thrift to flower in the sort of profusion rarely seen on the mainland. First the characteristic fine-leaved cushions, dull after the long winter, turned a spectacular emerald green, and then the pink flowers appeared in abundance, flowing down the sloping cliff edges until they disappeared from view. The only thing that disappointed me about the thrift was the smell. It was faint, but not particularly pleasant. I always wondered why such a beautiful flower could not have had a scent to rival that of the sea campion.

It is difficult to recall in words the visual beauty of Skomer, but it is even harder to describe the sounds that brought the island to life and the feelings that they evoke. These sounds are more powerful than any number of words and pictures. I have only to hear the cry of the kittiwake and I am at once back on Skomer, sitting at the top of the Wick on a carpet of sea campion looking across at a cliff crowded with seabirds just as I did so often during that first spring. The Wick is the largest and most impressive of the seabird cliffs on Skomer. It is an inlet tapering towards the landward end, and faced on its southern side by a vertical cliff of black basalt. This cliff is scored from end to end by hundreds of crevices which create perfect ledges for the nesting seabirds. On the northern side huge slabs of smooth rock slope down to the sea. The whole appears to have been created by some giant and playful hand which arranged these great rock slabs in such a way as to deceive the eye and distort all logical ideas of perspective.

It was possible, with care, to edge down this steeply-inclined rock slope to reach the shore below, but it was necessary to deny the evidence of our eyes and to lean sharply to one side in order to remain upright. The beach below was another optical illusion, for what appeared from above to be pebbles were in fact huge, smoothly-rounded boulders, like beach shingle magnified a hundred times. We were left wondering if, like Alice, we had eaten something that could effect a remarkable change in stature and had somehow shrunk on the descent to the beach. From the green, rolling banks above, the stone slabs were reached most

24

easily through a narrow gully in the rocks with steep, straight sides. On entering this tunnel we were cut off from the outside, and all was immediately silence and gloom, but stepping out at the far end was like entering a different world. First there was the sound, a deafening screech of kittiwakes as they flew out and back from the cliff in little circular sorties, repeating over and over again the cry of 'kittiwake'. These calls mingled with those of the guillemots and razorbills who, with their deep, guttural growls, seemed to vie with each other to produce the greatest volume of sound. All these calls echoed from the hard rock faces so that we felt totally enveloped in noise. The second sensation on leaving the gully was heat. With the sun reflecting all round on the rocks whitened by bird droppings, and sheltered from all breezes, the Wick felt considerably warmer than the world outside. Finally there was the smell, and, although the aroma of several thousand tightly-packed seabirds would admittedly not suit all tastes, it was so evocative of being completely surrounded by bustling bird life that I genuinely grew to like it.

It was here at the top of the Wick slabs that Mike and I came to sit whenever we could spare the time. The scenes that unfolded below us were always changing, always so busy and full of life that it was impossible not to feel happy watching them. The birds had evolved a fairly orderly way of arranging themselves on the cliff face so that competition for nest sites between the species was kept to a minimum.

Guillemots and razorbills are very similar in appearance; both tall, upright birds with dark backs and white breasts, bearing more than a passing resemblance to small penguins. The guillemots, with their chocolate-brown backs, nest on long, straight ledges standing shoulder to shoulder as if waiting in an endless queue that never grows any shorter. They benefit from safety in numbers, and present a united front to any marauding gull or raven intent on a meal of eggs or chicks. Unlike most birds they incubate their eggs standing upright, always appearing to be at attention and never conveying the impression of broody calm shown by their more orthodox neighbours who rest contentedly with their eggs at their breasts. The razorbills can seem indistinguishable from guillemots to the unpractised eye, but once I was familiar with the glossy, black back and heavy beak of the razorbill I never confused the two again. Less gregarious than the guillemot, the

25

razorbill seeks the relative tranquillity of a crevice, or cluster of sheltering rocks, to lay its single egg.

No kittiwake would deign to lay its eggs on to the bare rock. For these pale, delicate gulls only a large and elaborately constructed nest will suffice. Starting from the smallest of foundations the kittiwake gathers vegetation and mud from the island's ponds to cement to the cliff face a nest which appears to defy gravity. During spring the kittiwakes were constantly flying overhead to the ponds and returning with their beaks full of building material. As we watched one day from the top of the slabs a kittiwake returned to its nest site with long strands of grass flowing like ribbons from its beak. The point of rock on which the nest was to be built was so tiny that the bird found it almost impossible to land. Returning with grass streaming behind it, the bird almost managed, with a flurry of wings, to stop in the air while reaching with its feet for a safe anchorage, but was just too late, and began to fall away before making contact with the cliff. The determined little bird continued to circle back to the cliff with undaunted tenacity, repeatedly reaching out and then seeing the rock slip away from it, until at last, after ten minutes or more it reached its target. As it did so those precious, green strands fluttered slowly from its beak to the sea below. . .

The fourth bird to piece itself into this jigsaw of species clamouring for nesting space on the cliff face was the fulmar. This bird has the gift of graceful, effortless flight. With its straight wings outstretched it glides easily, soaring high as it is lifted by the rising currents of air. Only occasionally does it need a few strong strokes of its wings to maintain its position. I sometimes thought that nature could be unfair when I watched the fulmars gliding through the skies, apparently for the sheer pleasure of flying, while alongside the guillemots and razorbills worked hard at every rapid wing beat just to reach the cliffs above. The fulmars were relatively few in number, and their main nest site at the Wick was a deep, horizontal crevice set well back in the cliff. Their raucous, chuckling calls were a happy addition to the strident symphony of bird sound echoing from the Wick.

Together with the occasional raven, buzzard or chough these were the birds of the cliff face. But we could never climb the sloping banks and leave the Wick without stopping to watch the puffins, even though our house was set in a puffin colony and we could watch them daily from the windows. These lively little birds with a pert, upright stance and bright, red and yellow beaks clustered in profusion at the top of the Wick, and their burrows dominated the surrounding slopes. Whether strutting purposefully on the cliff top, or bobbing in the water below, we could never pass them by.

Looking down from the cliff top the sea at the Wick was a deep, translucent green, and as the water was shaded from the glare of the sun by tall cliffs it was possible to see far below the surface. We found endless pleasure watching the puffins, guillemots and razorbills diving in the sea here. As the birds slipped below the surface the air trapped in their feathers turned them to silver, and these unnaturally shiny creatures were easily visible as they darted through the water. The images were vivid enough to create memories that would last a lifetime.

THREE

THERE WAS SO MUCH TO discover, everything was so completely unlike anything I had ever known before, that time almost seemed to stand still and those summer days went on forever. The heat wave began in May, but for the first week we were shrouded in a thick, white, humid mist. It was strangely beautiful, and yet frustrating to know that above it all the sun was blazing in clear skies. But when the sun finally broke through and burnt away the mist we were quite glad to have had that extra week of moist air to stave off the scorching effect of the sun.

It was one of those rare times when it was possible to know with certainty that every coming day would bring unrelieved blue skies. Throughout this period the wind never raised itself above a whisper and the smooth sea became sparklingly clear. Every scrap of sediment seemed to have settled out of the still water, and it was possible to look right through to the rock and sand of the sea bed. The golden sand shimmered through the sea creating the sort of watery azure I had only seen before in pictures of tropical seas. During those hot, dusty days the water could not have looked more inviting, but it felt cold as ice. Nevertheless, we regularly fell victim to its temptations and snorkeled through the rippling weed and above areas of clear sand, creeping surreptitiously closer to the unsuspecting puffins, but the water was always too breathtakingly cold to make it a totally pleasurable experience.

Looking across the sleekly polished waters of North Haven we spent countless hours watching and waiting for the boat from the mainland. There was only one boat licensed to make the trip from Martin's Haven to Skomer, and it ran from April to early September. However, in early spring when there were few people wanting to make the trip, or late summer when the lure of the harvest was stronger than the pull of the sea, the timing of these crossings could be erratic. In the early years, when radio contact was almost non-existent, we had no way of knowing on which day, let alone at what hour, the boat might arrive, but if the boat was expected we had little choice but to wait. Our niche for boat watching, above the landing point, was a hollow on the cliff edge huddled into the shelter of North Castle which rose steeply behind. The east-facing cliffs tucked deep into North Haven were so sheltered that they were draped with the trailing leaves of ivy and honeysuckle. Here in the middle of the day the heat could be unbearable. Every ray of sun seemed drawn to that hollow, and the air was still and parched. When the stillness became overpowering we would often lean out over the cliff edge to try to catch a passing wave of sea breeze.

In this stifling heat the island felt vaguely tropical. The sound of faintly lapping waves faded into the rhythmic rasp of crickets and grasshoppers. I had never heard so many, or seen the air so full of tiny springing creatures. They were mostly green with an occasional streak of orange. When they took off from a resting place they sprang so rapidly it was as though they had disappeared into thin air. In this sleepy heat lizards came rustling through the grass to bask on the warm rocks. They were shy and rarely seen and if we wanted to take the chance to watch them closely we had to remain completely still and quiet.

Butterflies too swarmed around us soaking up the warmth. Meadow browns and graylings were the most common on the slopes above North Haven. These gave a general impression of dull brown, but some of the brighter individuals showed a strong flash of orange. Despite their drab appearance the sheer numbers made them spectacular. The graylings had pale, marbled undersides which camouflaged them perfectly against the sandy paths strewn with pebbles. They always rested with their wings closed in a straight line over their backs, tilted to one side so that they cast very little shadow. Sitting in this way they became almost invisible, but despite their apparent love of secrecy they often came to rest on us if we were waiting quietly in the sun.

When this sultry heat brought everything out of hiding it was comforting to know that there was no need to tread warily. There were, for example, no snakes on the island. The nearest thing Skomer had to offer was a slow-worm. These have all the appearance of small snakes, but are in fact legless lizards. They are beautiful creatures, smooth and warm to the touch, their golden skin often marked with black. Their fine little faces are beautiful and delicate; perfect features composed in a picture of calm indifference, with a tiny forked tongue which flickers occasionally into view.

The summer wore on and, in what seemed an impossibly short time, many of the seabirds were preparing to leave. Though the summer was still at its height, the fledging seabirds gave us our first sharp reminder that time was moving on and that this perfect season could not last forever. First to go were the guillemots and razorbills. By the end of June only the whitened ledges would be left to remind us of the teeming life that had so recently engulfed them. There can be few more moving moments than watching a chick, after weeks of careful nurturing, make its first tentative move into the world outside. And what harsher place can such a tiny creature face than the open sea? Close to the house in North Haven razorbills nested; we could watch them from the kitchen window. From the day the first egg appeared we waited anxiously for the arrival of the chick. The eggs were well guarded, and we glimpsed them only occasionally, but scavenging birds such as gulls and jackdaws were always hunting for eggs, and wasted no time in seizing these neatly-packaged morsels. From time to time a nearby fulmar might decide that a razorbill's nest-site was superior to its own, and edge the razorbill aside, leaving the egg to shatter on the pebbles below. We were therefore very relieved when the egg belonging to the pair whose fortunes we had followed most closely was finally transformed into a grey, fluffy chick. Although this tiny, vulnerable creature was by no means safe from the cruel onslaught of its natural enemies, with each day that passed its ultimate survival seemed more probable.

As the weeks went by a perfect miniature razorbill emerged from the ball of down, and we knew that it would soon swap its tiny, rocky world for the vastness of the ocean. That moment came, as it always does, just as the light was fading at the end of a long June day. In the grey, unwelcoming sea an anxious parent called the unwilling chick to join it. High-pitched, urgent notes filled the air, but the chick was hesitant, pattering to and fro, and looking down at the threatening world below. Tucked out of sight, in the dusk, Mike and I watched, willing the chick

30

to go, but wishing it could stay. Finally, summoning all the courage of its few short weeks of life, the chick threw itself into the unknown flapping its tiny wings, still insufficiently developed for flight. The bird landed, with an audible thud, on the pebbles below. Nature had intended that these chicks should fledge into the sea but, at the chosen moment, the tide was out. Mike and I both started and edged forward, with no idea how to help, but as the chick instantly struggled to its feet we cowered back out of sight. Fragile and valiant, the chick clambered awkwardly across the uneven beach to the sea, where its parents waited.

Unusually, this chick was escorted by both adult birds, and now all three were intent on fleeing unseen. Their main concern was to get the chick as far away from the island as possible, safe from predators. Overhead gulls wheeled and screeched idly, unaware of the tasty morsel that was making its escape in the dark waters below. Keeping the chick as close between them as possible the adult birds swam briskly to the mouth of the bay, constantly turning their heads in all directions and bobbing them frequently beneath the water to survey the threat from below. There was still a chance that the lingering traces of light in the sky might be enough to warn some unknown enemy of their presence. The chick, instinctively aware of what was required of it, used its untried muscles to the full, and we watched until the three were lost in darkness. Mike and I waited in silence for some minutes longer. We should have felt relief that the chick had fledged safely from our shores, but it was an inexplicably melancholy moment. We had grown very fond of that tiny bird, and now it faced an uncertain future. Even if it did survive it could be years before it touched land again.

Though it was the cliffs and seabirds that made Skomer so spectacular, the other birds added a gentler influence, and gave depth and variety to the landscape. When we were sitting in the stifling stillness above North Haven there was almost nothing more welcome than the arrival of the choughs. They are magnificent birds, now very rare, with sleek, black feathers, bright red legs and a red, down-curved beak. Not seabirds, these are birds of the cliff, with an unsurpassed mastery of flying. It took only their sharp, high call, a single exultant note, to cause us a flutter of excitement, and our heads were turned irresistibly skyward. Though unaware of their audience the choughs always put on

31

a flawless display. They soared above the cliffs, tumbling and diving, shouting to each other their loud, insistent cries. For a moment they eclipsed everything within their sphere, demanding notice, dominating the broad sweep of sky with their distinctive silhouettes, wings outstretched with feathers upturned at the tips, moving with perfect control. As quickly as they arrived they would be gone, remaining only as an echo in the distance, but taking something with them and leaving behind an emptiness in the air that had not existed before.

The character of the chough was so perfectly in keeping with the atmosphere of the island that I could never be sure whether the choughs were part of the island, or if the island was an integral part of the chough. There were many birds like this; so essential to the island that the two were inseparable. Some of these were ordinary, everyday birds; birds that might be found anywhere, not just those that sought out the rare sanctuary of an island to survive. They formed just one of the many layers of life that made up the island, adding their own subtle influence to it. I loved the peaceful drawn-out sounds of the central island, so different from the clamour of the cliffs and of the gull colonies. The curlews haunted the flat, marshy land. Their thin, bubbling calls rose from the rushes in a beautiful tuneless harmony that whispered in the mind long after silence had returned.

The call of the lapwing too lingered in the air. In spring and summer they were always to be found in the fields around the farm. Their backs were a dark rainbow of greens and purples, and their heads proud-crested. They climbed high on broad, blunt wings and then fluttered rapidly groundward, only rising again just short of impact. And all the time their shrill calls slid up and down the scale in short, regular bursts. When they were protecting their young the lapwings became consummate actors. If we passed close to a brood of chicks the lapwing put heart and soul into distracting us. Amid noisy calls the lapwing staggered ostentatiously across the ground dragging its supposedly broken wing in its wake, in the hope that we would be drawn by the sight of an injured bird away from the chicks. I always wished that there was some way we could communicate to them that we meant no harm to their young, and could save them their endless repetitions of this troublesome charade.

32

It was their silence that made the short-eared owls so remarkable. They could move without the slightest rustle of feather or rush of air. As day-flying owls they were seen frequently, often in late afternoon, hunting along the broad hollow of North Valley, watching, hovering, plunging. Their wings, rounded at the tips and shaded with subtle browns, had an appearance of softness which belied their strength, while their yellow eyes, stark and piercing, glared with a disconcerting intensity. As many as six pairs of these owls nested on the island, keeping themselves well hidden until they had produced their white, angry-looking chicks which hissed their strange sounds from deep within the undergrowth. Once the chicks had appeared the owls were conspicuous in their search for voles, and I could never quite come to terms with seeing these gentle animals plucked from the ground. But the owls did not have it all their own way. One was beaten from the air by mobbing gulls, and fell to the ground with its wing broken. Mike climbed down the cliff slope to rescue it and took it ashore to the vet, but despite everything the poor battered bird died. But for most of the time the owls moved stealthily about their business unhindered.

There was no bird that sang more clearly of summer than the skylark. It could maintain its ecstatic refrain to the sun seemingly without pause, the notes flowing in a continuous rise and fall like a stream over pebbles. And yet however high the skylark soared the song lost none of its clarity. I often looked up, incredulous that such a tiny bird could send its message from so far above. I would blink into the stark blue of the summer sky until my eyes were dazzled by the cloudless brilliance. Sometimes I gave up, and sometimes I was rewarded by glimpsing a dark speck against the sky, pouring its eloquence onto quiet green fields.

This seemingly idyllic summer was not without its disadvantages. The spring above the house which supplied our water ran very low. Baths were banned completely, and all other uses of water were severely rationed. Work carried on unabated, while the oppressive atmosphere drained us of all our energy. The bird censuses and research work could not wait for cooler weather, and earth paths and steps, baked by the sun, crumbled to dust necessitating endless repair work. When the smothering heat shimmering up from the earth became too overwhelming we used to launch the boat and drift out to where the sea breezes could reach us. It was a tremendous relief to breathe in air that was not thick with heat.

One of the projects Mike took on that year was actually made easier by the drought. There were two ponds on the island, North Pond and South Pond; both had shrivelled and finally disappeared in the heat. It was Mike's idea to create a third pond, large and deep enough to survive the driest summer. The marshy end of North Valley where the overgrown remnants of East Pond lay became dry and accessible. The ground was even firm enough for Mike to bring in the tractor and excavate the foundations for a dam wall, though most of the clearing and building had to be done by hand, and the work was hot and heavy.

The greatest problem was that the island was becoming scorched bare. The velvety green pathways had dried to dusty earth. In some places, particularly around North Haven, the soil was so light it resembled fine, golden-grey beach sand which trickled away down the slopes or was carried by the wind. The fragile network of vegetation that held the topsoil together was put under almost insupportable pressure by the rabbits. They had been introduced to the island about six hundred years earlier to be farmed, but had since become wild and, in the absence of ground predators, had thrived. They had woven an endless network of burrows and tunnels beneath the soil, and in the quiet of the evening they ventured above ground in their thousands. They were most obvious in the central fields where the ground was flat and open. Any evening, if we rounded the corner into the large field known as Calves Park, which gave us an uninterrupted view towards the farm, it seemed at first that only one or two rabbits were scurrying away at our approach. Then the domino effect became more apparent: as we moved through the field, rabbits further from us became aware of our presence. It was like a wave spreading out from us and rippling through the rabbits as one by one they took to their heels and fled for the safety of their burrows. Rabbits which had been almost invisible as they sat motionless suddenly materialised as they moved, and the distance teemed with grey-brown specks seeking cover.

Although the rabbits were obvious by their physical presence, their effect on the vegetation was even more overwhelming. They fed selectively, and so while their favourite plants could sprout only a tender green shoot above ground level before being chewed down, those that the rabbits did not care for sprang up with renewed vigour to fill in the gaps. The bracken, unchecked by hungry jaws, spread into every opening. By taking only the youngest, freshest shoots the rabbits sculpted heather plants into rounded humps. The grasses that they found palatable were cropped to form short, springy lawns, but now under the pressure of the drought the over-grazed vegetation was beginning to suffer. Once-green banks were turned to bare, crumbling earth. The burrows running down the cliff-top slopes looked dangerously close to collapse, and it would have been impossible to walk on them.

Beneath the heat of the sun and surrounded by singed grass fading to brown, the ragwort managed to thrive untouched by the rabbits. It was to be a ragwort year, and not even the drought could cause a set-back. The fields were ablaze with its flowers. It appeared in golden, billowing clumps, with one broad band of yellow cutting across the field behind the farm following the line of a crumbling earth-ridge wall. It is a plant often condemned as a weed, so common that it is almost invariably overlooked, but here it was impressive, bringing the island to life when, in that sleepy period between spring and autumn, it seemed to have forgotten every colour but dusty bracken-green. The hot sun intensified the ragwort with its own colour until it almost glowed under the stark blue of the sky.

Butterflies drifted on warm breezes, flitting sleepily through the ragwort, highlighting the yellow flowers with the iridescence of their wings. In the stillness, heavy with heat, the ragwort buzzed with the gentle sound of summer. A good year for ragwort was also a good year for the caterpillars of the cinnabar moth, startling little creatures boldly hooped with red and yellow, which scattered themselves across the plants, eating intently. The day-flying cinnabar moths were still more striking. With their wings of rich vermilion they dappled the air with flecks of colour.

I remember, perhaps because it was a plant she disliked so intensely, that it was at this time of year, when the ragwort was in full flower, that Wellington arrived. She was a young nanny goat who came to us from the feral herd on the neighbouring island of Skokholm. This is a small island, about one third the size of Skomer, and several of the young goats were removed

35

from the herd every year to prevent the island being overrun. The problem was finding good homes for these animals. When we heard that the annual Skokholm goat round-up was about to take place, Mike expressed some interest in giving a home to one of these goats. We discussed the proposition and both agreed that this would not be practical.

Nevertheless, when the boat left for Skokholm the following day to collect the unwanted goats Mike somehow found himself on board. When the boat returned to put Mike ashore, I watched from the house as he jumped the narrow gap from the boat to the rocks, followed by a small and very nervous goat. I thought at first the poor animal was just being allowed to stretch her legs, but when Mike lifted her across his shoulders and began to carry her up the cliff I knew different. Determined to put a stop to this I dashed from the house and ran along the path meeting Mike at the cliff top in time to see the boat, now shrunk to the size of a toy, disappearing towards the mainland leaving a V-shaped trail in its wake.

'What is that?' I demanded angrily, already mellowing at the sight of anxious, amber eyes.

'It's a present for you,' Mike replied disarmingly.

The name Wellington seemed to arise naturally (because she was such an old boot, according to Mike), and that was how she was known from the day of her arrival. With her rough coat and spindly legs she was never a pretty animal, not even in those early days when she had the softening charm of youth. She was the goat that no-one else wanted. She had the wide-eyed terror of a wild animal, and backed away in distress whenever we drew near. Her anxiety was painful to watch, but no amount of gentle coaxing would prevent her from straining at the tether as we approached. Finally we collected a bunch of the most succulent-looking plants we could find and brought it to her. She pulled away, but showed a glimmer of interest. I held this tempting bouquet at arm's length and edged slowly forward. She glanced cautiously all around, as if to check that no fellow goat was on hand to witness this betrayal of her species, and then tentatively accepted the offer of friendship, chewing delicately at the tenderest leaves. From this point on the relationship improved steadily, until we were finally accepted as honorary goats.

From these quiet, inauspicious beginnings we had no inkling of what a grand and dominant creature Wellington would become. She settled happily into the goat-house that we built for her, but had a tendency to wander. We spent long and miserable hours searching for her, fearing that she might have fallen over a cliff, although in truth this was unlikely since she was as sure-footed as an animal could be. Her greatest disappearing act occurred when she fell into the old lime-kiln. The kiln was full to roof level with tangled brambles. Wellington, tempted by this delicious growth, had walked out on to the insubstantial thatch, presumably mistaking it for solid ground, and had been plunged into the lime-kiln below. Had it not been for her plaintive cries she would never have been found, as she was completely concealed. Even the brambles had sprung back to hide the hole which swallowed her up. Although she was invisible, it took little imagination to guess where Wellington was, and sickles were quickly brought to cut away the offending bramble. Inside Wellington wailed as though the world was ending, and as we came into view through the slowly disappearing curtain of brambles she screamed with renewed vigour, now certain of her audience. Mike had to climb down and attach ropes to her, then she was carefully hauled to the surface.

It was eventually decided that Wellington should be kept on a long tether until she had learnt the extent of her territory. She was, however, set free to come on walks with us when she could be relied upon to stay close by. Wellington was always in charge on these outings, and insisted that we walk in single file, not side by side. The order in which we proceeded was also of vital importance; Mike first, Wellington second and me invariably bringing up the rear. If we strayed from these rules Wellington reared up threateningly on her hind legs, and if we continued to disobey she would administer a sharp butt. We tried to humour her, but if she became vicious she was sternly reprimanded. On these occasions she sulked, and instead of opting for open confrontation would gore us surreptitiously with a flick of her head as she walked past.

Wellington settled in well, though her oddest quirk remained her loathing of ragwort. She set upon innocent plants for no apparent reason and beat them mercilessly until the stems were broken and tattered. These attacks came without warning, and were launched against clumps of ragwort she had previously been quite happy to co-exist with. We never understood what triggered this obsession, but decided that she had made such concessions towards living peacefully with us we could allow her this one little oddity.

FOUR

THAT FIRST SUMMER WAS the sort of summer that everyone re-
members from their childhood, when no clouds marred the blue-
ness of the sky, and hardly a breeze ruffled the shiny surface of the
sea. Since I had never seen it any other way I almost believed that
this was what summer was always like on Skomer; that the sea was
always clear and blue and the water always met the shore with no
more than a gentle lapping motion. The weather had settled into
such a regular pattern it seemed impossible that it would ever be
broken, that it could ever be any different.

I have often heard talk of the 'calm before the storm', but
that summer did nothing to prepare us for the storm that was to
follow. It was a Saturday early in September, and we waited as
usual for the *Sharron*, the pretty little blue and white boat that ran
between the island and the mainland during the summer months.
A few people had been visiting the island, and Saturday was their
appointed day of departure, so we were in little doubt that the
boat would run, but by eleven-thirty we were wondering what
had happened.

Then we saw the storm approaching. Many miles away across
St Bride's Bay we could see the distant sea turning to white. That
white line moved towards us; the sea behind whipped into a foam.
The wind arrived with a suddenness we have never experienced
since, and within minutes we were in the grip of a gale. We
headed for the shelter of the house and watched, fascinated, as the
choppy surface of the sea was gradually heaped into huge, rolling
waves. The rain followed rapidly and mingled with the sea-spray
to bombard the house. The old metal window frames could not
withstand so much water driven by such force of wind, and the
rain bubbled through every tiny crack. I was fighting a losing

battle, hurrying from room to room with cloths and bowls, trying to stem the flow before it cascaded from the window sills. The walls of our wooden house shook, and the vibrations sent saucepans crashing from their shelves. The water in the sink splashed gently to and fro, and when the plug was pulled out the wind, howling up the pipe, sent the last dregs of water spraying up instead of down. As the waves grew I wanted to go out and see them shatter against the cliffs, to see the rainwater flow across the parched island, to experience my first real storm on Skomer. As soon as I rounded the corner of the house and felt the sea spray stinging into my face the sudden tearing strength of the wind pushed me to the ground. I retreated to the shelter behind the house and then tried once more, but again I could not stand, and eventually I contented myself with watching the weather through the curtains of rain streaming down the windows of the house.

Only one thing dulled our exhilaration. What had happened to the *Sharron*? If she had been moored at Martin's Haven it seemed impossible that she would have survived, and yet the storm had arrived so suddenly it was unlikely that there would have been time to move her to a more sheltered place. As darkness approached the weather continued to deteriorate. The screaming wind and crashing waves sounded so much more threatening without the benefit of daylight. We were relieved when at last dawn came and the wind slowly moderated. Throughout the day the sea grew calmer until, by the afternoon, we half wondered if we might see the *Sharron*.

The following morning, Monday, our fears seemed realised when a radio message sent via the coastguard asked Mike to take the three stranded visitors ashore. There was little doubt that the *Sharron* was out of commission, but we still clung on to the hope that she had suffered only slight damage. There was however a rather worrying problem. The outboard engine of our little open boat was on the mainland awaiting repair where it had been for most of the summer. Our reliable, old-fashioned Seagull engines served us well as a back-up, but they were not suitable for carrying passengers across the fast-flowing Sounds. Mike hit upon a solution. He would go ashore using the Seagull, borrow a more powerful engine, and return to collect the passengers. Within a few hours Mike was back, and I hurried down to the storm-scoured landing beach to meet him. Our fears were

40

confirmed. The *Sharron* had sunk at her moorings on Saturday night; her bright paint-work was now just visible beneath the shimmering water of Martin's Haven. Although it came as no surprise I felt stunned as Mike told me. I still do not understand how boats have the power to inspire so much affection.

With the three passengers aboard Mike set off again with Norman, a lighthouse keeper who used to visit Skomer when he was off duty, acting as crew. Before he left, Mike explained that the borrowed engine had to be returned that day, and so he might stay on the mainland overnight in the hope of getting our own engine back the following day. With the *Sharron* gone we needed some reliable form of transport and could not afford to be without our main engine. Mike did not return that day, and when early evening came I knew that he must be staying on the mainland. I still could not help watching for him, but when at last the dark shapes of the cliffs faded to be replaced by my own reflection in the window, I knew I need look no longer.

I finished the washing-up and turned to go and light the fire, but as I did so a glimmer of red caught my eye. I turned quickly; the room reflected in the glass was pierced by one tiny spot of red. I threw open the window and leaned out into the misty night. There was a flash of red low on the water, but as soon as I had focused on it, it was gone. I hesitated anxiously. Only the night before we had searched the cliffs until two in the morning after the coastguard had received reports of a red distress flare. Finally it had been conceded that the whole thing was a false alarm, and I had wondered how anyone could imagine they had seen a flare. Now I was in danger of doing the same thing. Perhaps I should ignore it; after all I had only glimpsed it for a second, and I would look very silly if nothing was found. I immediately dismissed these thoughts. Someone might be in real danger, and I decided I would rather be embarrassed than risk someone's life. I radioed the coastguard and explained that I had seen a red distress flare.

There was a pause before the decisive reply. 'Right, we're launching the Angle lifeboat.'

I had not expected such an instant response, and I pondered nervously over what I had seen. Was it a flare, or was it a trick of the light? It was nothing like the parachute flares I had seen before, but one thing gave me courage in my convictions. A few weeks previously Mike had disposed of some out-of-date flares by setting them off in a hidden corner of North Haven. It was the only other time I had seen a hand-held flare of the type I thought I had just witnessed, and it made me more certain that I had identified it correctly.

And then the awful truth dawned; that was the sort of flare Mike was carrying. Was it Mike who was out at sea? I called the coastguard again, explaining that Mike was not on the island, but that I believed him to be spending the night on the mainland. They decided to go to Martin's Haven to see if the boat was there. I don't know how long I waited before the radio crackled into life again.

'The boat isn't in Martin's Haven. Can you think of anywhere else Mike might be?' No, there was nowhere. We never used any landing point on the mainland except Martin's Haven. There were no other sheltered bays for miles, and in our little boat we always took the most direct route. From that moment on there was no doubt in my mind that it was Mike who had fired the flare, although the coastguard, not surprisingly, continued to make enquiries for him on the mainland.

I stationed myself on the cliff top where I could command a view of the whole of St Bride's Bay. A dense, drizzly mist reduced the visibility, and all I could see was blackness. I listened on the little portable radio as the operation grew. The St David's lifeboat was launched, and the cliff rescue parties were called out to search from the shore. The rain was very penetrating and I kept the radio well hidden inside my coat. It was the only link I had with the outside, and I was terrified of losing it. In time I saw the searchlight of the St David's lifeboat as it moved slowly through the water sweeping the beam to and fro. It was a long way off, but each time the light shone in the direction of my face it dazzled me, even through the heavy drizzle. It was comforting to have something to watch since there were long periods when the radio remained silent. I waited for hours watching, listening and thinking. It was 10th September; we had been married six months to the day.

The radio intruded into my thoughts. The voice was distorted and broken. I wondered if the batteries were running low. I finally made out the urgently repeatedly phrase, 'Please use land line.' They were going to communicate by telephone.

They did not want me to hear. I had a sick feeling of panic that something awful was being kept from me. (I later discovered that at this point one of the cliff-rescue parties had found wreckage of a boat which had fortunately turned out to be unconnected with their search.)

I was not alone on the island. A zoologist, Professor Bellamy, was visiting with a small group of undergraduates from Cardiff. I had told him what was happening, and tactfully he had not intruded on my lonely vigil, but at two in the morning he came and insisted that I return to the house. I protested but then realised that, being so deep in thought, I had not noticed how heavy the rain had become. Fearing for the safety of my radio I agreed to go home, and soon Prof and I were in the warm kitchen with the gaslights hissing cheerfully. I was surprised that everything felt so normal. I made tea, and we waited.

Eventually more encouraging news came through on the radio; a small boat had been sighted offshore. I listened, willing the radio to speak to me again, and at last I was told that they could make out two people in the boat.

'Are they both all right?' I asked anxiously. There was a pause.

'I think so. They're both shouting their heads off,' replied the coastguard with undisguised relief.

I was still worried. The wind had been picking up, and the sea was rough now. I wondered how they would get safely ashore on that rocky coastline in the dark. I heard over the radio that the coastguards planned to use parachute flares to illuminate the scene and guide the boat ashore. I longed to go and watch. I would not see the boat – it was much too far away – but I might just make out the flares in the sky. However, fearing Prof Bellamy's disapproval, I decided to stay put and be content with my radio. The minutes ticked past and nothing happened. Finally I heard that a flare had mis-fired and they were trying again. (I later learned that the flare had been fired into a nearby gorse bush setting it alight. It is strange how even the most desperate situations have their funny moments, and I was quite pleased to think that I was not the only person who could not fire a flare in the right direction.) Within a short time I was told that Mike and Norman were safely ashore. The radio faded into silence, Prof went back to his students in the research quarters, and I was left alone with my thoughts.

By the following morning the sea had grown very rough, and it was three days before Mike could return to the island and explain to me exactly what had happened. I had a long talk with the coastguards and assured them that I was happy to wait on the island until Mike came back. I think they were worried that after the trauma of the night before I might now be in need of rescue.

When Mike finally arrived back on Skomer he told me his story. Returning to the island the little Seagull engine which had been carrying them slowly but surely home spluttered to a standstill. This was not too daunting a problem as Mike never made the crossing without a spare engine. It took only a short time to put the second engine in place, but as soon as the boat was no longer under way it was tossed by the turbulent waters of the Sound, waves splashing over it from all directions. By the time it was secured on the back of the boat, the second engine was too wet to start. This was more worrying, but they did not despair. They had already made good progress; surely it would be possible to row the last leg to the island? In a conventional boat they would probably have rowed the distance easily, and there the story would have ended, but the flat-bottomed, blunt-ended dory was not made for rowing. They took turns with the oars but made no progress. Finally it was decided that they should sit side by side with an oar each. Their combined power, instead of propelling the boat forward, dipped the front under water, so they were in a floating bathtub. The baler was pressed into service for the tedious job of emptying the boat drop by drop. It was a very slow process which ended abruptly when the baler finally slipped from fingers numb with cold and was lost into the sea. At this point Mike and Norman knew they must seek help, and resort at last to their distress flares. It was not until the last flare had been fired that they saw the lifeboat maroons and knew that their signals for help had been seen. But, with no flares left, they had no way of indicating their position to their rescuers. They, like me, had watched the lifeboat move across the bay with its wide, dazzling searchlight scanning the water. They had shouted themselves hoarse when the boat passed within a few hundred yards of them, and then despair had set in as they realised it would be many hours before the lifeboat passed that way again. Cold, tired and hungry they had difficulty in staying awake. Fearing the onset of exposure if they drifted into sleep they buoyed up their spirits by singing.

As the wind freshened they were slowly carried onshore. With the wind came waves, and they knew that there would soon be a danger of the boat breaking up against the cliffs. If they could reach the safety of any of the rocks jutting from the water they knew they would have to take the option of dry land, however precarious, and leave the boat to its fate. It was at this point that they spotted the lights of the cliff rescue party. Aided by their lights Mike and Norman slowly propelled themselves inshore, until finally their rescuers waded waist-deep into the cold, dark water to drag them to safety. Although it was approaching three in the morning the Chief Coastguard, whom we had first met on the day following our wedding, took them to his house where his wife cooked bacon and eggs.

'And the rest you know,' concluded Mike. 'Except that while I was waiting to get back to Skomer I bought this for you.' He handed me a long brown envelope containing a life insurance policy.

Within a few days of Mike's return Prof Bellamy and his under-graduates left. They were the last visitors to the island that year, so we now faced the approaching autumn and winter completely alone.

FIVE

FOLLOWING THE DRAMA OF THE STORM which had come so unexpectedly out of the peace of an idyllic summer we looked on the prospect of our first winter alone with some trepidation, but we quickly grew to realise that it was our favourite season on Skomer. Spring and summer could be breathtakingly beautiful, but winter was exciting and exhilarating. We used the term 'winter' to cover the period when no boats crossed from the mainland and we were alone on the island, but this in fact extended from September to the beginning of April and so included autumn and early spring. During this period our access to the outside world was solely by means of our own little boat which was ill-equipped to deal with winter storms and the fast-flowing currents of the Sounds. This inevitably meant that we spent long periods in complete isolation with no access to fresh food supplies. This was when we understood the true meaning of being on an island; completely dependent on our own resources and beyond the reach of anyone. There were times, particularly in those early years when the more sophisticated helicopters had not reached our area, when we doubted if anyone would be able to come to our aid no matter how desperate the emergency.

Early in October, about a month after the storm that had so dramatically ended the summer, Mike had to leave the island for a series of meetings. He would be gone a few days, but warned me that it could be as long as a week. Nevertheless, I chose to stay on the island by myself – after all it was my home now. On that first occasion, and for the only time during our whole stay on the island, I found it difficult to come to terms with such total isolation. I would start at each unexpected sound or movement such as a pheasant hurtling screeching from the ground only a few yards in front of me.

I found myself one evening at the far end of the island as dusk began to descend rapidly. Looking out across the western sea the sky still looked quite bright, but as I turned inland to head for home a greyness loomed across the land and I realised that the light was almost gone. I knew that I must move quickly if I was to be back before dark. I had taken no more than a few steps away from Skomer Head when a horrific scream pierced the air. My heart pounded and my legs felt weak. I turned my head slowly, hardly daring to move, and in the failing light I was able to distinguish the silhouette of a buzzard struggling to rise from the ground, burdened by the weight of a young rabbit. It had been that poor animal's dying scream that had so terrified me. Although I knew I had nothing to fear, I did not stop running until I reached home.

As time passed I grew, in a strange way, to love this solitude; I began to feel completely part of my surroundings. Every living creature seemed like a long-lost friend; each rabbit or bird that disturbed the silence was a welcome sight. Our free-range chickens living at the farm always ran to greet me clucking cheerfully when I went to feed them, and it was a pleasure to find that at least something was pleased to see me. I could even forgive Wellington her recalcitrant, bad-tempered ways when she came walking with me. Sometimes, when I tried to speak to Wellington I found that my voice had all but disappeared through lack of use, and emerged as a barely-audible squeak.

Although the days grew pleasanter as solitude became more familiar to me, the nights still seemed interminably long. The gaslights, though comforting, always proved too gloomy for any serious occupation such as painting. The curtains that we had inherited with the house were only a decorative fringe which did not reach far enough to cover the windows, leaving black, gaping areas that cast back only my own reflection. When the night was full of strange noises I had to stop myself from thinking that, although I could not see out, anything outside might see in.

A week of isolation had stretched to ten days. Mike had just missed a break in the weather and now the storm was picking up again, so it seemed certain that he would not be back for several more days. Outside it had been dark for hours, and as the wind howled at the windows I could hear the waves tumbling the shingle on North Haven beach below. I settled myself down, resigned to spending yet another evening with only the mellow glow of the gaslight for company. I had not been sitting long when I heard a loud, insistent hammering on the door. I vaguely thought how strange it was that when the impossible happens we still have the ability to act with almost complete calm. I rose to my feet and, as I shaded the reflection of the room from the window with my hand, a quick glance revealed the obvious. There was enough moonlight to verify that no boat had ventured into North Haven on such a terrible night. I was quite alone, so how could someone be on the island, knocking at my door? With a composure that surprised me I walked up the dark hallway and opened the front door. There was Mike. I did not know whether to be delighted or annoyed, so I settled for a little of both. But I still didn't understand how he had got there. Mike explained that leaving our boat behind on the mainland to be collected in calmer weather he had persuaded a friend with an old lifeboat to approach the island on the southern side, which was sheltered from the present northerly winds, and to put him ashore in South Haven, not usually used for landing. Nevertheless, the long sea journey round St Ann's Head had been rough, and the huge waves approaching the open boat in the dark little short of terrifying.

We did not go to the island in search of isolation. We knew it would be part of life, and one that we would have to learn to live with, but it was not the main attraction. Had I known quite how much of our time would be spent in solitude I may have thought longer and harder about my original decision to go to Skomer. It came therefore as a very welcome surprise to discover how much we thrived on being alone; just us and the island.

We had known each other for about two and a half years by the time we were married, but I do not think that anyone knows another person well enough to claim with certainty that they could happily be isolated with them for months at a time. We took a gamble, but by a happy accident it would have been hard to find two people more ideally suited to being marooned together on a deserted island. The reason lay in the fact that we were total opposites in terms of character and temperament, and yet completely alike in our enjoyment of the same way of life

48

and our overwhelming love of the island. I worried and tried to analyse every potential problem; Mike could never imagine that anything might go wrong. I was endlessly patient and prepared to let things take their course; Mike could never accept any delay or hindrance to his plans. I always counselled caution when Mike tended towards recklessness. In short, there were so few areas where our personalities touched that there was little cause for friction.

With time these tendencies polarised, and our natural characteristics became more entrenched. The underlying reason presumably being that the harder we pulled in the direction of our own point of view the nearer the final solution was likely to be to our original intention. We were not paragons of moderation and good temper, but in the winter when we were alone arguments were rare, partly because we were so dependent on each other and valued each other's company, and partly because there genuinely seemed nothing to argue about. When we did have a row it was furious and short-lived; we could not afford long, rumbling bouts of ill-feeling.

There were only two subjects guaranteed to cause discord: eating and boating. We learnt from our initial mistakes how dreary food could become, but until I had experienced real shortages I had no idea how much the enjoyment of food influenced our feelings of well-being. We had to change the eating habits of a lifetime and look at food afresh. I had been used to shopping every day and buying whatever was in season, but I discovered that there was a whole range of food which had previously quite eluded me. Those mysterious dried peas that come with a soaking tablet and a little white net to cook them in we now bought by the case, but even in our most desperate moments we couldn't quite bring ourselves to finish the catering pack of dried cabbage that looked and tasted like seaweed. Tinned butter, dried soya meat, dried carrots and even dried egg; we tried them all and they quickly lost their appeal. It became obvious that there was no point in trying to find substitutes for the things we had left behind. Eventually I realised that there was no alternative but to ignore the recipe books and invent a completely new style of cooking. I must admit that a lot of this centred on disguising the things that came out of tins, but I did invent a whole range of dishes including pies, pizzas, soups and casseroles. Nevertheless, particularly

49

when supplies were running short, it was impossible to think of anything to turn our meagre ingredients into, and at the end of a cold, tiring day that could make us inexplicably depressed and irritable.

I would however have endured endless boring, tasteless meals rather than face a trip to the mainland. With our stocks beginning to run low I waited with dismay for the day when the wind eased and left the sea just calm enough for us to make the crossing. Finally the day arrived, and as I walked down to the concrete slipway to launch our boat I felt a cold, sinking dread somewhere deep inside. This was partly because after a long period of isolation I found the prospect of even a few hours contact with the mainland little short of terrifying, and partly because of a growing conviction that weeks of peaceful co-existence were about to be shattered in a few minutes. I arrived first, and began untying the web of ropes that secured the boat. A band of mist took the place of the horizon and damp specks hung in the air. The wind came only in gentle gusts, but a swell still troubled the sea and the waves lapped on to the rough, stony shore with rather more force than I would have liked. Mike arrived with the tractor and we carried oars, outboard motors, life jackets and all the other endless, but necessary, equipment down to the beach. Then, with some reluctance on my part, we began to launch the boat. It rolled easily on its trailer across the concrete, and had the tide been in we would have slid it smoothly into the sea without too many problems, but today an expanse of rock-strewn beach lay between us and the water's edge. We negotiated the first hurdle, the right-angle bend in the slipway without difficulty. Then we used the last straight stretch as a runway to pick up speed. We were treading a delicate path; too fast and we might lose control of the boat, too slow and we would not have enough momentum to carry us down to the sea. We hit the beach at a run, the boat bounced and slowed, we pushed harder, everything was progressing well until we came to a jarring halt. We dropped the front of the trailer and I rubbed my jolted wrist. One of the trailer wheels had hit a rock bringing it to an instant standstill.

'We'll have to lift it over this,' said Mike, angry impatience already colouring his voice.

We lifted and we pushed and nothing happened. I gritted my teeth, held my breath and strained every muscle.

50

'Come on, lift!' shouted Mike, as if to imply that I was standing watching with my hands in my pockets.

I continued to lift with all my strength.

'Oh, it's no good,' said Mike angrily, suddenly dropping the trailer without warning and letting the full weight of it fall back on to me. 'You're just not strong enough.' I should have been impervious to it. I should have let it drift over me like the damp mist trickling off my oilskins, but I didn't. I never understood why it was that if our combined strengths did not achieve the desired effect I had to take full responsibility for it, and I said so forcefully. Even as I spoke most of me was wishing that I would keep quiet.

We got the boat past the rock as we always did, but it was impossible to build up any speed again, and we fought the boat every inch of the last stretch to the sea. With every grazed knuckle and missed footing the atmosphere grew more oppressive. Once the boat was afloat at the edge of the water I tried to hold it still while Mike loaded it. The strong swell-waves tugged at it, drawing it out to sea and then throwing it back against the rocks. The sea snatched at the pebbles which surged in a clattering stream around my feet. In my anxiety to prevent the boat from being damaged on the rocks I gave up all attempts at keeping dry and waded deeper into the water, letting the cold sea flood into my boots.

'What did you do that for? You'll be wet all day now,' Mike said, with an air of exasperation that made me feel like a recalcitrant child.

As soon as we were in the boat and under way Mike was back to his usual cheerful self. Before we had even left North Haven he was grinning and pulling faces at me. These I studiously ignored, preferring to nurse my injured pride, but despite myself I felt a smile pulling at the corners of my mouth. I tried to control it but couldn't, so I turned away to hide my face and pretended to be examining the anchor chain intently. But the ice was broken and soon I turned and smiled back at Mike, and then at the whole expanse of sea around us. It was impossible not to feel happy moving steadily through the water with the waves lapping rhythmically at the side of the boat.

Mike interrupted my thoughts.

'Come and steer the boat,' he called, as a final act of

appeasement. I had to admit that he was never one to let an argument simmer. I picked my way unsteadily to the back of the boat and taking the tiller I perched myself on the stern. Staring ahead I felt the drone of the engine buzz through my clenched hand and cold sea spray spattered my outstretched arm. It wasn't going to be such a bad day after all.

I found the ever-decreasing day length the only aspect of approaching winter that was really difficult to come to terms with. Those almost imperceptible changes, as the sun seemed gradually to lose the strength to soar high into the sky and the light faded with only slightly unexpected promptness, were just about bearable. They were gentle developments that could be predicted and adapted to. What I hated was that awful day when the clocks went back and suddenly darknesss descended in the afternoon. It seemed to jolt life's natural rhythms out of sequence, and had a very unsettling effect.

It occurred to me that since our contact with the mainland was so minimal at that time of year there was no reason why we should change our clocks at all. To my surprise Mike did not think this an idea worthy of consideration. In fact all discussion of it had been so firmly dismissed that by the time the day arrived on which the clocks were due to be put back, the subject had not been mentioned again. I realised with a growing sense of amused anticipation that Mike had completely forgotten about changing the clocks, and when I woke the next morning it was with the guilty knowledge that we were now an hour out of step with everyone else. It became something of a game on my part to see how long the situation would prevail. I was encouraged by the fact that time meant very little to Mike. He was the sort of person who could 'just pop out for five minutes' and return two hours later. If I asked him to guess the time he might be wrong by several hours, whereas I was rarely more than ten minutes out. I knew the radio would be my downfall; it was the only opportunity Mike had of realising his mistake. We always listened avidly to the shipping forecasts, but I managed to hear these while Mike was out, and then casually relay them verbally without any apparent oddity in the timing.

It was several days before the truth finally dawned.

'You did that on purpose,' Mike said, mildly irritated at being on the receiving end of one of my jokes yet again. I grinned apologetically, hoping he might have realised how easy it was to live in our own time zone, but to my disappointment he immediately re-set his watch. He then got up to change our only clock, hanging on the kitchen wall. I watched in growing disbelief as he advanced the time one hour, so that we were now two hours ahead of the rest of the country. A surreptitious glance revealed that he had done the same with his watch. I wondered if I dared remain silent, and decided that I did. I would not have had the courage to engineer the situation, but now that it had arisen naturally I could not resist following it through. I knew that such a big time gap would be hard to maintain, but Mike did not realise until late the following day, and this time he saw the funny side of what had happened. It was harmless trickery, but it served a useful purpose. The next year it was accepted almost without discussion that we would not put our clocks back. From then on we spent much of each winter on summer time, or Skomer time as it became known, and it suited us much better.

We both adopted very different ways of coping with isolation. I withdrew further into myself; became more self-sufficient. Even as a very small child I had been content in my own company for hours at a time, and it was a skill I quickly relearned. Loneliness was an emotion that I did not recognise. I may have missed certain people, but I felt no general sense of being alone in any unpleasant way. I realised that a lot of my feelings of being at peace with solitude came from a shared contentment in our way of life, but even when Mike was away and I was completely alone I drew inner strength from an even greater degree of self-reliance.

I think that Mike adapted so well to isolation because he was a complete enthusiast. Whatever he did he immersed himself in to the exclusion of everything else around him. This was a quality I both envied and admired, and yet found very frustrating. When Mike embarked on a new project I knew that I had lost him for as long as it would take to complete, or at least until the first surge of enthusiasm had eased. I also found it hard to work with him since he was usually oblivious to being cold, hungry or tired, while the more I tried to ignore these minor irritations the greater importance they assumed. When he was not working Mike's obsessions usually centred on painting or carpentry. He did

53

everything on a grand scale, and only painted on large canvases. Once he had embarked on one of these works of art it was difficult to deflect him.

'It's such a lovely day, why don't we go out? It'll probably be raining tomorrow and you can finish it then,' I would suggest hopefully.

'What do you think of this blue? A bit bright perhaps,' was the only answer I was likely to get.

Even more frustrating was the knowledge that having used all his available materials on one painting, he would be quite morose when it was finished and he was confined to the house by bad weather.

Even when it grew dark Mike would not stop painting. Somehow the failing light lent enchantment, and each brush stroke seemed better than the last, urging him to keep going. It was only in the cold light of the following morning that the brush work seemed coarse and clumsy, and the colours muddy and ill-matched. As he painted out his elegant finishing touches of the night before he would criticise his own stupidity, but I knew that by the end of the day he would be doing the same again.

To conserve the precious hours of daylight for more practical uses we often walked the island in the grey of a late winter's afternoon. I was usually out by myself several times a day, perhaps checking the progress of seal pups or feeding the chickens, but I always felt slightly cheated if we did not get out once a day together. I was never happier than when I was walking; there was no day, however windswept or rain-soaked, that did not seem welcoming after a few minutes' acclimatisation. When we did go out together I always hoped to make it through the front door without hearing the dreaded words, 'I think I'll bring the camera.' 'The camera' usually came accompanied by a companion or two, a large, heavy bag of equipment and a tripod. Inevitably these came into my possession, leaving Mike free to go in pursuit of his quarry. The perfect picture was rarely there, waiting to be captured. We usually had to wait for it to arrive. We would wait interminably while the fiery orb of a setting sun sank a little lower in the sky, or while the clouds drifted a shade further to the east, or while the silhouette of a lone gull moved itself into a more acceptable position.

One sparklingly cold winter day we found ourselves on top of the stark promontory of North Castle. As we looked down, everything spreading below us was illuminated by a pale, silver light, so different from the golden warmth of summer. The waves in North Haven flickered with an inner glow and the grass-covered slopes had a rich, mossy softness. In the centre of it all our house, normally so exposed, from this angle appeared to nestle beneath the protective slope of Captain Kites. Mike immediately saw the potential for a photograph, but one look through the viewfinder had him shaking his head.

'It's no good,' he pronounced. 'It needs some sun on the house.'

Pools of sunlight were spilling from between the clouds and drifting across the island, so we waited for the right moment. Sometimes the pools of light overflowed and ran into each other, sometimes they faded and disappeared as though they had soaked into the ground. Occasionally the warm light bathed us in a momentary respite from the cold, but it did not once touch the house. As the minutes passed the cold seeped through our coats, but I knew that Mike would not give up however long it took.

'My toes have gone numb. I'll get chilblains,' I complained, stamping my feet.

'Run up and down,' Mike said helpfully. Then without warning, from the midst of this mundane chatter, Mike said,

'I'd like to have my ashes scattered here.'

'Why here?' I asked, as much surprised by the choice of location as the subject matter. It was not one of my favourite places, in fact we rarely went there. It was high and empty, and was not on the way to anywhere else, so it easily got overlooked.

'You can see everything from up here,' Mike tried to explain. 'There's the house, North Haven, South Haven, the Neck, and you can see right down to the sounds in that direction.'

I was beginning to understand. I certainly could not think of anywhere better. I realised that in a strange and unexpected way Mike had put into words the unshakeable conviction we both had that whatever happened in the rest of our lives nothing would ever supplant Skomer in our affections. Suddenly it seemed unthinkable that we would not finally come back here. I opened my mouth to agree, but in that instant the long-awaited shaft of sunlight swept across the house and the urgency of the moment banished all such thoughts from our minds.

Winter highlighted all the flaws in a house that seemed principally designed for summer occupation. The only heating was a small open grate in the living room and an ancient paraffin heater that belched black smoke and sooty smuts. The fumes from the heater were so disgusting we used it only for occasions of real necessity, such as keeping warm the batches of bread dough that I made two or three times a week and which definitely needed molly-coddling. Other than that, when the house became too cold to bear we went out for a walk, and it always felt comparatively warm when we came home. The fuel for the open fire was driftwood collected from South Haven and dried in the cellar. When the wind was strong the fire roared fiercely, spitting and crackling and spraying us with glowing embers. The roaring heat was sucked straight up the chimney leaving us as cold as ever, and it was almost a full-time job keeping the fire stacked with wood. I sometimes thought the fire made the room colder; it pulled in so many drafts, the wind even whistling up through the gaps in the floorboards, that I could often feel my hair wafting gently in the breeze. We occasionally resorted to sitting by the fire shrouded in coats and blankets.

Despite the inadequacy of the fire, it was often difficult to leave its illusion of warmth and go to an ice-cold bedroom, so we often talked late into the night as the spluttering fire sank to ash. The evenings were long, and we passed them mostly in reading and listening to the radio. Mike is a voracious reader and, despite our sizeable collection of books which was added to at every opportunity, he often ran short of reading material. When he got a new book he set upon it and devoured it in an evening instead of rationing it and saving some for leaner times. The result was that he was often to be found searching the bookshelves for anything he could bear to read yet again.

We listened to Radio 4 as our way of keeping in touch with the outside world. It was one thing I would have really hated to lose. If we were in danger of running out of batteries, our last few hours of listening were carefully eked out to avoid being cut off completely. The worst problem was that although the gaslight was golden and warm, it was very dim, and cast deep shadows. It meant that painting, or anything that needed clear illumination, was barred to us as soon as the natural light failed.

Despite the inability of the gaslights to cope adequately with the gloom of a winter evening I did not miss electricity at all. In fact it rarely occurred to me that we did not have any. The only thing I regularly longed for wistfully was a washing machine. I could think of no greater waste of time than standing for hours at the kitchen sink with my hands in soapy water until they were white and crinkled and sore. Because we led such a messy outdoor way of life our clothes were always filthy, and I had to take the scrubbing brush to everything. I found a wonderful flat-topped ship's flagpole, about three feet long, washed ashore in South Haven, and I used it as a makeshift washing machine. I put all the clothes in a tub of hot, soapy water and used the flagpole to plunge them up and down for some time before transferring them to the sink to be finished off with the scrubbing brush.

By way of compensation, I was mostly spared the chore of ironing since our gas iron, spurting flames out of the sides, was so alarming that I only used it in cases of real necessity. All in all our life was much more comfortable than I had imagined it would be, and the presence of running water, to me, made up for every other little luxury we might lack, despite the fact that our water supply had barely survived the summer drought.

On stormy nights, when the whole house shook in the wind, and we were huddled round our spitting, driftwood fire, Wellington seemed quite comfortable in her goat house. But, I must admit, she would have much preferred to live with us. She lost no opportunity to come into the house, even discovering that the front door would open if she hurled herself at it with enough force. We were more than once startled by a crash on the door followed by the noisy clatter of hooves up the wooden hallway. As she was being evicted Wellington always made a last ditch grab for the wall, attempting to strip off a section of paper with her bare teeth and curling lips, and thus cause maximum irritation.

One very cold night Mike went to the now deserted research quarters next to our house for a shower; a luxury that we did not possess. While he was gone I decided to settle for the more leisurely enjoyment of a bath. I turned on the taps, watched the water splash and gurgle against the white enamel, and waited while the bitingly cold air filled with warm steam. I switched on the radio, turned up the volume so that I could hear it above the bubbling waterfall from the taps, and lowered myself into the tingling-hot water. From outside, above the noise of the taps and the radio, I could hear loud and persistent wailing. I decided that it was only the seals howling, but they seemed exceptionally noisy that night.

Alone in the house I felt just a little uneasy, and splashed the water loudly as I washed, to blot out all trace of the sound. Eventually, with sudden alarm, I realised that above the distant call of the seals was the louder sound of a human voice. I leapt out of the bath, sending a wave of water across the floor, and turned off the radio.

'Help! Help!' Mike's pained cries filtered through loud and clear now.

Stopping only to grab a towel I ran outside. The cold air swept across my wet skin causing me to catch my breath. The night was without the faintest glimmer of illumination and I could see nothing. I felt my way along the wall of the house, sliding one foot carefully in front of the other, and all the time dreading what I might find. As I entered the research quarters I was greeted by another weak cry of 'Help!' from Mike, and made my way to the far end as quickly as I could.

'What is it?' I gasped anxiously, still breathless from the cold.

'The gas cylinder's run out, my shower's gone cold, and I'm freezing.' said Mike petulantly. 'Can you put a new cylinder on for me?' I was very far from pleased, but preferred to get back to my warm bath rather than stand arguing and so went outside. I carried the heavy cylinder into place and after some minutes groping round in the dark managed to connect it to the supply, and then went back to the house.

Although my eyes must now have been fully accustomed to the darkness, I could detect no hint of light in the hallway. I felt my way through the open front door, and then stopped in barely suppressed panic. I had heard nothing, I had seen nothing, but I had the distinct impression that something had moved in the hallway just ahead of me. I waited, frozen in terror, and listened. In the silence I could feel my heart beating very hard and fast, but everything else was calm and still. After a few minutes

I breathed a long sigh of relief, relaxing my tensed muscles as I did so and half smiled at my stupidity. I stretched out my hand to begin groping my way up the hall again, and touched something warm and hairy. I felt my stomach lurch sickeningly. Above my scream I heard the familiar rattle of hooves on floorboards, and abruptly fell silent.

'Wellington! Don't come in the house again,' I called furiously. But Wellington knew she was in trouble, and was gone.

One of our greatest winter pleasures was beachcombing. Hardly a day went by when we did not make our way down the slippery winding track to South Haven. It was something we rarely found time for in the summer, and besides the winter storms were much more fruitful in casting their jetsam on to our beach. We found useful things such as buckets and mooring buoys, but what we really went in search of were curios, things of no practical value that excited our interest. One of my favourites was a Russian pencil, brand new and unsharpened with its strange, unintelligible lettering. I loved to think that such a mundane object had travelled so far finally to be found by us. We wondered by what meandering route it had made its journey, and kept it as a souvenir. We found only two glass fishing floats, one green and one amber. Mike could remember a time years ago when they were common, but now they were remnants of a passing era. These too we kept. Their glass was coarse and flawed, but with the sunlight streaming through them they still looked too fragile for their intended purpose.

An emergency ration pack from a lifeboat was one of our more unusual finds. The container was battered and rusty, but we could not resist a look inside. Mike prised it open, and to our surprise the polythene-wrapped contents seemed perfectly preserved. There were boiled sweets and biscuits and some sickly white chocolate. Mike was all for tasting them but I hesitated. He sampled them regardless, and once he had pronounced them edible I felt bound by curiosity to follow his lead. The biscuits were impossibly hard, and everything was very sweet. Perched on one of our favourite rocks we unwrapped a boiled sweet and stared out across the open sea. I loved sitting there, everything silenced by the deep echo of the water. We watched the seals watching us; grey heads motionless but for the rise and fall of the waves. I turned my face to the sun and felt its faint warmth on my cheeks. The tide crept up the beach, the larger waves threatening our feet, until eventually, as it always does, the tide won and a surge of foam sent us fleeing from our rock. The sun had slipped behind the cliff filling the bay with cold evening shadow. The sea was reclaiming its territory and it was time for us to leave. But tomorrow there would be another day and another tide and everything that might bring.

SIX

O UR LATE ARRIVAL THE FIRST YEAR meant that we missed one of the most exciting events of the spring; the return of the puffins. But it became one of the most eagerly awaited highlights of the following year. Spring came slowly to the island, with the last remnants of winter clinging tenaciously and refusing to release their grip. There was a barren, battered appearance to the land after a season of storms rolling in from the open ocean. Everywhere the dried and broken remains of summer growth covered the ground so thickly that there seemed no possibility of new, young shoots breaking through. There was an overall impression of nondescript brown, as though all colour had been leached out by the driving rains. Spring still seemed so far off that the arrival of the first puffin took us almost by surprise. A solitary bird came in before the rest, appearing silently, unexpectedly, just a black and white speck drifting in the empty bay. It had come through all the seething anger of the Atlantic storms to find itself in North Haven on a still, dull day when no waves moved across the water.

Although we had waited so keenly for the first puffin to return, it came so quietly, so unostentatiously, we might have missed it completely if we had not been walking back to the house from the farm down the slope above North Haven. Had the sea not been so calm the single bird would have been lost among the light and shadow of the waves, but as it was it stood out clearly on the flat surface of the water. For a moment we could hardly believe what we were seeing: it was as though a bright memory of last summer had come to this misty, wintry day. We walked on until we were standing at the top of the cliff, but still the bird was no more than a fleck on the vast expanse of greyish water. For a moment the sun broke through beneath the heavy sky. The sea gleamed metallic

61

grey and the distant clouds looked black and threatening, but the pure white of the puffin's breast almost glowed. Its reflection shimmered in broken bands across the water and the brilliant red of the beak was highlighted. Then the sun was again subdued by the clouds and the bird on the sea almost disappeared.

When we looked again there were forty or more puffins huddled in a small group close together. They seemed nervous after their long winter spent at sea. They did not come flocking back to the cliffs as we would have imagined, to take up exactly where they had left off last summer. Instead they stayed in the bay, gathering in clusters on the surface of the water. As evening approached they began to take to the air, trailing their ephemeral footprints across the sea as they ran over the still water in an attempt to give impetus to their take-off. The splashing of feet, the whistle of air rushing against the determined beat of their sturdy little wings permeated the stillness. A purposeful clamour filled North Haven as the puffins circled high above the cliffs, dusting the evening sky with their dark outlines. The puffins did not fly easily; their bodies are thick and muscular, while their wings are relatively short, so the air was a frenzy of rapidly beating wings. Though we watched patiently for the puffins to land, not a single bird touched the island that night. Many came tantalisingly close, dipping down towards the burrowed surface of the isthmus and hovering momentarily as if considering the prospect, before flying past. But eventually they retreated further out to sea and disappeared into the growing darkness.

The following day the whole process was repeated. As the afternoon drew on the puffins slipped silently into the bay, their numbers increasing almost imperceptibly as the rafts of drifting birds grew. Late in the day they again took to the air, wheeling round and round above the cliffs, soaring over the house, but none came to land, and with the dusk they vanished. It was not until the third evening as we watched the birds skimming across the isthmus, slowing as if to land and then passing on, that one brave bird finally touched down. It landed very gingerly with its wings stretched out behind but, after a second or two, it folded its wings against its back and stood upright, as if in final confirmation that it had left the sky. Fidgeting awkwardly from one foot to the other it looked round constantly, apparently certain that something was about to pounce. Crouching low it made a short run, picking out one burrow from all the identical ones around it. The bird lingered only long enough for a brief glance down its burrow before anxiety forced it into the air again. But it seemed that once that first red, webbed foot had touched Skomer's soil the curse was broken, and other puffins now felt free to pay the island a fleeting visit.

Puffins are true seabirds. On land they are out of their element, as the nervousness they displayed on their return to the island clearly showed, but, as no bird has the ability to incubate eggs at sea, their annual pilgrimage to dry land is a necessity. Puffins are not shy birds however, and once their initial uneasiness was overcome, it was possible to approach within a few feet of them. If we sat motionless on a cliff top the curious puffins came so close that our outstretched hands could have touched them.

If they breed successfully, puffins return to the same burrow each year, and remain with the same mate. Their first job of the spring was to restore their old burrows to pristine condition after the ravages of winter. Some would have been damaged by winter floods, or collapsing earth. In some cases, it might even be necessary to evict invading rabbits. Most of the burrows used by puffins were originally rabbit burrows, and although they could dig their own, they did not waste unnecessary energy in this tedious pursuit. By now most of the burrows were so old that their original ownership was long forgotten, and the rabbits occupying them were just opportunistic intruders seeking shelter for the winter. The rabbits were no match for the puffin's powerful beak and claws, and the matter of repossessing their burrows was no more than a formality. Each year the puffins liked to do a bit of tunnelling, whether the burrow needed it or not. This meant that the underground passages annually grew a little larger, increasing the risk of burrow collapse and soil erosion. Once the puffins had re-established themselves the cliff tops were characterised by the sight of clouds of earth spraying into the air from burrow entrances as the birds set about spring cleaning. Often an inquisitive mate, attracted by the flurry of activity, would find itself showered with earth if it chose the wrong moment to peer into the burrow. In wet weather the puffins presented a sorry sight as they emerged from their labours with their perfect, white breasts stained with mud.

A period of settling-in and courtship followed, combined

63

with a little perfunctory nest-building. The birds were often seen tugging at nearby flowers and strutting round with their beaks brim-full of tangled plants, as though proudly displaying their finds to their neighbours, but the resulting construction was really no more than a handful of dried vegetation at the bottom of the burrow. When the egg was laid, and incubation began in earnest, there came a slightly quieter period at the puffin colony, with the birds spending long periods either underground or out at sea feeding. In common with many seabirds the puffin lays only one egg so that both parents can devote all their energies to raising a single, sturdy chick, strong enough to face the rigours of the open sea.

When we saw the first puffin return to the cliff, its beak overflowing with a neat row of glistening sand eels, we knew the chicks were beginning to hatch. The birds worked furiously now to supply enough food for their rapidly growing chicks. From dawn to dusk they could be seen darting down their burrows with their prized catches. This was also a good time for the gulls. These lazy, scheming birds had realised that there was no need to find their own food when they could wait on the cliff top for the puffins to return with fish. A little puffin could not hope to fend off an attack from a gull, and so relied on speed or stealth to deliver a feed to the waiting chick. Some would fly with incredible precision straight down the mouth of the burrow. Others would land some way off, and then run at full speed to safety while the gull was not looking. The gulls were tenacious in their search for food, and were sometimes seen to grab the tail of a puffin as it disappeared below ground, drag it to the surface, and shake it until the fish fell from its beak.

It was at this time of year that immature puffins swelled the numbers of breeding birds. Usually between the ages of two and four years they return each summer to the place of their birth to look and learn. It is a relatively relaxed period in their lives, culminating in the serious business of choosing their own burrow in preparation for breeding the following spring. Distinguishable by their narrow, unridged beaks, these birds are fascinated by everything that happens around them. Forming themselves into little groups they would run en masse to the scene of any excitement. Fights were a favourite spectator sport, and the youngsters would encircle the tussling pair, leaning forward and poking their beaks as close to the action as they dared, to ensure no fragment of the drama was missed. Although puffins may appear docile, even comical, fights between them can be fierce and furious, but fortunately rarely result in serious injury. We often watched as the birds wrestled with their beaks locked tightly together, wings and feet flailing in the air. It was not unusual for the struggle to end with both birds plunging over the edge of the cliff, and continuing the fight undaunted as they hurtled towards the rocks below. At first we found this very alarming until we realised that they always broke off the combat and flew to safety a split second before crashing to their deaths.

Our house was built at the edge of a puffin colony, and was not considered out of bounds. Throughout the breeding season our roof resounded to the patter of puffin feet from the scores of birds which lined its apex. When a fight broke out overhead the noise was quite deafening as the birds clattered across the wooden shingles. I was once startled by a thud on the roof of the garage which extended to one side of the house. It seemed that the quarrelling pair had fallen from the main roof above and, mistiming their descent, had met unexpectedly with the garage while still locked in combat. Ruffled, but unhurt, they beat a hasty retreat.

When the house was first built the puffins had apparently considered the chimney to be the ultimate burrow, and surprised birds would occasionally emerge, via the fireplace, into the living room. Fortunately this practice had almost stopped by the time we came to the island, but one day I heard a strange noise coming from the wood-burning stove which had replaced the open fire. I opened the door and looked inside, but it was quite empty. Passing the room some hours later I again heard a scrabbling sound emanating from the stove, and again close inspection of the interior revealed nothing. When Mike returned I told him, and we both examined the empty stove which contained only a thin layer of ash. Mike had obviously put it all down to my imagination, but was too polite to say so, when the noise came again. A further check of the inside of the stove proved fruitless. Eventually Mike lifted off the lid. Before we knew what was happening a flurry of soot shot past us into the room, and a thin and very dirty puffin landed in the corner. It had obviously come down the chimney, entered the pipe to the stove, and become stuck in the small gap above the water heater. Quickly retrieving the puffin before it could spread any more soot across the carpet, Mike studied the bird carefully. It seemed none the worse for its ordeal, apart from having lost some weight, and Mike decided that the best medicine for this casualty would be to get it back into the fresh air as soon as possible. When the bird was released it hurtled off without a backward glance, determined, I am sure, never again to set eyes on the inside of a chimney.

As the time approached for the puffin chicks to fledge we watched the colonies carefully each evening, and were usually rewarded by the sight of a young bird emerging from the entrance to its burrow. In the last few days before leaving the island the chicks would stand at the front of their burrows to stretch their wings and survey the world. Considering that their lives had been spent in darkness, they greeted their first sight of sea and sky and cliffs with remarkable equanimity. They were rather drab little birds, having already attained the shape of an adult puffin, though still only about six inches tall. They had black legs, and a dark grey face from which protruded a small, black beak. The young puffins waited until nightfall so that they could fledge, unseen, from the island. If we ventured on to the cliffs early on a July night we could see the determined little creatures scurrying about in preparation for their plunge into the darkness. Their wings were sufficiently well developed to allow them to flutter gently to the sea. A young puffin does not have the advantage of a parent bird to guide it through its first bewildering weeks of freedom. As the fledgling splashes into the cold sea it has reached independence, and must learn by its own resources to sink or swim. It is not surprising that perhaps only one in five of these chicks will live long enough to return and breed on the island.

One evening, as Mike was working on the dam wall of the new pond started the previous year in North Valley, a puffin chick, fledging rather early in the day, found itself in the small, muddy pool at the bottom of the uncompleted pond. Overhead gulls wheeled and called, hoping for a taste of young puffin, but disturbed by the human presence. The puffin should have escaped in darkness, and been well away from the island and its gulls by daybreak. Now completely disorientated and far from the cliffs it would never have run the gauntlet of gulls to the sea, so Mike picked it out of the dirty water and brought it home. In common with many young birds it had not learnt to fear people, and happily explored our kitchen until darkness fell.

When the time came for the puffin to leave we decided to spare it the ordeal of plunging over the cliff edge, and carried it to the beach. As we walked down all was quiet. The gulls, no longer able to hunt in the dark, had settled down for the night.

'You'll be safe now,' we told the bird, but it seemed un-impressed.

When Mike placed the chick gently down it pattered rapidly over the wet pebbles with its strange, upright gait and hopped into the sea. It seemed momentarily surprised by the sensation of floating in the water, but soon found its feet, and paddled furiously into the night, until all we could see were the ripples it had left on the smooth sea.

The chicks fledged in July, and by August the last of the immature puffins, seeking burrows for their first breeding season the following year, had left. For us this was a sad time which hinted at the end of summer.

Whenever I was watching the puffins with their immaculate black and white plumage and ludicrously over-sized beaks as they strutted with jerky, jaunty movements across the cliff tops like rows of identical clockwork toys, I was sure that they must be my favourite birds. But deep down my greatest admiration was saved for the shearwaters, who thrived on a staggeringly arduous way of life. Skomer is the breeding site for 100,000 pairs of Manx shearwaters, about one quarter of the world population. We were therefore acutely aware of the importance of the survival of the Skomer colony, and held these birds in special regard. For the day visitor to Skomer no sight or sound of the shearwater could be detected, and only the astonishing honeycomb of burrows covering every acre of the island bore silent testimony to the vast shearwater colony. During the daytime the birds would be deep underground with their eggs, or far out to sea feeding, well away from Skomer's airborne predators. Below ground, in the darkness of their narrow burrows, the shearwaters were safe; there were no wingless aggressors stalking the island, and this was the secret of their success. Skomer is one of the few places completely free of ground predators, with nothing more threatening than a rabbit.

Rats, foxes or any sort of predator capable of entering a burrow to take eggs or young, or able to hunt shearwaters on the ground at night, would very quickly destroy the colony.

The shearwaters confined their visits to Skomer to the night-time, when avian predators such as great black-backed gulls and ravens were grounded by darkness. Even a bright moon would guide an airborne raider to its prey, and so this pale light alone was enough to still the calls of the shearwater. On a moonlit night all was silence, except for the occasional rapid flutter of a shearwater forced by necessity to return to its burrow. If the visit had to be made on a moonlit night it was done quickly and noiselessly, the burrow located and entered with unhesitating precision. On a dark, foggy or overcast night the situation was completely different. No sooner had total blackness descended than the relative tranquillity of the daytime was shattered by thousands upon thousands of calling, tumbling, crashing birds. It seemed that the exact degree of darkness was critical, and as soon as this point was reached the birds emerged from the obscurity of the sky as if from nowhere. The air reverberated to a hundred thousand discordant calls. It is a cry impossible to describe, but once heard it is never forgotten. It is harsh, high-pitched and very loud; a few discordant notes repeated endlessly. But for me its sheer exuberance made it perfect, and if there were one sound that I could choose to hear again now it would be the cacophonous serenade of the shearwater.

The shearwaters did not confine their activities to the outside, but nested in the cellar of our house. It was felt that as the house had been built on shearwater territory, it was only fair to return the land to its rightful owners. To this end numerous holes were left around the base of the house leading to nest boxes in the cellar, which replaced the stolen burrows. At some point before our arrival the nest boxes had been removed, and the shearwaters now had the run of the cellar. They put this to good use, and one enterprising pair established its nest just below our bed with only a layer of floorboards separating us from our noisy neighbours. When the calling began the noise was so powerful it was hard to believe that the birds were not in the room with us. Often it was only the first hint of dawn that lulled these night-birds into silence. When I first heard these discordant noises bubbling up through the floorboards I could not imagine ever being able to sleep through them, but I quickly grew accustomed to the sounds and, if I was lying awake, found them quite comforting. It was only occasionally, after a night of tossing and turning and frayed nerves that Mike cursed them for their choice of nesting place.

Venturing out at night had to be undertaken with extreme caution, especially if the night was windy or foggy. The air was so full of birds that the chance of being hit by a low-flying shearwater was very high. I tried to keep alert at all times, and always ducked if the rush of wings sounded uncomfortably close. It was necessary to rely on ears and instinct, since by the time visual contact was made in the darkness it was already too late to avoid a collision. Some mystery surrounds the shearwater's amazing navigational abilities, but I suspected that their eyesight was little better than mine, and was therefore happy to share the responsibility for taking evasive action. I had never heard of anyone being seriously hurt by a shearwater, but I imagined that being struck in the eye by a sharp beak would be dangerous, while Mike and I could both testify that a direct hit on the head or stomach was a stunning experience.

Once settled on the ground the shearwaters are very approachable, and can be observed at close quarters. They are relatively small for seabirds, having a body only about the size of a pigeon's, but with very long, slim wings. Black above and white below, they have round, dark eyes and a thin, black beak, curved down at the tip. One of the most unusual things about their appearance is the fact that the legs are set so far back on the body that the shearwater is unable to walk, or even stand. Although this makes the birds ideally suited to swimming, on land they seem awkward and cumbersome as they shuffle their bodies along the ground. This also means that once landed the shearwaters have great difficulty taking off again, which makes them very vulnerable, and explains their highly developed strategy for avoiding predators. The easiest method for take-off would simply be to launch from a steep slope close to a cliff edge, but as the birds nested over the whole island, including the interior, this was usually not possible. The favoured methods for achieving the required uplift were to clamber on to a wall or high rock and launch themselves from an elevated position, or to use an open patch of ground or footpath as a makeshift runway, and to scramble along these, wings flapping, until at last becoming airborne. These valiant attempts often ended in exhaustion, with the bird stopping so abruptly it tumbled forward beak first.

The shearwaters were among the first birds to arrive on the island each year, and were the last to leave at the end of the breeding season. Although this was just their breeding pattern, it was easy to convince ourselves that the shearwaters showed some special loyalty towards Skomer. We listened avidly for the first shearwater call from the beginning of March, and the last of the fledging young were still with us in October. Distance seemed to have no meaning to the shearwaters, choosing as they did to overwinter each year off the shores of South America. Arriving back on the island in spring they appeared as fresh from their 6,500 mile journey as if they had just hopped across from the mainland. And when the time came for them to find food for their young they did not, like other birds, plunge into the well-stocked waters around Skomer and return, with beaks laden, in twenty minutes. The shearwaters took several days to fly to the Bay of Biscay and back, so that the chick could be treated to a diet of sardines. Sometimes, looking down at a shearwater, I found it hard to believe that this little bird had probably travelled further in one year than I would travel in a lifetime.

The shearwaters are the most assiduous of parents. Having the longest incubation and fledging period of any bird on Skomer, the adults are kept occupied in producing their chicks for a large part of the year. Like the puffin, the shearwater keeps the same mate and the same burrow providing they rear their chicks successfully. Since a shearwater can live well into its thirties, some of Skomer's burrows would have been occupied by the same birds for many years. Shearwaters spend a long time settling in and feeding themselves until they are in peak condition. When the egg is finally laid both birds share the incubation. This must be a very tedious time since the incubation period is almost two months and while one of the pair is away feeding the other will remain sitting on the egg for long periods without a break.

Cramped in the confines of a dark burrow without food the birds would become restless, and the degree of frustration was obvious among the residents of our cellar as the calling grew more continuous and more insistent each evening as they tried to attract their returning mate.

The effort expended in rearing the newly-hatched chick is

enormous. The adult bird remains with the chick only for the first few days, and then both parents work full-time at providing food. The young bird is able to survive long periods without eating, as feeds carried such long distances are few and far between, but the chick grows rapidly on so rich a diet. The fish are swallowed by the adult bird and then regurgitated on to the burrow floor for the chick. We quickly learned the importance of not handling adult shearwaters during this period. A disgruntled bird was likely to shower an unwitting meddler with a cascade of warm, partially digested sardines. The smell was disgusting and clung for days, the oily residue defying the onslaught of soap and water. Worse still was the knowledge that the poor bird had lost the feed it had travelled so many miles to catch.

When fully grown the young shearwaters were approximately one-and-a-half times the weight of the adult bird; no half-grown creature could be expected to face the test of endurance these birds would undergo. By the middle of August many birds were reaching peak weight. They were enormous and soft, enveloped in a thick blanket of grey down, the first wisps of which were already beginning to moult. A long, black beak with down-curved tip, a perfect replica of the adult's, emerged from the profusion of fluff, and glittering black eyes were just visible. At this time the colony began to grow quieter as fewer and fewer parent birds were returning to their chicks. The clamouring cries of the adults faded, to be replaced only by the occasional squeak of a chick. The chicks were abandoned by the adults up to ten days before fledging. They spent the intervening period living off their fat, and shedding their down, until they were reduced from balls of fluff to the sleek, streamlined shape of an adult shearwater. At this stage chicks and adults were indistinguishable, except under the closest scrutiny. A slight difference in colour, a lack of abrasion on feathers or legs, or a scrap of remaining down might be enough to distinguish adult from chick. When it came to censusing the fledging youngsters it was important to know the difference, not only in the interests of scientific accuracy, but also to avoid an unwelcome dousing in warm sardines. I discovered that my first impressions were usually right. The young were soft to touch, still padded by excess fat, while the adults felt hard and muscular, indicating that their sturdy wings had already carried them many thousands of miles.

Although peak fledging was in late August and early September, some would remain on the island for a further month. On any dark night from mid-August onwards it was possible to see young shearwaters preparing to leave. The colony looked little changed, the missing adults having been replaced by tens of thousands of almost identical youngsters, but the uncharacteristic silence gave it a sad, end-of-season feeling. The young shearwaters, however, were a delight to watch. Many were still in the latter stages of moulting, and retained incongruous tufts of down. The last down to be shed was often on the head, giving the faintly ludicrous impression of a wig. The birds were very active at this stage, enjoying for the first time the freedom to stretch their wings, after a short lifetime confined in a burrow. High points such as rocks and walls were much in demand and in the densest parts of the colony disorderly queues formed around these projections. There was a small, pyramid-shaped rock above North Haven where I knew I would always find a crowd of birds. Clambering to the top with difficulty, the youngsters would flap their wings energetically until toppled from the perch by their own lack of balance or an impatient onlooker anxious to take its turn. Inevitably there would come a time when this was no longer just an exercise, and in an ungainly scramble the fledgling would launch itself into the air. For a moment it could be seen held aloft for the first time on its slender wings and then it disappeared into the darkness.

No matter how many hundreds of times I saw this, I always felt overawed by the courage of the young bird. A shearwater who had never flown before, never even seen the light of day, was embarking, quite alone, on a journey of many thousands of miles to the South Atlantic. I looked at the young birds, incredulous that at a few weeks old they knew things I would never understand. I wondered by what communication the parent birds forewarned the chick of the journey it must make, or whether there was an inbred knowledge, already firmly implanted when it hatched from its shell. And how could a bird whose whole life had been spent in the dank, earthy walls of an underground burrow on a tiny Welsh island find the shores of South America? These were thoughts that troubled me often, but I knew that it was their mystery that made shearwaters so special, and part of me hoped that no-one would ever answer these questions.

After two long years at sea the birds would return, with the same unerring accuracy, to the place of their origin, to touch land again for the first time since fledging. The navigational skill of the shearwater is incredible, whether on a scale of thousands of miles or just a few feet. From the tens of thousands of burrows on Skomer a returning shearwater could always locate its own, even on the blackest of nights.

Despite their delicate streamlined appearance, the shearwaters were among the sturdiest of birds. In the darkness they covered the ground so thickly, and seemed so intent on placing themselves in the path of a hapless walker that, however careful our attempts to avoid them, I occasionally had the heart-stopping feeling that one was underfoot. Dismay would turn to relief when invariably the birds emerged unhurt and completely unperturbed. On a foggy or very windy night it felt as though our house was under siege. Disorientated shearwaters battered our walls and windows with remarkable force. As it seemed that under these confusing conditions the lighted windows attracted them, we were often left with no option but to turn out the lights and go to bed. However, when we surveyed the battlefield in the light of day, it was very unusual to find that a single bird had been killed. One evening we were startled by an unusually forceful thud, followed by a noisy tumble down the roof and a crash onto the garage. We looked at each other and then went to look outside. Through the window we could see the lifeless form of a shearwater lying on its back on the garage roof, wings outstretched and head lolling to one side. We clambered through the window on to the roof to examine the bird, and were amazed to find it still alive, though completely unconscious. No trace of injury could be found so, placing it upright and folding its wings over its back, we left it in peace. When we went to check its progress half an hour later it had staged a remarkable recovery and left. We often wondered how a shearwater could find its way from one end of the Atlantic to the other, but not manage to avoid our house.

I was standing in the kitchen late one night by the large window that overlooked North Haven, finishing a few last-minute chores before bedtime. A northerly wind sprang up quite suddenly, and within minutes the familiar sound started as shearwaters, driven by the wind, bombarded the house. It was such a regular occurrence that I hardly noticed it until I was jolted by a splintering crash. The window two feet in front of me caved in, and I ducked, covering my face, as glass rained over my head and down my neck. It felt

73

as though it would never stop. When at last the noise subsided I remained with my muscles tensed and hands over my eyes for some seconds, unsure whether I had been cut and afraid to find out. As I eased my hands away I could see no blood, but just a tiny white feather resting on the worktop. I turned to find that a shearwater had entered with such force that it had come to rest against the far wall of the room. I also noticed that it was shaking even more than I was, but not a drop of blood stained its feathers. As Mike arrived, bleary-eyed from bed, I began to recover my senses, and realised that I was standing in a sea of broken glass. How could so much glass come from one window? Mike took the shearwater out and placed it on the doorstep, and we then set about clearing up the mess. It was at this point that we noticed my freshly-baked pies arrayed on the table, their foil covers pierced by shards of glass. There was no option but to consign them to the bin, but first Mike went outside and found the shearwater still sitting by the door. He picked it up and returned it to the scene of its crime.

'Look what you've done,' Mike said, holding it in front of the glass-strewn pies. The shearwater appeared unrepentant.

Ideally, shearwaters should be encountered for the first time at sea. I spent months thinking of them as noisy, clumsy creatures after my introduction to them on land, and when I first saw them at sea I was amazed by the transformation. They gathered in large rafts out at sea during the daytime, gradually moving inshore, in anticipation of the darkness that would secure their safe passage to the island. By late evening these rafts were usually only a mile or two off the coast of Skomer.

I can still remember clearly the first evening when we put to sea in our little boat to visit the rafting shearwaters. The sea was calm, just gently ruffled by the breezes, and in the evening light its daytime blue had faded to grey. The sky was dominated by a huge, red sun low on the horizon, its fiery glare paled to a smoulder. The rosy light dappled the sea with an ever-changing kaleidoscope of colour, and set the wispy clouds alight. The damp chill of the sea breezes belied the golden warmth of the light. We scanned the horizon in search of a raft of shearwaters, and when we saw the dark pool of birds we headed rapidly in their direction, the boat leaving a trail of sun-lit ripples on the water.

As we approached the birds Mike stopped the engine, and I was stunned by the unexpected silence. The only sound was the gentle lapping of waves against the boat. Having always associated shearwaters with the strident medley of calls that continued unabated throughout their visits to Skomer, I had never considered that at sea they would be silent except for the occasional high-pitched squeak. We rowed the last stage of the journey to the shearwater raft to preserve the stillness of the evening and the tranquillity of the birds. The oars cut smoothly through the water, rising and falling with a shower of golden drops. When we were as close as we dared venture we stowed the oars and watched the elegant, noiseless birds as if seeing them for the first time. Eventually, as though at some command inaudible to our ears, they rose in unison, churning the surface of the sea and shattering the silence. As they circled repeatedly, the flock so large it seemed to enclose us, I knew that I was seeing shearwaters as they should be seen. They flew very low over the waves with graceful ease, their long, elegant wings almost breaking the surface. They moved swiftly, turning as they went, dipping first one wing and then the other towards the sea, flickering from black to white as they twisted. It was easy to see how they justified their name and how they could cover such remarkable distances. But the spectacle was short-lived, and quickly the birds moved off and landed again, a united group on the distant sea.

These visits to the rafting shearwaters were comparatively rare, and so inevitably it is the noisy night-time birds whose memory is etched most indelibly on my mind, but I try never to forget these birds as they should be seen, at sea, in their own element.

SEVEN

W HEN SEPTEMBER CAME and the shearwaters were fledging I knew
that we were almost certainly due for a period of storms. (The
young shearwaters caught up in these storms could face serious
problems. They were sometimes blown off course and deposited
exhausted in streets and gardens on the mainland, often to the
amazement of the residents who had never seen such a bird before.)
It was at this period as the shearwaters were leaving that any late visitors abandoned the island and all boating activity between Skomer
and the mainland came abruptly to a halt. And this was when we
began again what we could not help but refer to as the winter; our
period of solitude.

Our second winter was undoubtedly the worst. This was due
to two factors; the first being long, unbroken periods of stormy
weather, and the second being our boat. After Mike's narrow
escape at sea the previous September we had decided that we
did not want to keep the dory any longer. On land it was
heavy and unmanageable; barely possible for the two of us to
manhandle down the beach. In the water its flat bottom meant
that it bounced over the waves instead of riding through them.
Not only did this make the boat uncomfortable and difficult to
control in rough weather, but it meant that we took on board so
much water that it was impossible to keep our stores dry on the
journey from the mainland. Finally, we needed a good, powerful
engine and a reliable back-up to carry such a boat safely across
the sounds, and these we did not have. We decided instead
to buy a new boat. The one we chose was small, only thirteen
foot, and made of fibreglass, but built to a traditional design

so that it rode the waves beautifully. It was light enough to be driven safely by Seagull engines which, while lacking in power, were simple enough for Mike to repair and service on the island, which meant that we were not left stranded while our unreliable old engine was away on the mainland for repairs. Of course it was not ideal. New, powerful engines and a bigger boat would have been better, but the finances of the West Wales Naturalists' Trust would not run to that, and I have to admit I loved the little blue boat. It took a great deal of the trauma and tantrums out of boat launching, but although it battled through anything we and the weather asked of it, crashing determinedly through the waves, the engines often had barely enough power to carry us through. Worse still, they could be temperamental, and my heart always missed a beat when they spluttered and died, leaving us wallowing helplessly in the sounds. Consequently, we needed to wait for reasonably calm weather before we dared make the crossing to the mainland.

As the autumn wore on we went through the whole of October without being able to get fresh supplies from the mainland. We were so well prepared for this, both mentally and practically with good stocks of food and fuel, that I greeted this isolation with a resignation bordering on enthusiasm. The weather had been so bad throughout this period that, to my relief, the possibility of going ashore had not even been discussed. The thing I dreaded most was Mike deciding that we should make the crossing to the mainland when I was sure that the sea was too rough.

We were cut off in our own little world, even enjoying the storms that proceeded one after another, but as October stretched into November I did not realise that there was a cloud looming on the horizon. During our first few years on Skomer Mike was a heavy smoker and, although he found it an irritating and distasteful habit, all attempts to stop had failed. With the slight sense of guilt common to many smokers Mike would not admit the size of the problem, even to himself, and would not buy enough cigarettes when the opportunity was available. Inevitably, his stocks of tobacco began to run low. He had been cheerfully burning his way through the rapidly dwindling stockpile of cigarettes until he was down to the last packet, and there was still no sign of the weather improving sufficiently for a trip ashore. Suddenly panic took over, and Mike's cigarette intake was drastically reduced to three a day. With this severe rationing the remaining packet was eked out for a week. As the last cigarette was smoked to a tiny, grimy stub and storms still raged outside, despair set in.

I had anticipated such a catastrophe, and in the days of plenty had smuggled a single packet of cigarettes from the store, and kept it hidden. The following morning, taking the box from the drawer where it had lain concealed under a thick jumper for many weeks, I tied it with a pink bow and placed it on the breakfast table. Some time later Mike shuffled despondently into the kitchen to face his first cigarette-free day. Throwing open the window he hung his head outside and stared menacingly at the long, rolling, white-crested waves, obviously blaming them for his fate. It was not until some minutes later that he closed the window and turned towards the breakfast table. He froze for a moment in disbelief, perhaps suspecting that it was only a mirage, uncertain whether to throw his arms round me or the cigarette packet first.

At a miserly three cigarettes a day the packet lasted for a further week. During this time we listened avidly to the weather forecasts. It was weeks since the predicted wind speeds had been below gale force. By now I was beginning to share a little of Mike's anxiety to get ashore. We had enough supplies to last for many more weeks, but mealtimes were becoming tedious, and all the food we had left was very unappetising. I wasted a great deal of time thinking about chocolate sponge, filled with cream and smothered with rich icing. My collection of cake recipes was so well thumbed that the ink was wearing from the pages.

By the time the last fragment of the last cigarette was smoked Mike was very dejected and irritable. The next morning he looked at me hopefully, half wondering if I might be about to produce another packet of cigarettes from concealment, but I had to tell him honestly that there were no more. This was not the first time Mike had run out of cigarettes. There had been the time when he had fallen in the sea with the last packet in his pocket, and the occasion when he had gone to his cigarette drawer to find that a mouse had beaten him to it and shredded the lot. But this had been a particularly long period of deprivation.

When, for the first time in many weeks, we woke to hear that the wind was no longer beating against the house Mike leapt excitedly out of bed. After a few minutes he returned and announced that the sea was calm enough for us to make the crossing. I followed after him gloomily and padded barefoot across the cold kitchen floor to the window. I protested, as I always did unless the sea was mirror-calm, that it was too rough. The sea was steely grey and threatening, but it was no longer scattered with white-topped waves, and I knew that I had no hope of dissuading Mike, so I prepared to leave. Dressed in boots and oilskins we trudged down to the beach, and the boat was soon launched. The boat handled beautifully on the slipway, but in that sort of weather it did not inspire a great deal of confidence at sea.

The moment we left the shelter of North Haven we felt the first wave. It was dark and solid and, approaching rapidly, it towered above us. At first I thought we were going to be swamped, but the wave slid beneath the boat, lifting it on to the crest and propelling it forward with alarming speed before releasing its grip and allowing the boat to sink slowly down the other side. I thought perhaps we had just met a freak wave, but before I could recover my breath I saw another bearing down upon us. Sunk in the trough between two waves, watery walls rose steeply on either side of us, and we could see nothing but deep grey sea. Moments later we rose again to the wave top, and the boat was swept forward like a surf board. It was as though all the power from weeks of gale force winds was now locked into the sea. The foamy, white, wind-tumbled breakers of the storms were gone, but these moving mountains of water had a terrifying force.

From the cliff top, in the dull half-light of morning, the absence of white water had made the sea appear relatively calm; from where we now sat it looked awesome. But there was no turning back. If we caught one of the waves side-on while we were trying to turn we were afraid it would flip the boat over. We could only go forward, and let the waves meet us steadily from behind. We put on our life-jackets, and I took some distress flares from their waterproof canister and held them tight. Gripping the handle of the outboard hard Mike stared doggedly ahead. Neither of us spoke, and I listened anxiously to the steady sound of the engine, terrified that it might falter.

The further we went the rougher the sea grew as the huge, rolling swell met the turbulent waters of the sounds. We knew however that the most perilous part of our journey would be off Wooltack Point, the mainland promontory which stretched out towards Little Sound. By the time we reached this passage of water the waves had increased in size tremendously, and one glance into Martin's Haven, where the waves were shattering against the beach in a haze of white spray, told us we couldn't land. Quickly Mike spun the boat round, glimpsing as he did so my horrified expression. As the waves had grown in size, so too had the gap between them, and Mike thought there would be just time to turn the boat in the trough between two waves. The manoeuvre seemed agonisingly slow as the mass of water rushed to meet us, threatening to roll us over, but the boat was almost straight as the first wave hit us head on.

The return journey was grimmer still as the swell was surging in from the west straight towards us. Meeting the oncoming wave the boat slowed almost to a halt as the engine struggled to force it up the steep slope of water that pushed relentlessly in the opposite direction. Reaching the top of the wave the bow of the boat fell forward with a jarring crash as it crossed the peak of water, and slid rapidly down the other side as the wave moved away from us. I felt tiny and powerless in the face of the invincible strength of the waves. The boat seemed like a cork bobbing at the whim of the sea. I was sure that if the engine failed now we would have no chance of escape and be smashed into the rocks. I could feel the fear aching deep inside, and yet I remained calm, willing the boat over every wave. Our progress was painfully slow, and the succession of climbs, which the engine barely had the power to make, and plunging descents continued interminably until we reached the calm of North Haven.

As we moved towards the slipway I turned back to watch the huge waves sweeping from west to east across St Bride's Bay, and I felt enormously relieved to be back in the shelter of Skomer. The boat touched the shore and I climbed tentatively out on to the stones, making sure my trembling legs would support my weight.

'And I didn't even get my cigarettes,' groaned Mike.

I gave him a long, sideways look, just to make sure he was joking. Thankfully Mike did eventually give up smoking, but I have to confess that during the transition period we made one or two wet and bumpy crossings in pursuit of wine gums before he was finally cured.

Now that we were back on the island with no addition to our

supplies, though, even I had to agree that we were in desperate need of a trip to the mainland. We had been cut off for a month and a half, and the lack of cigarettes combined with a lack of appetising food were whittling away at Mike's temper. One of the biggest problems was actually coming up with ideas for something palatable to make out of the limited ingredients we had left. One night, when we were totally stumped for ideas Mike retired to the large, walk-in food cupboard with a chair, lit the gaslight, and sat surveying the half-empty shelves in the hope that they would provide inspiration. When even this failed to produce a solution he emerged defeated and snapped at me in accusing tones, 'Can't you think of anything?'

Unwilling to take the blame for a situation that was beyond my control I leapt to my defence, but before the situation escalated into a full-scale argument we decided on a joint expedition to the food cupboard to review the situation.

We were both standing in the larder pondering the vexed question. A small group of tins was clustered half-hidden on a high shelf. They were the things we didn't much like that had been pushed out of sight in the days when we could afford to be selective. Now they offered a glimmer of hope. As Mike moved the tins into view, one by one they were dismissed as useless. We both hated butter beans, and what could we do with evaporated milk? One last tin lurked at the back, its label tinged with spots of rust. Mike spun it round and a dish of pallid pear halves came into view. I wrinkled my nose in disgust, but Mike was suddenly animated by a flash of excitement.

'Why don't you make us a pear sponge?' he said, clutching my shoulders and obviously quite smitten with the excellence of the scheme.

I hesitated a moment since dinner, to me, meant something savoury, but brushing aside my preconceptions I hastened to agree.

'Yes,' I said, already feeling enthusiastic, but before the words had left my lips I realised the problem. 'There aren't enough eggs,' I said, fumbling with the egg box. Then, 'Yes there are. There are two here.'

'And you could flavour it with cinnamon,' Mike continued, eyeing the shelf of spices – the only one that looked respectably full.

81

'And I could make some chocolate sauce to go with it,' I joined in, really warming to the subject now.

It was not long before the sponge was made and in the oven. I began to tidy the kitchen, placing the mixing bowl by the sink ready to wash and picking up the empty pear tin to throw away. As I did so I noticed one last half of pear forgotten in the bottom. Not wanting to waste it I retrieved the dish from the oven and pushed the extra piece of pear out of sight beneath the layer of sponge. The mixture was hot now, and the aroma had been brought to life by the cooking. I thought it was the most delicious thing I had ever smelt. As I was replacing the sponge in the oven my hand touched the hot metal shelf. Involuntarily I jerked it back, banging my elbow on the leg of the table behind me. The cake tin flew out of my hand and hit the floor in a cloud of fresh-baked fragrance. The heat had turned the sponge mixture to liquid and on impact it all slid from the tin leaving me unable to salvage anything. Hearing my anguished howl Mike immediately came running. One look at the golden, cinnamon-scented pool spreading across the floor and me slumped in the chair, head in hands, negated the need for words. Quickly and silently Mike set about clearing up the mess.

'I can't make another one, there's nothing left to make it with,' I wailed.

'It doesn't matter,' Mike said bravely, still scraping at the sticky smudge on the floor.

I almost wished he'd been angry. At least then I could have soothed my conscience with injured innocence. As it was I only felt doubly guilty.

By now we had used up everything that made food inter-esting. I discovered a dozen different ways to disguise instant mashed potatoes, until all the ingredients were exhausted, and we were forced to eat the unadulterated mixture by the bowlful, with very little to accompany it. To make matters worse we were running short of food for the chickens, and I had to sort through the larder regularly in search of something to supplement their diet.

'Shall we give this to the chickens, or eat it ourselves?' I would ask Mike, holding up one of our less tempting store-cupboard items. I condemned a highly suspect sack of wholemeal flour with some relief, and allocated it to the chickens. I think the damp had got to it; it tasted bitter and I found tiny white caterpillars lurking in it. Using this I baked loaves for the chickens every day, and allowed the hot bread to cool on the way to the farm. These, together with some tinned butter which had not stood the test of time, were a great delicacy for the hens, and I almost envied them their wholemeal sandwiches.

Our hens had multiplied, but still we knew them all by name, and had grown very fond of them. The bold and aggressive Henrietta had numerous offspring. One of her daughters, Zuleika, was a complete contrast to her mother. She was a beautiful bird, almost jet black, but so shy we had to feed her away from the other hens, otherwise she would stand timidly on the sidelines, not daring to compete for her share of the grain. They were all watched over by Rover, a huge, white cockerel we had been given, who fussed solicitously over the hens and always saved the tastiest morsels to lay at the feet of his charges. Their egg production had declined dramatically for the winter, and eggs were in short supply. Sometimes we actually stood and waited for one of the hens to lay so that we could have an egg each instead of one between us. Fortunately, although they were completely free range, they usually obliged us by laying in the straw-lined boxes in their shed, saving us the trouble of hunting round the farmyard for eggs.

Occasionally in the summer, however, the urge would take one of them to build a nest in one of the thickets of bramble around the farm. Although we strongly discouraged this, it was often hard to detect, and if we found a hen sitting proudly on her clutch of eggs we did not have the heart to turn her off. So it was that that year we had a fine batch of growing, but unproductive, hens and eighteen cockerels. The latter were a problem. They had to be disposed of one way or another, and common sense told us we ought to eat them. From the first we tried to treat them with detachment; not calling them pet names, and trying not to notice their individual characters developing, but it was not easy. Faced, as we now were, with a shortage of food for ourselves and the chickens, it was impossible to delay any longer, and we decided that cockerel would feature on our menu. We planned to make it a special meal to relieve the tedium of weeks of tinned and dried food, and so we spent half a day digging over our vegetable plot to unearth a dozen small potatoes that had lain undiscovered in the ground. When the bird was cooked I hardly knew whether to laugh or cry; it looked totally unappetising. Being free-range, it had developed huge, muscular legs which refused to lie flat. We ate the meal with difficulty, and tried not to think of its origins. As soon as we managed to get ashore we gave away the other seventeen cockerels. I could easily guess their fate, but I preferred not to be responsible.

At least our isolation spared us from the usual winter problems we might have encountered; we had no fear of coming into contact with colds or flu. Nevertheless, there was something about the knowledge that we were out of reach of medical help that had a tendency to magnify minor ailments. I countered this with the certain knowledge that every complaint disappeared of its own accord if I waited long enough, and fortunately in my case it did. Mike sometimes became quite concerned about his health, but I cheerfully dismissed all his symptoms, convinced they would get worse the more he dwelt on them. There came a point when Mike had been complaining for several days of a rather vague collection of symptoms. As usual I tried to brush these aside, and glossed over the ones that refused to budge, but eventually even I became quite concerned. In desperation I turned to the rather old-fashioned medical section of our encyclopaedia and began to flick through in search of an explanation to the problem. I found some likely-sounding symptoms and began to read them out.

'Yes, yes,' Mike enthused in agreement as each new revelation seemed to describe his plight more accurately.

'Well, that's it,' I said with an air of mock solemnity, slamming the book with a satisfying echo for an added note of finality. 'I'm afraid you've got beriberi.'

We both laughed, although Mike did not seem to quite share my enthusiasm for the joke. I never heard any more about the beriberi symptoms, although afterwards I felt quite guilty, and even began to wonder if our limited diet might not lead to vitamin deficiencies, but decided that it was a subject best left to die a natural death.

We knew that if we were ever really ill or in need of help everything humanly possible would be done to come to our assistance, although there were of course times when the weather was so bad that we knew it would be impossible for anyone to reach us. The willingness with which this help was offered had been clearly demonstrated to us back in the summer. Mike had been smashing rocks with a sledgehammer when a splinter of stone flew into his eye and became embedded in the cornea. Although the weather had been rough and we had been cut off for some days, the boating season was not quite at an end and we felt certain that the passenger boat would still be in Martin's Haven. As the weather was growing more settled Mike called up the coastguard on the radio to see if the boat would be making the crossing to the island that day. His message was intercepted by a friendly helicopter pilot who happened to be passing, and help was on the way. Mike entered the helicopter with his eye carefully bandaged to indicate the location of the injury, since his ability to walk to the rescue helicopter unaided added little to the drama of the situation. As soon as he was strapped into the back of the helicopter and they were under way the pilot passed back a note scrawled on a message board. It read simply, 'The things you do for cigarettes'.

Transport seemed to be a perennial problem; if we were not struggling with the boat, we were struggling with the tractor. Problems of this sort were always intensified during periods of isolation because whatever went wrong we had to sort out by ourselves. The tractor was an essential ingredient of our lives, and was in almost daily use, carrying everything from gas cylinders to building materials, or bringing our supplies up the cliff from the landing beach. It was also used for towing the boat, digging ponds, clearing blocked tracks and to power our ancient cement mixer. In fact the list was endless, and we certainly could not have imagined being without it.

I was very fond of our first tractor. It was small and manageable, quiet and well-behaved, and being the original tractor brought over when the island first became a reserve had, I felt, a certain sentimental and historical value. Unfortunately, as time went on it developed more and more faults, and spare parts became increasingly unavailable. Old parts were mended, new bits were made, but some faults could not be repaired.

One day, having loaded the tractor to carry some fencing materials across the island, we could not start it. Mike tried everything, but eventually we resigned ourselves to the fact that there was no option but to manhandle the tractor up the steep track behind the house. By means of a small hand winch and ropes attached to stakes driven into the ground we dragged it inch by inch up the slope. As Mike worked the winch handle back and forth the rope stretched and strained, and only after several minutes of hard effort did the tractor begin to edge up the track. We could only progress a few feet before the heavy metal stakes had to be moved, and the whole process began again. While Mike toiled hard with the winch I strained against the tractor wheels, gradually rolling them up the slope. The grit from the tyres ground so deeply into my palms that it remained for many months. We progressed with painful slowness, but after an hour and a half we had moved the tractor somewhere in the region of a hundred yards up the slope. We convinced ourselves that that was far enough, and we set about rolling it back down the hill to get it started. The tractor picked up speed, and I pushed hard at the back. The tractor coughed and spluttered. Black smoke churned in irregular clouds from the exhaust. The engine turned more quickly and I pushed with all my strength, willing it to start, but the slope was running out, the speed died away, and the tractor slid to a gradual halt, as dead as when we had started. An hour and a half of hard work was wasted in a few seconds. The disappointment was indescribable. We just looked at each other and, with hardly a pause, began the long haul again.

We knew that this time we would have to get the tractor even higher up the slope, and in a little more than two hours we had achieved what we believed to be sufficient height. This time the prospect of failure made us almost afraid to try again. The tractor careered down the slope, the engine turned reluctantly and slowly, again spraying black smoke into the air. We were running out of time; we were not going to make it. Then, with only a few yards of track left, the engine burst into life. It whirred for a second, and then it roared, as if in triumph. It was one of the most welcome sounds I have ever heard.

By the time we had reloaded the tractor and set off to start work we had been delayed almost four hours, and were already exhausted. We were building a rabbit-proof exclosure at the Wick to monitor the effect that rabbits were having on the vegetation. This involved cordoning off a large area with a fence whose bottom edge was buried three feet into the ground, or at least until it reached rock, to prevent the rabbits from digging their way in to the greener grass inside the fence. The soil at the Wick was thin and stony; digging through it was blistering work.

I set off walking behind the tractor with a distinct lack of enthusiasm. When we had come as far as the tractor track would take us it was necessary to strike out across rough, bracken-covered ground to reach the cliff top destination where we were building the exclosure. We were almost there when the tractor began to descend a slope. The underside hit a rock concealed in the bracken. The front tipped forward down the slope, lifting the back into the air. The tractor was stranded, pivoted on the rock with its back wheels off the ground. It was the sort of extraordinary occurrence that would be almost impossible to create deliberately, but somehow happened all too easily by chance. Mike leapt to the ground and strode round the machine staring in angry disbelief. I stood back, trying to make myself as invisible as possible, and uttering silent thanks that I had not been driving at the time.

We hauled and pushed, and it soon became obvious that we were not going to extricate ourselves from this mess without a struggle. There was the added problem of not being able to re-start the tractor, so we had to leave the engine running. We tried everything to no avail, and were very conscious of the fact that time was running short.

'Of course you realise that if we run out of diesel now, this tractor will never move again,' Mike fumed. He was never much comfort at times like this, but I did see his point. It was one thing pulling the tractor a few hundred yards up a track, but it was quite another to drag it over rough ground to the flat central fields, and then another half mile to find a slope steep enough to start it. As it was now November we knew that we could not expect any help before well into the next spring. Fortunately we had spades and fence posts in the back of the tractor which we put to good use making ramps and levers, but all our efforts invariably ended with the wheels spinning uselessly. Mike tried to drive the tractor while I strained against the lever until I felt sick. When this did not work we swapped places, and I reluctantly took my turn at the wheel of the tractor, with warnings against stalling it so dire as to be unrepeatable. Mike's extra strength on the lever helped, but still success eluded us. Time and again we came tantalisingly close, before the engine threatened to give up under the strain and we were forced to ease back. Eventually Mike gave an almighty wrench on the lever, born of sheer fury, and the tractor broke free. Much as I loved the old tractor, we sadly agreed that an island was no place for a vehicle that would not start, and that the time would come when we would have to consider the daunting problem of how to get a new tractor on to Skomer.

EIGHT

THE AUTUMN, when all the birds had abandoned the cliffs and the interior of the island leaving behind an empty stillness, marked the beginning of a new breeding season. During our early years North Haven was one of the most successful seal breeding sites on Skomer. It was also an important haul-out site. On autumn and winter nights, when everything else was quiet, the silence was broken by the sound of seals; not just the long, drawn-out howls, but the rattle of shingle as they moved up and down the beach and constantly rolled over to find a more comfortable position. Inevitably fights broke out, and we heard low, breathy snarling and the sound of pebbles being scattered as they lunged angrily at each other. Sitting by the fire in the glow of the gaslight, these sounds had a way of demanding our attention, and, as we invariably did on a moonlit night, we eventually found ourselves compelled to take a closer look.

Leaving the flickering warmth of the fire and stepping outside, the startling chill in the air was almost tangible. The night was still and cloudless, and a bright moon illuminated the silver sea. This starkly beautiful night came as an unexpected finale to a storm-battered day, and we paused a moment to breathe the still air and stand quietly without having to bow our heads against the buffeting wind. From the house we crossed the short distance to the cliff edge, proceeding with extreme caution as we came closer in case any careless sound disturbed the seals below us. The more carefully we moved, the more noise we made. Every stem of dry vegetation that we trampled underfoot cracked with a resounding echo, and even the rustle of our feet through the dewy grass sounded deafening. The moonlight was so strong it cast shadows, and its blue-grey light complemented and enhanced the natural colouring of the seals, giving them an ethereal quality rarely associated with so solid an animal. From our perch sixty feet above the colony we were able to watch unnoticed, something that was impossible in daylight when the ever-watchful seals would have detected our presence and fled in panic.

The seal pups that were born in North Haven were our special favourites. We watched them through every stage of their development, and grew very concerned for their safety, particularly when vicious northerly winds smashed the waves against the cliffs of North Haven. Although we tried not to be sentimental about these wild animals they became such a familiar part of our daily routine that they often developed nicknames. In the autumn of our third year a seal was born of which we grew unusually fond. He grew so rapidly that each day the change was remarkable. From a scrawny animal whose skin hung in loose folds he became gently rounded and then fat before progressing to positively obese. Not surprisingly we began to refer to him as The Barrel. Frequently we thought he must have reached peak weight, but each day he grew a little more, and still his mother kept on feeding him. He was a wonderfully contented animal, and was never heard to cry. Despite his vast size he still enjoyed a leisurely swim when the tide was in and he did not need to make the troublesome journey down the beach. Although I am sure it was just an illusion created by the layers of fat, he seemed permanently to have a huge grin on his face.

After about ten days The Barrel was joined by a second pup. This one was small and lively, in sharp contrast to The Barrel's sluggish contentment. The new arrival became known as Nipper. He was always on the move, and spent many hours swimming. Nipper was so agile in the water his mother could hardly keep up with him. Sometimes he plunged deep and then surfaced behind the cow seal leaving her still searching. On the Sunday when Nipper was about a week old we had a quick look at the pups before setting out to walk round the island. As we returned, the steep track above the house gave us a clear view of the eastern end of the beach, and we both thought we could see an extra white speck on the pebbles. As we came closer it was obvious that it was, as we had thought, a newborn pup, still damp and bloodstained. We were delighted to see the pup, but frustrated at having so narrowly missed the birth. At first glance all pups appear the same, but to the practised eye they differ greatly in size, shape and facial characteristics. This new arrival was unusually attractive; her fur golden and silky, her face blunt and delicate. In recognition of her beautiful colouring, and after Sunday the day of her birth, she was called Sunny.

The following day was one of those when summer returns for a few fleeting hours before winter takes its immovable grip. The sea was still, the sun shone with surprising warmth, and no hint of haze blurred the horizon. Although reluctant to leave the island on so perfect a day we had to take advantage of the opportunity, and were soon preparing to cross to the mainland to collect our post and some extra supplies from the village of Marloes. We launched the boat easily into the calm sea and left North Haven, the chugging of our engine the only sound to intrude upon the silence. On such days the crossing to the mainland was a pleasure. We were not wondering where the next wave was going to hit us, or staring anxiously ahead to the swirling waters of the sounds uncertain if it was safe to pass, or frantically rushing in the hope of returning to the secure haven of the island before the forecast gale arrived. Today we took our time, gliding slowly over the shiny water, stopping to watch the curious entourage of seals that followed us.

Mooring the boat in Martin's Haven and travelling three miles inland to the village we had time to take in the sights and smells of a mainland autumn, always very different to our own. Then there was that special excitement of receiving weeks of accumulated letters all in one day. We returned to the island at a gentle pace, making our way quietly up the coast exploring all the hidden bays and inlets. I always loved returning to the island; even a few hours' absence seemed too long. I could think of no more wonderful feeling than setting foot on my own beach again, with a bundle of letters to read, a newspaper that was not out of date, and fresh food for dinner.

That evening, however, our homecoming was shattered when we learned on the radio that an oil tanker had run aground on the Hats and Barrels, a reef of rocks about fifteen miles to our west, and that an oil slick had resulted. The tanker, the *Christos Bitas*, had apparently freed itself from the rocks and continued its passage up the coast with oil streaming from a hole in the hull. It was not until a plane had spotted the oil slick that the ship had been halted. The days that followed were very tense. Numerous boats were engaged to spray the oil in order to disperse it before it reached land. This method was proving reasonably successful until the autumn weather returned with a vengeance. Although the sea remained calm, a dense fog settled over the area. The plane that was co-ordinating the operation from above, guiding the spraying boats to the oil, was rendered sightless. The boats were left to continue their haphazard battle unassisted.

On the first evening we walked to the western end of the island and stared into the blankness. The grey was so intense we could not even distinguish rocks from sea on our own shore. On the second day the menacing stench of oil reached us. Enclosed in grey walls of fog we felt helpless and isolated, knowing only that the oil had to be moving closer. Towards the end of the third day the wind increased, lifting the fog slightly. We walked the north coast and saw traces of oil drifting along it. The wind changed to a more northerly quarter and, as darkness ended our anxious vigil, the first streaks of oil were pushed into North Haven.

By the following morning the wind was blowing at gale force straight into North Haven. In the half-light of dawn I tried to see if the pollution had reached us. I could not see any oil, but a thick, grey foam filled the eastern side of North Haven along the tide line. I thought at first that it might be a collection of weed and debris carried in by the storm. I called Mike.

'That's oil,' he informed me, without hesitation.

As the light improved I could see that the foam was not grey but dark brown, and that patches of this dark scum were still drifting into the bay. We were later told that this substance was an emulsion of oil and water caused by the action of the waves, and that it was known as 'chocolate mousse'. It was a very apt name. It had exactly the colour of milk chocolate but, although it looked light and fluffy, it was in fact thick, sticky and clinging. As the sea level fell the oil was deposited on the beach in a layer several feet thick in places.

Mike and I went outside to look for the seal pups. We could not see them although the mothers were clearly visible. The three cows were just offshore, where they often drifted watching their pups. Today they thrashed wildly, obviously in agony. Their eyes were being burnt by the oil, and they clawed at them frantically with their flippers. Their coats were stained a uniform brown. No other seals were in the vicinity, obviously having left at the approach of the foul-smelling, stinging oil, but these three mothers loyally refused to move.

It was not until we heard a cry that we were able to locate the pups. They were so thickly coated in oil that they were almost completely camouflaged. Not one tiny portion of their bodies remained uncovered, and as they moved pebbles from the beach clung to them, increasing the weight of their imprisoning strait-jackets. They were soon exhausted, unable to move, and with barely the strength to hold their heads above the deep layer of oil that surrounded them. Mike and I watched from the cliff top like participants in a nightmare over which there was no control. Mike shook his fist helplessly in the air and shouted his abhorrence of the disgusting pollution to the echoing cliffs. I could not speak, I just felt the wind chill the warm tears as they rolled down my cheeks.

There was nothing we could do. The gale force winds made any approach from the sea impossible, and the sheer cliffs afforded no access from the landward side. We returned to the house and Mike called the coastguard. In those days we had only a small, portable radio, and communication was difficult at the best of times. Today, because of the oil spill, the airwaves were buzzing with calls, and in the confusion only scant attention was paid to our plight. There seemed little prospect of getting any help until the weather was calm enough for us to go ashore and demand the assistance we needed. In the meantime Mike considered the idea of shooting the pups to put them out of their misery and to prevent the cows from enduring the torture of the oil any longer, but he knew he could not do it while a glimmer of hope remained. The only thing we could do was to walk round the island to see if there were any more oiled seals. A tinge of grey still lingered in the early morning light, and the wind was raw and biting. As we walked briskly towards the farm a buzzard rose from behind a wall only a few feet in front of us, the wind obviously having carried away all warning trace of us until we were almost upon it. As its huge wings unfolded and beat powerfully against the air I was amazed by its size and strength. I had never been so close to a buzzard before, and it imprinted itself clearly on my mind as one bright moment in a very black day. But to our relief we found no more oil around the island.

As we returned to the house we were startled to see two men

standing on our front doorstep. Our initial surprise subsided into relief when we realised that one of them was Eric Cowell, an old friend of Mike's who now worked for BP and, we discovered, was involved in the clean-up operation. They had monitored Mike's call to the coastguard on their own radio, and then come out to the island by helicopter to see what help they could offer. They surveyed the oil and talked cheerfully of the whole thing being cleaned up in a day or two, which felt almost like a miracle.

The most pressing problem was the need to reach the seal pups as quickly as possible. As soon as the weather eased we approached the beach by boat. It was too late for Sunny. She was only a few days old and did not have the strength of the other two. She fought hard against the smothering oil which tried to drag her down into black oblivion. As she struggled she became exhausted, and gradually let her head sink until the sea of oil stifled her last feeble breaths. Not a single strand of her soft, yellow fur penetrated the layer of oil. Her body was as smooth and as lifeless as if it had been carved in polished stone. She appeared as a perfect memorial to all the wasted lives sacrificed to the lethal tide of oil.

Nipper had fared slightly better. Being that much older he had greater reserves of strength and resilience to carry him through. He was so thickly coated in oil and stones that he was barely distinguishable from the surrounding oil slick, but he had struggled to hold his head up despite the weight pressing down on him, tempting him to give up the fight and allow himself to slide into the suffocating oil. The exertion, together with the quantity of oil he had undoubtedly swallowed, had taken their toll, and he was extremely weak. Nipper was taken to an animal hospital on the mainland where he died a few days later.

The Barrel was a survivor. He had the solid determination to come through anything. Although as severely oiled as the other two, his general condition was good. He was wrapped in a blanket and carried to the western side of North Haven, which was miraculously unpolluted. North Haven was divided naturally into two by a promontory of rock jutting out into the sea, and it was possible to cross from one side to the other on foot only at the lowest of tides. The western side, where The Barrel was taken, was known as the landing beach, where we launched our boat; the eastern side, by virtue of the weather conditions, had trapped all the oil. The Barrel was scraped clean. The worst of the oil and pebbles were removed, leaving his coat blackened and matted. He was spared the ordeal of chemical cleaning, the efficacy of which was doubtful. The whole operation was greatly simplified by The Barrel's relatively calm temperament. From the beach The Barrel was transferred to the edge of the concrete slipway where he could rest undisturbed. Within a few days the residue of oil dried and hardened, and as the once white coat was shed by the natural moulting process, the whole outer layer cracked and peeled away like a protective shell, revealing a grey velvet coat hardly damaged by oil. Although weak, he was obviously healthy, but slowly his condition seemed to deteriorate. The problem was found to be an abscess under one of his foreflippers caused, almost certainly, by the oil. Once this was treated The Barrel's condition quickly improved. Despite his torment he showed no fear of people and was happy to remain on the slipway with only the occasional irritable hiss at all the coming and going. The Barrel's survival was a key factor in maintaining our morale in the long dreary days that followed. He remained steady and unshakeable, like a placid island of sanity in a world turned upside down.

Although we had no love for the oil industry in general, we held those individuals who came to organise the clean-up operation on Skomer in the highest regard. Their determination to see Skomer restored, as far as possible, to its original condition was every bit as strong as ours. As the weather settled, and we knew there was no more oil to come, the full extent of the pollution could be seen. A brown, shiny slick of oil filled the whole of the eastern section of North Haven between high and low water. When the tide was out it covered the entire beach to a depth of about a foot, with deeper pools forming in the hollows. When the tide was in the whole mass was afloat. The oil was deep brown in colour and had the consistency of petroleum jelly, but was much heavier and stickier. It was estimated that about two hundred tons of this oil had arrived on North Haven beach but, apart from some pollution at Martin's Haven, the mainland had been little affected. Now that the oil had come to rest it was decided that it was neither desirable nor practical to use chemical dispersants on it. Despite all the sophisticated technology at the oil company's disposal, the method of removal finally settled upon was a manual one. Dozens of men with thigh boots and spades arrived to shovel the oil into plastic sacks. It was a very slow process, with the bags of oil being transferred to a small boat, and then to a waiting barge. The barge was not built for speed, and each evening undertook a journey of many hours to transfer her cargo to Milford Haven. The men started each day in brand new waterproof suits, but within an hour or two they were brown from head to foot, as though they had been coated in chocolate.

Machines designed to skim oil from the surface of the water were brought in to try to speed up the process, but they completely failed to cope with the thick, greasy emulsion of oil and water. And so, as a temporary measure, the drifting patches of oil were trapped and encircled by booms before they could do any further damage. The booms were brightly-coloured, inflatable tubes that floated on the surface. These miniature slicks enclosed by booms looked rather like huge, oil-filled paddling pools drifting in the sea.

The days were so full of activity there was hardly time to think, but left alone in the evenings we found it hard not to succumb to black depression. BP had made sure that plenty of fresh food was shipped over to us, but for the first few days we had no appetite at all. The smell of oil lingered everywhere. I could not escape the feeling that Skomer had been so horribly violated it would never be the same again, and always at the back of our minds was the haunting memory of the pups.

Even amid the awfulness there were brighter moments. Gradually the lighter fractions of the oil evaporated, and it lost not only its smell but its burning properties which had caused the cows to writhe in pain. As this happened the seals gradually returned to see what had become of their favourite beach. Finding that the oil no longer stung their eyes or offended their nostrils they came closer, and slowly made their way on to the beach. Heaving their way laboriously up the shore they found that they could slide down the beach in a matter of seconds. They continued to struggle up and ski down the oily slope, obviously enjoying this newly-discovered sport. Although their coats became stained brown they did not become thickly covered in the way the pups had done, and appeared to suffer no ill effects. Nevertheless this activity worried us, and the next day a bird-scarer was sent out. In the quiet of the evening when the workmen had gone home this was set up on the cliff top to keep the seals out of the oil.

It fired at regular intervals with an ear-splitting crash, but we seemed to be the only ones bothered by it. The seals quickly grew accustomed to its sound and continued with their new-found pastime unperturbed. We had to admit defeat, and much to our relief dismantled the bird-scarer.

The booms also attracted inquisitive attention. The enclosed oil formed a thick, impenetrable skin on the surface of the sea, and acted rather like a floating skating rink. Watching carefully we saw bulges appear on the surface of the oil as the seals dived underneath and pushed at the strange substance from below. Growing bolder still, they clambered onto the booms before launching themselves onto the oil with enough force to slither right across the surface and off the other side.

However distressing we found the whole experience, we had to acknowledge an overriding feeling of relief that the spill had happened outside the bird breeding season. Had the accident occurred in spring or early summer Skomer's seabird colonies would have been devastated, or possibly even completely destroyed. During the three days that the oil was at sea the water around Skomer was smothered by a sheet of oil stretching for miles. It covered the areas where the auks would have been feeding, and where the returning shearwaters would have been rafting. In October the island was fortunately almost devoid of seabirds, but thousands of birds were caught up in the oil out at sea and died. The true numbers will never be known. Mike told me how they had discovered barely recognisable corpses buried deep in the oil, and that many more must have been cleared away with the oil unnoticed. I remember seeing a gull land in the oil on the beach. It realised its mistake immediately and tried to take off again, but it was already too late. Its feet were held fast, and all the power of its wings would not lift it. The more it struggled the faster the oil dragged it down until, in less than a minute it had gone, vanished without trace as though it had never existed.

Eventually it became obvious that this was a desperate situation calling for a desperate remedy, and we began to feel renewed hope of seeing some progress when we heard that the *Bay Skimmer* was to be called in. The *Bay Skimmer* was a brand new weapon in the battle against oil pollution. It was an extremely costly and innovative piece of technology in the shape of a boat whose front opened up to reveal a revolving belt, like a conveyor belt, which lifted oil from the water and deposited it in the hold. It should have been able to devour our relatively minor problem in no time at all, but first it had to be brought across from Ireland. It was at this point that the BP officials in London decided that the whole operation was becoming ridiculously expensive, and should be called off. Fortunately, those who were working on Skomer had become extremely involved in the battle they were sent to fight, and replied in no uncertain terms that the island would have to be cleaned no matter what the cost.

The *Bay Skimmer* duly arrived. It was a beautiful ship of which the captain was justifiably proud, and was in pristine condition, never before having come face to face with an oil slick. One minor problem was that the captain was determined that his immaculate new boat would stay that way, and was adamant that it should not get dirty. He therefore rushed forward in horror, arms waving, to fend off the slimy, brown people who came to discuss a plan of campaign, and insisted that they keep their distance. He spent a lot of time hurrying round with a cloth wiping off oily fingerprints, which seemed to us a very strange way to treat a boat whose job was to plough into the heart of the oil pollution and swallow it up. It must be said that this unfortunate man did eventually enter into the grimy spirit of things, and entertained everybody with his attempt to walk on water. He tried to take a shortcut to a nearby boat by walking across one of the floating booms, which immediately buckled under his weight plunging him into the oil. After that he could hardly ban anyone from his ship for being too dirty.

The *Bay Skimmer* was not a success. The revolving belt refused to lift the oil, in fact it seemed to have a remarkable ability to repel the sticky mess which clung so tenaciously to everything else. The boat was not without its uses however, and pumps were brought from the mainland to suck the oil on board. The *Bay Skimmer* had separation tanks so that the excess water could be removed leaving the oil behind. Using our little boat Mike weaved close inshore between the rocks towing a boom, and then hauled the oil that was encircled by the boom over to the *Bay Skimmer*. Pumping the oil from boom to boat was less straightforward than might be imagined. The oil had become so thick and solid that it had the consistency of soft cheese, and had to be chopped into chunks with an oar and fed piece by piece to the pump. It seemed a very primitive solution amid so much expensive equipment, but it was effective and speeded up the whole operation considerably. In the meantime our boat was taking a terrible battering. It was constantly being smashed against the rocks, and its fibre glass hull was cracked and crazed. Its original blue colour had disappeared under a sticky, brown film. Its deck grew dangerously slippery, and any slight jolt was likely to send the occupants flat on their backs.

The only light relief in all this gloom was the helicopter that buzzed regularly back and forth to the island. It was a tiny but beautiful bright blue and orange machine, which seated four in a space about the size of a very small car. The pilot revelled in the opportunity for adventurous flying offered by the island, its cliffs and its gale force winds. He had ferried the BP officials down from London on the first day, with the intention of returning the same evening, but had been persuaded to remain throughout the emergency on condition that he was supplied with a change of clothes.

On the day the oil arrived we had been taken round the island by helicopter to see the extent of the problem for ourselves. The wind was blustering towards gale force and the island looked breath-taking from the air, encircled by foaming waves. The front of the helicopter was fitted with a glass floor which gave a sickeningly spectacular view of the cliffs underfoot. We flew right up the Wick and, completely disorientated by its tumbled, sloping rocks, I had the stomach-churning feeling that the helicopter was flying on its side. When we returned to land on the isthmus next to the house the helicopter hovered for some moments above the ground as the strong winds which held it in their grip refused to set it down.

We made several more flights in the helicopter and the pilot, Jim, was so unpredictable that these rides were always far from dull. His usual method of starting was to let the helicopter drop over the edge of the isthmus and plunge towards the sea, pulling out of the dive only at the last possible moment. I can still remember the panic-stricken expressions on the faces of the men on the boats in North Haven as we hurtled past them towards the sea at breakneck speed. Jim's official explanation for this strange manoeuvre was that it was necessary to pick up speed. I suspected that it was necessary only to alarm the passengers, but I did not really object to being alarmed.

One evening, while he was waiting to take his passengers home at the end of the day, both Jim and his helicopter disappeared. We knew from the deafening roar of rotor blades that they could not be far away and, sure enough, after a few minutes they surfaced just below the cliff. After parking his helicopter on the isthmus Jim came to tell us that he was trying to fan the oil away from the cliff with the rotor blades so that it could be recovered more easily.

We took our final trip in the helicopter on the last day of the clean-up, when we went to the mainland to choose a new boat to replace our old, battle-scarred model. I would have liked another exactly the same, but to Mike's relief we were persuaded to settle for a larger, more seaworthy craft. We were also promised a new and efficient radio so that we would never again be stuck in an emergency with no-one to listen to our calls.

Although it felt like an eternity, the whole incident was over in less than two weeks. The beach was not left perfectly clean, but only streaky patches of oil remained. Unsatisfactory though the idea of using men with shovels might have seemed, it was in fact a great success. On Martin's Haven, where greater accessibility allowed the use of machinery together with chemical sprays, the results, although at first impressive, soon began to show flaws. The oil which had been ground down into the pebbles by the heavy equipment continued to surface for many months.

The removal of those two hundred tons of oil to restore Skomer to something like its original condition cost a staggering £400,000. Although we admired the determination of those who saw the whole thing through, we could not help but imagine what that money could have done for the island in other circumstances. The hardest things of all to accept were the wasted lives of birds and seal pups and the suffering, on which no price could ever be put.

NINE

O VER THE YEARS WELLINGTON had settled in to become almost part of the island. Her bad behaviour did not moderate with the passage of time; she simply became more headstrong, and her stubbornness grew more entrenched. From the first year she had gone to live on the mainland during the cold, hungry winter months at the smallholding owned by our boatman, Terry Davies. We had put much of Wellington's antisocial behaviour down to loneliness, and so when she returned to the island the following spring she was accompanied by Togs, on permanent loan from the smallholding as a companion. Togs was a pretty, good-natured Toggenburg nanny who was sleek, sturdy and very affectionate. We discovered that Togs' only vice was cigarettes. These she stole by the packetful from the pockets of unsuspecting visitors, and devoured them ravenously as we tried to prise them from her mouth.

Togs and Wellington got on well together, but her new companion did nothing to curb Wellington's wicked behaviour. In fact Togs' gentle nature served only to highlight Wellington's wilfulness. Wellington was playful, and she certainly enjoyed company, but she was prone to unprovoked fits of temper, during which she became very aggressive. Togs was often on the receiving end of one of these tantrums. The poor, gentle animal accepted vicious blows from Wellington's horns with stoic calm. Assuming this to be normal goat behaviour we rarely interfered, but occasionally Togs was seen limping badly after one of these attacks, and Wellington had to be firmly rebuked.

Throughout that year Wellington continued to rule the roost, and organise our daily outings. Togs was slotted into the pecking order behind Wellington, leaving me, as usual, bringing up the rear.

101

The following spring, after their annual winter holiday, we noticed a remarkable change. Togs had grown still sleeker and sturdier, while Wellington, by comparison, looked even more spindly and ragged. We quickly realised, to our amazement, that Togs was now head of the herd. She exercised her role with dignity and tolerance, never hitting Wellington harder or more frequently than necessary. Wellington accepted her subservient position with surprising indifference, and made no attempt to assert her former dominance. There followed a year of complete harmony, in which Wellington was as amiable and obedient as we could have wished.

After her third winter on the mainland we noticed a more alarming change. Wellington was pregnant. True to form, Wellington did nothing by halves. She grew to enormous proportions. Unsure exactly when she was due to kid, we followed her anxiously for several weeks, certain that the birth was imminent. During this time Wellington remained stubbornly unco-operative, and simply expanded still further. When the momentous day finally arrived Wellington was settled into the garage which had been prepared with bales of straw. The first arrival was stillborn. We consoled ourselves with the fact that it was a billy, and that it would have been impossible to find a home for it. We had little time to grieve over it since it was obvious that another was on the way. Time passed, and nothing happened. Equipped only with his childhood memories of delivering lambs, Mike decided that he must give a hand. An internal examination revealed a tangle of legs and, after long and complicated manoeuvring, a second stillborn billy was finally delivered. The third was trickier still. It was facing forward, but the head and one foreleg were bent backwards, impeding its movement out of the womb. It seemed to take forever to rearrange the head and leg to allow delivery of the kid. Wellington was growing weak and distressed, making speed essential. Each stillborn kid had been hurried away from Wellington's sight in the hope that at any moment there would be a live birth to distract her, but as we waited for the third kid there was no doubt that it too was dead. When it finally arrived the only consolation was the fact that it was yet another billy.

Despite her obvious exhaustion, Wellington was distraught. Instead of settling down for a rest she searched incessantly through the straw, bleating weakly. We wanted her to sleep, but it seemed she would be quite inconsolable until she found her

102

kids. She continued in this fruitless quest for a further two days until, gradually, the memories of what should have been began to fade. In her state of pathetic misery she seemed far removed from the arrogant, strong-willed creature of former times, and we spent long hours talking to her and comforting her. She was given daily injections, prescribed by the vet, to guard against infections, and within a week the old Wellington began to emerge, boisterous and belligerent. We actually welcomed her tantrums, telling ourselves that she must be feeling better to behave so badly.

The rest of the year passed without incident, and Wellington's trauma seemed completely forgotten. Wellington went to the mainland as usual for the winter, but when she returned early in the spring we discovered to our dismay that she was pregnant again. This was not an accidental happening, but had been carefully arranged to compensate us and Wellington for the distress of the previous year. While appreciating such a considerate motive we did not relish the prospect of seeing Wellington through yet another pregnancy, and we had no idea what we would do with the kids if any should survive. Wellington, however, was very contented, and so we decided to look on the bright side. Her mate had been a travelling gipsy's goat, a magnificent white Saanen guaranteed to produce only female kids. The latter claim we greeted with some scepticism.

We read everything we could about kids and kidding. We had a strong idea of when the kids were due, but, according to our book, the expectant mother could select the precise day of birth, with a leeway of about two weeks. That seemed slightly ominous to us, since any decision in which Wellington played a part was certain not to be straightforward. The expected day of arrival came and went, as did several subsequent days, until one morning Wellington went missing. It was very unusual for Wellington to be out of sight of the house, and she was invariably within earshot, and always came running if we rattled her food bowl loudly enough. This day, however, was an exception. No amount of calling or bowl-clanking would entice her back to the house, and so we began searching. We finally found her, not far away, in a shallow cave on the slope of Captain Kites overlooking the sea. The floor of the cave had been scraped and hollowed, and the earth was soft. Wellington had obviously visited this cave many times before, and prepared it as the site in which to have her kids. If this was Wellington's choice, this was where she would stay.

We settled ourselves at an unobtrusive distance, to be on hand if we were needed, but otherwise to leave Wellington in peace. It soon became obvious that a kid was on the way. Wellington was struggling, but remained sitting down. We had read that she should not only be standing, but standing on a slope, to have the kid successfully. Gently we lifted her to her feet, but she strained violently against us and planted herself back on the ground. After several more attempts Mike sent me back to the house to fetch the goat book. I left the scene reluctantly, and when I came panting back up the hill a few minutes later one tiny kid had already entered the world. When I first glimpsed the kid it appeared to be enclosed in a punctured pink balloon. The pink membrane was removed, and a small, white, female kid emerged, damp and scrawny, but already able to take its first stumbling steps. Meanwhile, Wellington was obviously about to produce another. This she accomplished with only a minimum of effort. Obstinate to the last, Wellington had managed to give birth to two kids while remaining sitting down, leaving us to retrieve them from the hollow of soft earth beneath her.

The second kid was also a nanny, and virtually identical to the first, which made us wonder if the gipsy owner of the billy really was correct. The two white kids had the gangling, gambolling charm of new-born lambs, and at a quick glance could easily have been mistaken for such. Having taken a few minutes to compose herself, Wellington was now fascinated by her offspring. The three animals were taken the short distance to the house and settled into a warm, straw-lined shed. We named the two kids Boojum and Snark. I could recognise Snark by the small, black markings on her nose, but to everyone else the two were indistinguishable. Wellington became a devoted mother, and for the first few days her eyes hardly left the kids. Throughout the first night she stood over them in awed admiration, and did not appear to sleep at all, or even relax from the standing position.

The kids took unprecedented liberties. Whenever their mother settled down peacefully they scrambled on to her back. Having attained the summit they jostled each other for the best position, often resulting in one losing its balance and sliding down the furry slope, attempting to halt the descent by digging in its

104

miniature black hooves. This was just the sort of behaviour guaranteed to trigger Wellington's sensitive temper, but she remained a model of placidity throughout. She did, however, let herself down a little when it came to feeding time. She quickly lost patience, and would walk away leaving the hungry kids bleating behind her. As the magic of the first few days of motherhood was beginning to wear off, Wellington was occasionally seen to give Boojum an irritable butt as she tried to feed. Boojum was by far the least outgoing of the two, and so usually fed last, since they were rarely able to cope with the complexities of feeding together. As a result, Wellington usually decided that feeding time was over just as Boojum took her turn, and Boojum grew noticeably thinner than Snark. We offered her bottled milk which she rarely took, but soon the imbalance sorted itself out, and the two became, once again, identical. With Wellington now so preoccupied with the kids, Togs returned at the end of the summer to live with the other goats on the smallholding.

After the arrival of the kids we could never again sit outside without a goat each on our laps. This was very endearing in the first weeks, but less so when they were approaching full size. When they were small they had a 'king of the castle' mentality. This meant that they always made for the highest point of anything, and if they reached this coveted position together would attempt to dislodge each other. Consequently, they were never content to sit on our laps for more than a few minutes before clambering on to our shoulders. From there they usually tried to scale the dizzy heights of head level before being brought firmly back to the ground. Snark, always the most adventurous, would jump from the ground on to Mike's shoulders if she saw him bending down. This became something of a favourite trick, and she would sit tight as he stood upright, and then ride round standing on his shoulders. This was another of those habits that became more irritating as she grew in size. . .

In the early weeks the kids looked so tiny and fragile that we could not bear to see them playing near the cliffs. We would call them anxiously as they teetered precariously on the edge, but they ignored us, springing into the air with a sideways flick of their back legs. Mike used to get up several times each night to check that they were safe and bring them in from the cliffs, but I had no doubt that they would be back in their favourite haunts

105

before his head touched the pillow again. Finally we managed to convince ourselves that for all their frivolous gambolling they were very sure-footed, and gradually returned to our normal sleeping pattern.

If we had any lingering doubts about their acrobatic abilities Snark quickly put an end to them. She invented a somersault that involved charging at the house, springing off the wall with all four hooves, turning full circle in the air, and landing back on her feet again. We were so impressed with her powers of invention we could hardly believe what we had seen. In the softly-lit hour before dark a trace of wildness entered the kids. Their lively behaviour often culminated in a game of chase, with the young goats pursuing each other on a circular route around the perimeter of the house. As the two were well-matched there was never a winner until one wily contestant changed course and doubled back. No matter how many times this happened there was always a start of complete surprise as the pursuer came face to face with the pursued.

Summer drew on into the golden days of early autumn. The kids had grown rapidly. Their bony figures had become strong and rounded. The soft baby-fur had coarsened into a thick, warm coat. Autumn brought with it the eagerly-awaited mushroom season, and the goats joined us on long walks in search of this welcome supply of fresh food. First to appear were the parasols. They emerged dome-shaped on long stalks before opening into huge, shaggy-topped discs, often the size of small plates. They looked temptingly succulent, but in practice were disappointing. The large caps disappeared to almost nothing in the frying pan, and the grey remains were soggy and bland-tasting. After identifying the edible ones carefully, we tried many of the wild mushrooms, but quickly learned that if the true field mushrooms were available nothing else could lure us away from them.

In all but the best years we had to search hard for mushrooms. Our first year had been exceptional, with a damp autumn following the hot summer. Then we could take out a huge bag and half fill it. We could enjoy a meal that consisted of a plate piled with fried mushrooms and almost nothing else. But we learnt to our disappointment that it was not to be the pattern of every year, and we never again saw such a good mushroom season. The ideal time to look for mushrooms was on mild days, following rain. On days like these the island looked refreshed after the dusty summer. The dying fronds of bracken glistened red in the sunlight, and the grass that had been spared by the rabbits was a luxuriant, paint-box green. Hidden by stalks of bracken and blades of grass were the first unblemished, white curves of the field mushrooms. The goats quickly learned the object of these outings. They watched as we sighted our quarry, picked it, and turned it upside down to examine the powdery, brown gills. Before long the goats too developed a taste for mushrooms. As we sighted one in the distance they took off, and we usually arrived just in time to see our intended breakfast being enclosed in prehensile lips and delicately plucked from the ground. It quickly became apparent that the goats were only interested in mushrooms intended for our own consumption. In order to avoid returning empty-handed, a routine developed in which one of us would make a great display of pointing at some unwanted mushroom, such as a parasol, which the goats would instantly seize, while the other quietly picked the field mushrooms. I am glad to say that in some instances goats never learn.

Early in November Mike went to the mainland for the usual meetings to plan management and new projects for the island during the coming year. While I was alone the goats were good company. When I was walking it was nice to have two cheerful companions and one who, mellowed by motherhood, deigned to accept my presence while launching only sporadic attacks against me. Mike returned, having been held up by bad weather for only a few days. The extra time had given him an opportunity to do some shopping, and the almost unknown luxuries of a chicken and a bottle of wine immediately suggested to us the completely rational idea, as it seemed at the time, of having an early Christmas dinner, just in case there was not another chance later on. After dinner we played cards and finished the wine. I could never raise much enthusiasm for card games, and soon found myself struggling to stay awake. When I finally went to bed, well past midnight, Mike was still wide awake and continued to play patience.

I sank very quickly into sleep, and was oblivious of everything until I heard a loud, hoarse whisper from the door-way.

'Are you awake?'

I remained non-committal, hoping my silence would be taken to mean no. Mike was undeterred.

'I've seen something outside, and I think I must be imagining it, so I'd like you to come and have a look.'

Startled, I leapt out of bed and hurried to the open kitchen window. Undoubtedly something was there; a light, low down on the rocks, to the north-east edge of North Haven. It was moving and flashing on and off, its long, straight beam reflecting across the hard, black water towards us. I stared in disbelief. There was no logical explanation; the rocks were inaccessible from the land, and the weather was too stormy for any boat to have approached. For a moment I suspected Mike of an elaborate practical joke, but dismissed the idea as impossible. We had no idea what to do. Mike finally decided to call the coastguard, probably as much for the reassurance of an outside voice as for the hope of any practical help. By now it was three in the morning. The coast-guard answered rapidly, slightly startled, his voice betraying his surprise at hearing a call pierce the silent hours. Mike launched a little sheepishly into his request.

'There's a light low down on the cliffs off the tip of North Haven. Have you any idea what it might be?'

The coastguard hesitated and then proffered rather lamely, 'Perhaps it's somebody fishing.'

That was not much help since there was no-one else on the island who could be fishing. There was obviously no explanation the poor man could offer, but we still felt rather disappointed, and were quite at a loss as to what to do next. After some discussion Mike called the coastguard again and asked for permission to fire a white parachute flare which would illuminate the whole area. This was readily granted. We dressed in warm clothes and, finding the necessary flares and torches, set off.

The goats were instantly woken by the disturbance as we left the house and, never willing to miss any excitement, they left their shelter and ran after us. As soon as we had crossed the isthmus we felt the full force of the wind. We were running hard now, struggling against the wind, and stumbling through long grass and deep, hidden burrows. Rising panic, and the effort of running uphill caused a tightness in my chest that forced me to gulp hard for every breath. As Mike ran beside me an unspoken fear hovered between us. Struggling through the darkness we were thinking not of the events of that night, but of a day several years ago. During a routine morning radio check the coastguard had enquired about a bright light seen on the island the previous night. Mike had explained that this was impossible, that there was nothing on the island capable of generating such a light. The coastguard however had been so persistent in his questioning, and so certain about the presence of the light, that we had grown quite anxious. The position he had given for the source of the light was just the other side of Captain Kites. This was the ridge that rose steeply behind the house, and the light would have been hidden from us by the high ground in between.

As the radio conversation had finished the room was momentarily silent. The implication was obvious to us both. At that time Pembrokeshire was rife with stories about UFOs, and large, silver-suited men were supposedly roaming the mainland. Skomer fell within what had become known as the Broad Haven triangle, the centre for these activities. We gave these stories little credence, but as we had climbed the hill behind the house to examine the scene of the occurrence I had half expected to find a circle of scorched grass. Of course we had found nothing, but it had been sufficiently unsettling to make us lock our door at night for the first time.

As we now ran through the cold night air we were terrified that the whole thing would be repeated. The light was so definitely there that if it disappeared before we reached it we knew it would leave behind an almost incurable unease. At the same time, logic told us that there could be no light.

Running into the wind we seemed to make hardly any progress, and all the time the goats hampered every movement. Windy weather brought out the worst in them, making them frisky and boisterous. In addition they always considered that when we ran we were inviting them to play. The kids gambolled around us, pressing as close as they could, tangling their legs with our own, and hindering every step. Wellington was more of a problem. Excited by the atmosphere, and taking advantage of our preoccupation, she lost no chance to gallop close to us, flicking her head round as she did so to strike a powerful blow with her horns. She was challenging us to a duel, but we were in no mood to play. Frustrated by the lack of response she frequently raced on in front and turned to meet us head on, rearing up on her hind legs. In the torch light her eyes glowed red, giving her horned head a very sinister appearance.

In spite of the goats we made headway, and drew close enough to see that the light was moving backwards and forwards, as though someone was holding a torch and sweeping it in a wide arc above their head. When we had reached the best viewing point Mike informed the coastguard that he was about to fire the flare. It soared through the air and exploded into a searing white light. The whole of North Haven was aglow, patterned by brightness and deep shade. We blinked into the unaccustomed brilliance, but before we could focus our eyes the flare fizzled and died. Mike called the coastguard and then sent a second flare screeching into the sky. This time we saw our mystery light. It was mounted on a long metal rod supported by a buoy and was obviously some sort of marker that had broken free in a storm and become trapped on Rye Rocks. Following the first wave of relief there was a slight sense of anticlimax, and as we trudged slowly back to the house with the goats, now exhausted, trailing behind us, I knew that I was very far from the peaceful sleep I had been enjoying an hour ago.

With hopeless inevitability the winter set in, but this year we could not welcome it with any enthusiasm. Knowing that we were unable to keep three goats, winter was the time when we had agreed the kids must be found a new home, but as the season drew on we knew we could not part with them. They were found a temporary home on the mainland for the winter, and returned in the spring well-fed but disgraced, having caused chaos on the farm where they spent their winter holiday. The culmination of their misdeeds came the night they gatecrashed a New Year's Eve party at a nearby house by entering through the French windows as the proceedings were in full swing, causing havoc among the guests.

The following summer was a happy one, increasing age having done nothing to moderate the goats' playful behaviour. As winter approached we knew that we could not keep three fully grown goats, and they were too much of a handful to board out on a temporary basis. We had hoped that the kids would have grown more independent, but the three were still inseparable. Finally and reluctantly we decided that Wellington should go with the kids to a new home rather than stay alone and lonely on the island. The kids thrived on the mainland, and eventually had kids of their own, but the island was never quite the same without them.

TEN

WINTER DID NOT SEEM TOO LONELY without the goats since we were used to losing them for the colder months, and despite all its hardships it was a season that we never liked to see coming to an end. With the first signs of spring, as we waited for many of the seabirds to return, we knew that our way of life would soon be changing; that boats and people would come from the mainland imposing routine and reality on us. But even in the winter visitors occasionally reached us, mostly by helicopter. We gained a great deal of security from knowing that RAF Brawdy and their rescue helicopters were just across the water on the other side of St Bride's Bay. But fortunately, it was not only emergencies that brought us into contact with the RAF, and many of those that we met came to be close friends. Two or three times a year they gathered together a work-force of a dozen or so men and spent a long weekend on the island helping with some of the major building projects, and even with the annual census of thousands of pairs of breeding gulls.

As we got to know the crews of the rescue helicopters they often made a point of flying over the island to give us a wave as they travelled to and from their training exercises, particularly in the winter when they knew we were alone. One of the pilots was exceptionally enthusiastic in these greetings. If he spotted us out walking he charged at us so low that we were forced to throw ourselves face down on the ground, and sometimes at night we were startled by a helicopter search light beaming through our kitchen window.

It was early on a Sunday morning in the last week of March, with the island still deserted but for us, when the house was suddenly engulfed by a deafening noise. We both hurtled to the front door, half expecting to find the roof being torn from the

112

house by a freak whirlwind. We were greeted instead by a man in a yellow flying-suit dangling outside our door on a cable with a pint of milk in one hand and the Sunday newspapers in the other. Our initial incredulity turned to laughter as the explanation became obvious. A helicopter had approached the island high, so we could not hear it, and then descended over the house, at the same time lowering the winchman on the cable. We looked up to see the crew waving and grinning broadly, no doubt satisfied with the obvious success of the mission. Within seconds they were off again, the winchman dangling precariously on the long cable. As they reached the cliffs the helicopter swooped downwards, plunging the winchman towards the sea. It may have been only a practical joke to them, but for us the unexpected luxury of fresh milk and Sunday newspapers brought the sort of pleasure that is almost impossible to describe.

As March was almost over and with it, we hoped, the worst of the gales, we began to think again about fishing. We put one or two lobster pots out around the island during spring and summer, but without access to the right bait our success was limited. On hearing of our disappointing results Jim Aldred, one of the local fishermen, took to baiting our pots whenever he was passing, and if we caught anything he always brought it ashore for us. Despite this the catch was low, and so he began to fill the pot with his own crabs. This way we knew that if we wanted a crab we had only to row out to the pot and there would be one waiting.

Jim was always there to help. In the winter he kept an eye on the weather, and if it looked good enough for us to make the crossing, there he would be on Martin's Haven beach waiting to give us a hand. Often, of course, his journeys were made in vain, but this never seemed to deter him. This was typical of the attitude we met with throughout our time on Skomer. Though we loved our isolation we relied heavily on the support that was always available from the mainland, and without it our way of life would have barely been possible. Help came from all quarters; given so freely that we sometimes felt embarrassed that we could never adequately repay it. The villagers of Dale and Marloes were always ready to come to our assistance, whether we were stranded on the mainland and needed a bed for the night, or whether we needed a tractor to help us pull our boat up the beach. In addition we received a steady stream of fruit and vegetables from local farms and gardens. We valued, too, our contact with the coastguards who were always present on the end of the radio, and who patiently answered our routine calls twice a day, every day.

Already, with spring no more than a fleeting illusion, that came in for a few days and then retreated into winter, the ravens were finding their nest sites. It was not unusual to see a raven, or perhaps a pair, moving across the sky, their deep, resonant calls echoing from the cliff. I admired the ravens. They seemed to me true birds of the wild, building their nests on the highest and loneliest cliffs. I began to learn the knack of finding ravens' nests, and it was something I quite prided myself on. There was one nest we did not have to look far to find; it was nearly always in the southern entrance to the Lantern, a cave on the furthest tip of the Neck, overlooking Little Sound. Although it was easy to find, there was nowhere that afforded a good view into the nest. Early in the season we liked to see into each nest just to check that things were progressing properly. For this particular nest we had developed a technique which involved me lying face down on the cliff top and Mike holding tight to my ankles. Then, with the supposed reassurance of Mike's firm grip, I would lower myself head first over the cliff until I could see into the nest. It worked so well that we repeated the operation whenever we needed to check the nest. One morning we came to the nest as we had every year before to see if the raven had laid its eggs.

'I don't think we had better dangle you over the cliff any more,' Mike said quite seriously, and to my surprise I agreed.

It was rather sobering to think that we must be growing up.

As spring got under way a boat service began, erratically at first, from the mainland, and people came to Skomer both to visit and to work. It would be easy to give the impression of an island that was always cut off by storms and where we were always isolated because they were the dramatic times, the ones that stay in the memory, but in fact as the year drew on the island was full of activity. During the summer months we were joined by a variety of post-graduate students, voluntary helpers and an

114

assistant warden. From these people we could never have asked for greater support. They always put our needs above their own, and although the students were there to carry out their own studies on the island, usually working towards a PhD, if we needed help they abandoned everything to come to our assistance. Mike always liked to have some major project on hand, and I joked that he was only happy when he was up to his elbows in cement. But whether he was re-roofing the house or building a flight of concrete steps up the cliff from the landing point, the help was always there.

Over the years there was very little that Mike did not tackle, from creating a huge dam to form the only deep-water pond on the island, to building a new boat-shed. One of the greatest problems in our island situation was the transportation of building materials. Everything had to be carried down Martin's Haven beach, then transferred from beach to dinghy and from dinghy to boat. Once Skomer was reached the whole process was repeated in reverse. At very busy times it seemed that only a week or two would pass before another five tons of sand or cement was needed. Every time Mike told me the bad news I felt a flicker of despair.

One of our most memorable feats of transportation was to transfer fourteen tons of building blocks from the mainland to the island. I think even Mike was rather shattered when he saw the quantity he had ordered, as the mechanical arm of the lorry began to unload them on to the side of the dusty track down to Martin's Haven beach, and did not stop until the lorry was empty. It took three days to carry the blocks across to the island, the last loads being brought ashore by torch light at eleven or twelve o'clock at night. At times like these everyone rallied round, putting aside their own work, and joining us to form a human chain to move the thousands of blocks one by one down the beach. At the time we felt that we could happily live without these days of non-stop punishment, but the end result was invariably such an overwhelming feeling of achievement that we were soon planning the next project.

Between all the demands of managing the island we tried to work on our garden at least occasionally. In common with previous residents we had taken the sheltered, walled garden to the north of the farmhouse for our vegetable plot. We knew after the first year that it was a lost cause, and our enthusiasm waned as it became obvious that we grew our produce only as a sacrifice to wind, drought or voles. But we persevered, spurred on by the prospect of fresh vegetables as a relief from the tinned and dried variety. The vegetable garden was well fenced against rabbits, but the voracious Skomer voles could squeeze through such tiny gaps that there was no hope of fencing them out.

This summer the garden was looking more devastated than ever. No matter how many times we checked the fence for signs of holes or burrowing and assured ourselves it was still rabbit-proof, our vegetables disappeared so fast we were sure rabbits had to be the culprits. Eventually, while working in the garden we spotted the villain; a tiny rabbit that would fit comfortably into the palm of a hand was gorging itself on tender, young lettuce seedlings. Immediately the hunt was on, and we careered across the garden in hot pursuit of the despicable sneak thief. It darted up and down the rows of broad beans leaving us floundering helplessly, before charging head first at the wall. We waited, horrified for the crash, only to see the rabbit disappear before our eyes. Incredulously we went to examine the scene of this miraculous escape, and could only assume that it had squeezed through the tiny space between the fence and the wall and vanished into the dense bramble beyond.

These dramatic chases became a regular occurrence in our garden. Each time their entry hole was blocked the baby rabbits found another. However successfully we had fenced out full-sized rabbits in the past, these tiny ones seemed unstoppable, and in the meantime our vegetable garden was looking decidedly depleted. When yet another of the beasts was caught plundering, Mike responded with renewed vigour, and was within inches of catching the perpetrator as it reached its bolt-hole. In a life or death leap the tiny creature misjudged the distance and hurled itself with full force into the fence post. It fell to the ground and lay motionless. Mike was overcome with remorse, and quickly picked it up. It remained perfectly still, stretched out on its back on Mike's hand, its little face framed by soft, white paws. We were beginning to fear the worst when its eyes flickered open, but it remained too dazed to move. Mike hurriedly selected our best lettuce, and hand fed the rabbit leaf by leaf until it revived.

Early in the summer arrangements had been finalised for the

116

replacement of our ailing tractor. The local RAF base at Brawdy would have been happy to help, but they did not yet have a helicopter capable of carrying a tractor, so a Sea King had to be called in from Culdrose. This took a lot more time and planning, and when it was finally settled the arrival of the tractor was anticipated with great excitement. The day dawned wet and windy, which did little to dampen our enthusiasm, but did raise doubts as to whether it would be suitable for flying. When at last the helicopter appeared through the drizzle I was amazed to see that our new tractor looked no bigger than a toy dangling below the enormous helicopter. The tractor was set down on the grassy track leading to the farm as gently as if it were made of glass.

The problem of lifting our old tractor back to the mainland had to be considered with care. The points at which the lifting strops were attached were critical, to ensure that the tractor was correctly balanced. We had been warned that either tractor might start to swing back and forth on its cable as it was being carried. If the swinging became too violent it would endanger the helicopter, and it would be necessary to jettison the tractor. Mike and I were secretly hoping that the old tractor would be dropped in Jack Sound. After so many years of faithful service on the island, a burial at sea seemed much more fitting than a return to further drudgery on the mainland. The old tractor, however, had a safe passage across to the mainland, and we watched sadly as it faded to a speck in the distant sky.

I never really took to the new tractor. I could forgive it for being large, difficult to manage and excessively noisy, but I could not forgive its inefficient brakes. It was not in fact new, but a well-worn second-hand, and gave nothing but trouble from the day it arrived. It always seemed to be in pieces while some repair or other was under way.

Over the years, whenever anything had gone wrong Mike had always managed to put it right without being able to call on the services of a plumber, mechanic or any other skilled help, so when he told me that the tractor needed a new clutch I had every faith in his ability to do it, despite the fact that he was complaining bitterly. When the required parts arrived work commenced in the garage. It was necessary to split the tractor into two halves to gain access to the clutch, and I had to agree that this did sound rather daunting. The choice of the garage as

117

a work place was made necessary because it provided the only level surface on the island. It was not the ideal situation since once the tractor was in place there was barely enough room to squeeze round the outside of it. Given the lack of space, and a certain amount of cowardice on my part, I decided to leave Mike to tackle the job with the help of Richard, our assistant warden. The sounds coming from the garage were less than encouraging, but I resisted the temptation to investigate.

Finally, at about two o'clock in the afternoon when I heard that the new clutch was in place I popped down to offer my congratulations, and there I remained for the next seven hours. I had not realised that the worst was yet to come; the two halves of the tractor still needed putting back together. Richard and I were stationed one on each wheel, while Mike guided the operation from the front. On the command 'Now' we eased our respective wheels forward, but we never managed to get it quite right, and the back half never met the front with perfect precision. It was heavy and awkward to manoeuvre, and all we could do was roll it back and start again. The garage floor was by now awash with oil, which had an effect reminiscent of a skating rink. We slipped and slithered, and occasionally fell.

Despair grew as the hours passed, and we began to suspect the task to be impossible. Time and again we thought we had made it, only to find that inside two parts had not quite matched up. As the evening wore on, and darkness followed, we seemed on the brink of success. Everything was in place, and the tractor was back together, but a tantalising quarter inch gap remained between the front and back halves, which just would not close. We were too desperate to concede defeat yet again, so we eased, and we strained, and we tightened the bolts until, fraction by fraction, the gap disappeared. It was now nine o'clock in the evening, we were extremely oily and irritable, and wondering why we had ever given up our dear old tractor whose only fault was refusing to start.

When the day to day frustrations became too great there was no better place to escape to than Skomer Head, at the edge of the endless Atlantic Ocean. Here it was possible to forget everything else and to sit perched on the brink of the island

118

gazing out to sea as far as the imagination would allow. It was one of those places where the wind was rarely still, where the weather chose to do its worst, but when it was calm it was idyllic. I particularly liked to watch the gannets fishing offshore. With huge wings outstretched they moved effortlessly through the air, gliding, searching. Their white feathers caught the light, showing bright against the sea as they turned into the sun. When, from a seemingly impossible height, they spotted the shimmer of a fish moving through the water they folded their great wings and plunged. Neck outstretched, beak pointing downwards, they fell from the sky. Hitting the surface of the sea and shattering it into spray, they did not halt their downward dive until they reached their prey.

Watching the gannets diving always reminded me of the time we had been taken to Grassholm, an island gannet colony to the west of Skomer, in a small inflatable boat. We reached Grassholm in a solid downpour of rain, and it was not until the boat slowed to a halt close to the island that we realised it was not just raindrops breaking the surface of the sea; the water around us was boiling with an enormous shoal of mackerel. Suddenly the air was full of gannets plummeting from the sky. They struck the sea so close to the boat that the water they displaced added to the rain already showering over us, and I wondered anxiously if the precision of their aim ever failed. But despite this unnerving experience or perhaps because of it, I never tired of watching gannets, even from the comparative remoteness of Skomer Head.

If there was nothing to watch out at sea we could turn our attention to the herring gulls that nested on the rocky slopes below Skomer Head. There was always activity in a gull colony, eggs hatching, chicks begging for food, adults squabbling. I both loved and hated the gulls. I loved their powerful flight, the pristine perfection of their feathers and even their cruel, yellow eyes. I hated their raucous screeching and their insistence on harassing other birds and robbing their nests.

When we first came to Skomer this distant tip of the island was bleak and desolate. There was only earth, enveloping the area in a cracked and flaking crust, and threaded through it a terrifyingly fragile web of burrows. The area could be crossed only by one narrow path which over the years had been hardened by compression. Leaving this route-way skirting the cliff edge, it

119

was impossible not to shatter the thin shell of soil that covered the burrows and crash through into the nest chamber below. Not only did this destroy nest sites and endanger the inhabitants of the burrows, it also hastened the process of erosion. The loose fragments of earth were waiting to be carried away by the wind, depleting the thin soil layer.

The final destruction of plant life had been triggered by a violent storm raging in from the west to Skomer Head. Huge waves scaled the cliff, flooded the burrows, and bathed everything in reach with the shrivelling lick of salt water. Plants that dared venture so close to a cliff open to the full force of the Atlantic naturally had some degree of salt tolerance, but not even these hardy species could withstand total immersion. They blackened and died.

The part the rabbits played in this devastation was outlined by a single square of luxuriant green, splashed across the brown earth. This was a small area from which rabbits had been excluded by a fence, buried deep in the ground to prevent burrowing. Like the exclosure at the Wick this had been established to provide some understanding of the effect the rabbits were having on the vegetation of the island. Within this compound red fescue grew knee-high. This is a grass which is quite resistant to salt, but which presents such an irresistible temptation to rabbits that not a blade of it was to be found outside the protective fence. Growing unchecked the red fescue forms a thick mattress which is freely draining and prevents the salt water being trapped in puddles around the plant, and it had once grown strongly on Skomer Head. The protected plants were able to recover rapidly without the unwanted attentions of the rabbits to check their progress. The rest of the headland remained a brown desert.

At that time Skomer Head seemed a sad place, barren and forsaken, but gradually the first brave pioneers emblazoned flashes of green on to the dead earth. In sheltered hollows one or two tiny, nibbled cushions of thrift appeared. Fighting against such adverse conditions the plants were too beleaguered to produce flowers, but it was a valiant beginning. It was the scentless mayweed that finally brought the headland back to life. A pedestrian name for a plant that seemed little short of miraculous in the way it revived that fringe of the island. Gradually, from scattered pockets, the mayweed spread until it had covered the once bare ground. It had a flower like a daisy, white petalled with a yellow centre, and soft, feathery leaves, but compared to what had been there before it was a riot of colour. Disdained by the rabbits the mayweed thrived, binding the soil, trapping moisture and providing the opportunity for new plants to grow in its shelter. In fact the mayweed proved so good a host to new growth that by degrees it was replaced, and sorrel eventually smothered the headland, stippling it with pale red. And so the succession would continue, slowly repairing the damage, until the next catastrophe of nature.

Although its sensitivity to salt spray prevented bracken from growing on exposed promontories such as Skomer Head, it thrived in the more sheltered areas to the point where it had become something of a problem. In spring the island was alive with colour, in a mix so vibrant it would have been thought unreal if it had come from a paint-box. Red and blue flowers growing too close smudged into purple, drifting back and forth in the breeze to complete the mixture. Pink and white ran together but retained their identity in pools of clean, clear colour. But beneath the blue and the red slowly the bracken was unfurling, and soon it would wash over everything with its own dull green. When it was young even I could find the bracken attractive as it emerged, tight-curled, and still bright and fresh. As the fronds unrolled and spread open they still had that crisp, pale green of new leaves, and mixed harmoniously with the other plants, but as they grew and smothered everything with their blanketing dowdiness, my dislike of them also grew.

It would be wrong however to suggest that the bracken was all bad. It played its part in the scheme of things just like everything else. The bluebells on Skomer were magnificent. They were remarkable above all for their sheer numbers and the expanse which they covered. They were large, sturdy, deep blue and overflowing with scent, and yet in a sense they looked out of place under clear skies, spilling their fragrance in the heat of the sun. Bluebells after all are woodland plants, to be glimpsed in clusters between trees in the shade of overhanging branches. This was where the bracken redeemed itself. Reaching up over the fading bluebells it spread itself above them offering deep, green shade. In the cool of this shelter the bluebells were preserved, the bulbs waiting patiently in the damp soil for spring. By mimicking the sheltering effect of

121

trees the bracken helped to create ideal conditions for the bluebells.

In weighing up any possible benefits from bracken against its
generally unwelcome smothering effects it was difficult to know
how far we should go in trying to control it. There was such a
complicated network of life surviving in and around the bracken
that any changes might be far-reaching. How, for example, were
the puffins affected as the spreading bracken reached down to
their cliff top burrows? Would they be driven from their nesting
places as they became swamped by the ever-rising green tide?
Mike instituted a long period of study into this problem, and
reached the conclusion that while established puffins were unaffected, young puffins seeking their first burrows would not enter
the bracken. The reason for this apparently being that young
birds learn by watching mature birds, and that in entering the
bracken and losing sight of their guides the imitators no longer
knew which were safe or desirable nest sites. Once this fact had
been established the bracken was removed from these areas by
the slow, old-fashioned method of scything to avoid disturbance
to the birds, and the puffins were once again free to spread over
the cliff top slopes.

But that was only one small piece of the jigsaw, and there were
many more to fit into place. While the shearwaters managed well
on most parts of the island it seemed inevitable that a very dense
bracken growth would eventually make some burrows unreachable.
Then there were the Skomer voles. As creatures unique to the
island they certainly deserved our protection, but was it possible
that bracken was their ideal habitat? Even when these questions
were answered they needed to be balanced in relation to all
species, and the way forward was never clear cut.

In spring the island was so overwhelmed with flowers that
it was almost impossible to look in any direction without being
greeted by colour, but even as spring matured into summer and
the bracken became dominant the beauty was still there, it
was just broken into smaller fragments and was sometimes a
little harder to find. Even the tiniest flowers could match their
more ostentatious rivals, having a quiet dignity all of their own.
I often marvelled at the miniature perfection of tiny flowers such
as the soft blue forget-me-not, each with a speck of gold in the
centre. The scarlet pimpernel, only a little larger, redeemed its

122

lack of size with strength of colour. With its low, creeping leaves and cluster of flowers the scarlet pimpernel was a brilliant fleck of colour against the smooth green of a grassy track, and yet individually it was too small to be noticed. But gathered together around the springs above Pigstone Bay, the plants uniting to form a carpet over the damp ground, sweeping towards the cliff in a flush of deep red, it refused to be ignored.

Many plants, which singly might go unremarked, grouped in profusion took on a whole new character. The silver weed, unexciting and pale-leaved, pressing close to the ground, shimmered with all the life of a stream flickering in the sunlight as it poured smoothly down the waterlogged bank above Tom's House. Even Yorkshire fog, which in wet years grew strongly, could look spectacular when it enveloped broad, open areas such as the low land sandwiched between South Plateau and Wick Ridge. The seed heads were ordinary enough, pale cream tinged with green, maturing to dark gold, but when they spread across the ground in a soft mist with the wind rippling through them there seemed to be a hundred different shades of ochre swaying through the grass.

As some things thrive in the wet, so others flourish in drought. An exceptional year for foxgloves should follow two years after a drought, and accordingly two years after our first rainless summer foxgloves had abounded. Banks where once only one or two foxgloves grew had been obliterated by tall, purple flower heads. Now the cycle had moved on again, and once more the foxgloves were scattered sparsely along the banks and walls. Showing their dappled interiors the bell-shaped flowers hung open in welcome to the insects. Bees hummed lazily among them, drifting right to the depths of the bloom, dusting themselves gold with pollen.

The two valleys were completely different from the rest of the island, and also contrasted sharply with each other. Here in the valleys, shelter and the trickling moisture of the streams changed everything. Plants grew tall unbowed by the wind, cutting a swathe of luxuriant growth through the island. South Valley's slopes caught the best of the summer sun, and descending the inclines on a hot day the air that gathered in the valley could seem oppressively still and humid, but the plants thrived in this atmosphere. Hemlock water-dropwort followed the course of the stream, colouring the banks with its own strong green before bursting into a cloud of white flowers. It grew so prolifically that it completely filled the shallower parts of the valley, like a morning mist trapped in the hollow. As the pale, carefree colours of spring gave way to the stronger hues of the maturing season South Valley was streaked with purple. The purple loosestrife fought its way through the throng of plants to emerge tall and bright above the greenery. Finally the flowers of the water mint appeared, small puff-balls of colour, whose own version of purple leant much more strongly towards blue. The leaves of this plant had long been growing along the margins of the stream, now shrunk by summer, and the aroma of mint often encouraged us to pick a few of these fresh-tasting leaves to chew on as we walked. The thistles added yet another shade of purple, but they soon sacrificed their colour to the soft, white down that drifted in the air.

All these plants held an irresistible attraction for the butterflies, particularly in late summer when South Valley clung most tenaciously to the remnants of the season. Peacocks, small tortoiseshells and red admirals meandered across the water mint, many battered and faded from the rigours of their short lives, some showing the unmistakable v-shaped scar that signified a very narrow escape from a bird's beak. But all seemed at ease, gliding carelessly among the flowers, giving no hint of watchfulness for predators. Among the green and purple the tiny, orange wings of the small copper shone like precious metal. These butterflies were replaced by new arrivals so frequently through the summer that their colours always looked fresh and their wings had the bloom of new velvet. Occasionally common blues found their way to this sheltered haven. They did not breed on the island and, though plentiful on the mainland, to me were a rarity and therefore wonderfully exotic. Just one tiny, wandering butterfly that had ventured too far afield seemed to transform the whole atmosphere of the valley into something colourful and exciting. I would watch, not daring to move in case by disturbing this visitor I might hasten its departure. Instead I would remain transfixed by the metallic rainbow sheen of its wings until the butterfly drifted out of sight into the distant tangled chaos of plants.

Further upstream South Valley opened out to a marshy hollow, and the tall plants gave way to a dense covering of rushes and grass. It was among this greenery that I first saw ringlets, drab grey butterflies with dark eye-spots on their wings, but for me they had a unique appeal. Once plentiful on the island they had for some reason disappeared and been absent for decades, but following that first sighting I discovered more, until I was certain that these butterflies were becoming re-established. Though they had less pretensions to beauty, the return of these lapsed residents meant more to me than all the showy visitors that drifted briefly into view.

It was in this hollow, where the stream barely moved, that we found frogspawn in early spring. It clustered so thickly that there seemed little room for the water. Gradually some of the black, beady centres whitened and died, while others emerged into the freedom of the still water with tiny tails. The tadpoles grew and their tails with them. They gathered into great wriggling masses; the ponds were blackened at their fringes by the sheer quantity of tiny lives in perpetual motion. It was a testament to how few of these would ultimately survive that the island was not overrun by frogs. But those that did escape the countless hazards of being a tadpole grew into some of the most beautiful frogs I have ever seen. Some were bathed in a wash of fine, translucent red, while others were story-book green.

North Valley was totally different in character to South Valley. From North Pond the stream followed a swampy course until, still and rush-lined, it opened into the smooth reflections of Mike's creation, Green Pond. Where the peaty brown stream gushed from the motionless water of the pond North Valley suddenly took shape; steeply inclined and filled with an impenetrable thicket of blackthorn. Beneath this natural curtain North Stream babbled unseen. It was a pleasant place just to sit and listen to that evocative whisper of fresh water across polished stones, trickling softly towards the sea. And from within the shelter of gnarled branches, sculpted by the wind, came the song of birds, clear and melodious above the rush of water. Hidden from sight whitethroats and sedge warblers skimmed from twig to twig, and we marked their progress only by brief bursts of sound as their wings hammered rapidly against the air. Occasionally the birds emerged briefly from the smooth dome of knotted branches; tiny creatures whose voices had the power to fill the air with music. Elsewhere the sound of bird song was usually lost to us in the roar of the wind or the harsh persistent call of seabirds. It was a favourite place of ours; so different to the rest of the island that it stirred vague thoughts of another

125

time and another place, but still made us happy to be where we were.

Towards its seaward end the valley became a wild confusion of brambles. Progress was slow, and the thorns snagged and tore at our clothes, and so it was a journey that we made too rarely, but reaching the sea at last and seeing a fresh view of our familiar coastline was always enough of a reward to bring us back. In early autumn the brambles that surrounded us dripped with blackberries. Over-ripe fruits fell from the bushes, staining the leaves below with dark juice. The temptation to taste one was always irresistible, and one led to another until our fingertips took on that unmistakable shade of crimson-blue.

After six summers on Skomer we realised increasingly that it was a mistake to look only for the obvious, to see only the seabirds and miss the quieter corners of the island. Even at night there were many different aspects to Skomer. At first the shearwaters seemed to overwhelm everything, crashing haphazardly to the ground amid a deafening riot of calls. Just to avoid a dangerously close encounter with the fast-moving birds seemed to demand total concentration. But gradually, with familiarity, the noise receded and I became less disconcerted by the wings whistling past my head, and another smaller, less spectacular world emerged. As well as shearwaters, toads too scattered themselves across the paths. Grey-green and lumpy with sulking mouths they still managed a certain grotesque charm. In mid-summer the glow worms appeared. I had never seen them before, and was amazed to discover so many. They studded the blackness with points of luminous green, and the light they produced had a surprising intensity. At this time of year too the scent of honeysuckle oozed into the night air. As summer drew to a close even the sea came alive with sparkling phosphorescence. We kicked our feet against the black waves and trailed our hands through the dark water just to watch the sea momentarily spangled with a blaze of white sparks. We never grew tired of the island because the more we knew of it, the more we realised how much there was still to be discovered.

ELEVEN

I NEVITABLY ON AN ISLAND so full of life death, too, was common-place. It was something we had to accept; a balance of nature in which we played no part. We could only do our utmost to ensure that conditions on Skomer were the best possible for the breeding birds, and reconcile ourselves to the fact that not every chick emerging damp and bewildered from its shell was meant to survive. Sometimes it was hard to maintain this philosophical attitude, and we grew very fond of certain creatures, particularly those that lived close to the house.

The attachment that we developed for the rabbits that came to the surface outside our kitchen window was something that surprised even ourselves. We discovered that any vegetable waste was devoured ravenously by the rabbits, and from then on all peelings and scraps of vegetables were deposited straight out of the window. To our amazement we realised that crusts of stale bread, thrown out for the birds, were a particular favourite of the rabbits. As dusk gradually turned everything to grey the rabbits emerged. Slowly and tentatively at first, drawn by the food-scented air, they crept forward and nibbled anxiously at the discarded leaves furthest from the house. Gaining confidence in the growing darkness they came further forward and were joined by others, twitching their noses and cautiously sniffing the offerings before choosing between a cabbage leaf or a rosy twist of apple peel.

At first I was surprised to see disputes breaking out over a particularly choice morsel. I was so used to seeing rabbits chewing contentedly at the grass that I had never imagined they would fight over food. I soon grew accustomed to seeing a tug of war take place over a slice of bread until the victorious rabbit broke free and hurtled down the slope. Slowed by the bread trailing from its mouth it would soon be caught by the second, and another struggle would follow. The slice of bread might break in two, or change hands several times, before eventually being dragged down a burrow.

Under cover of darkness even the most timid of rabbits ventured out, and leaning silently out of the window we heard the cool night air come alive with the munching of tiny jaws. No matter how much food we put out for them it was always gone by morning. The only things that they would not eat under any circumstances were leeks!

Most endearing of all were the young rabbits, which emerged sometimes as early as February. When they first left the security of the burrow they were tiny, and appeared frighteningly vulnerable. Their fur was fluffed out from their bodies giving a softly rounded appearance, and with the low morning sun lighting them from behind they seemed to be surrounded by a golden halo. The kittens appeared singly or in family groups, sometimes as many as four together. Still less wary than the adults, the youngsters came above ground throughout the day and, provided we remained quite silent, we could watch them without fear of causing disturbance. In the quiet of the day, with little competition from the older rabbits who would have driven them away, the kittens were able to take full advantage of the vegetables they found outside our house. When startled they darted for cover, diving underground through holes that looked far too small for rabbits, or scurrying into our cellar through the shearwater holes.

It is easy to imagine that all wild rabbits look the same, but a small proportion of the Skomer rabbits, probably about one in every hundred, were jet black. When one of these tiny, black creatures made its first appearance above ground on the grassy bank outside our house it was an instant favourite. Its fur was fine and glossy, and it was characterised, as were many of the rabbits in that small area, by a tiny, white spot on its forehead. It appeared so small and fragile I found myself watching anxiously each day to make sure it would show itself. Every time I saw it it appeared to have grown a little more, and I began to feel increasingly hopeful about its survival. One evening we returned to the house just as the light was going. Entering the kitchen we heard a scream from outside and hurried to the window. We arrived just in time to see the black rabbit being carried off by a gull. At times like that we found it very hard to accept the justice of nature, even though we knew that everything had to eat to survive.

The most unforgettable of all rabbits was not one of those that we watched daily from the house, but one which lived far away on the north-west coast of the island, on the steep, grass-covered slope above Bull Hole. This rabbit was pure white, and we strongly suspected it to be at least eight years old. Although this seemed to be an impossibly great age for a rabbit, we knew that there had been a fully-grown white rabbit at Bull Hole for this length of time. We had never seen more than one white rabbit in the area, and so could only assume that the same individual had reigned throughout the years. He (or possibly she) was usually above ground unless the weather was really terrible. His white fur stood out like a beacon on the distant green bank, and gave him the appearance of being twice the size of the other rabbits. He seemed almost fearless, and when an inquisitive raven sweeping too low over the ground sent the others scrambling for their burrows, the white rabbit remained impassively chewing the grass. Possibly his odd colouring was his protection in that predators did not recognise this strange, white animal as food, and perhaps unthreatened he became unafraid. His presence was so welcome and so dependable that he became an important landmark for us, and we dreaded the day when he would not be there, or worse still that we might find him dead. Each year we felt he would not survive another winter, but he always did. During our last year on the island we stopped seeing him regularly. Whole weeks would pass, and we would decide that he must definitely be dead, only to see him again a few days later. In the few months before we left Skomer we did not see him at all and, although logic tells me he must have perished, in my imagination he will always be there.

Of all the birds we encountered, none had a character to compare with the Raven. He was about two months old when he was found, his wing having been broken by mobbing gulls. He was large, but not quite full-grown, and his feathers were dull, lacking the oil-slick shine of a healthy adult's. He arrived dejected and aggressive, and had to be put in a cardboard box while a cage was built for him. Built on the bank behind the house the cage was about six feet square, and inside were a variety of perches and runs, and a small wooden shelter. It was the best we could manage in the time, and certainly adequate for a bird without the use of its wings. The Raven was taken ashore to the vet, who strapped his wings together with sticking plaster, which was to remain in place for six weeks, and said that there was about a fifty percent chance of him flying again. When transferred from the cardboard box to the freedom of his cage it took the Raven only about half an hour to remove the strapping from his wings. Fortunately, the vet had shown Mike how to replace it; the only problem was retrieving the Raven from his cage. He cowered back into the little gap beneath his shelter and hunched his shoulders menacingly, his thick, blue-black beak glinting from the darkness. Armed with a pair of strong, leather gloves Mike entered the cage and seized the angry bird. The wing was secured with heavy, green tape which proved so impervious to attack that eventually the Raven gave up trying, and it remained in place throughout the recovery period.

The Raven never had any other name. It was our firm intention that once his wing was healed he would return to the wild, and therefore it was important that he did not become tame. To this end he was fed, watered and ignored. He settled down quickly, and seemed contented as he hopped from perch to perch. Shortly after dawn each morning he greeted the day with a beautiful melodious song. It was so different from the characteristic, harsh 'kronk, kronk', which was the only call I had ever associated with ravens, that I could hardly believe it came from the same bird.

Six weeks passed quickly, and when the time came to remove the strapping I felt a sense of foreboding. It was hard to believe that a piece of green tape could work a miracle, and that the Raven would fly again. If it had not worked, the disappointing discovery was something we would rather have put off until another time. We allowed an extra few days, just to be sure, but could hesitate no longer. The indignant Raven was removed from his cage, and the tape carefully cut. The feathers were very ragged where the tape had been, and the broken wing drooped a little lower than the good one. He was returned to his cage to recuperate and exercise his wings before we put him to the test to see how well he had recovered.

On his first excursion from the cage it was obvious that the Raven would not fly. Even so, to be sure we had not judged him too hastily, he was given another try after a few days, with the same spectacular lack of success. One thing was certain; he would never return to the wild. With this fact sadly established there was no longer any advantage in treating him with aloof reserve, and we set about making friends with him. We had noticed from the start what an extraordinarily intelligent creature he was. He never appeared bored or dejected as caged animals often do, but was alert and active, always finding something to do, and watching the world around him with endless interest. Now that the ban on associating with him was lifted we spent many hours standing by his cage and talking to him, which he seemed to enjoy enormously.

We were constantly on the lookout for new toys for him. He seemed particularly to like small objects which he could hide in his cage. He had already built up a good collection of stones in various shapes and sizes, and was delighted to add to this. His collection was carefully secreted, possibly buried or hidden behind a piece of wood, and at regular intervals was resurrected and transferred to a new place of concealment. His most precious items were kept separately in various secure hiding places. These included a rabbit's ear which he had stolen one day from his mealtime offering, and the original sticky tape that he had removed from his wings. Just when we thought he had forgotten about these distasteful trophies he would make unerringly for the spot where they were hoarded and examine them proudly for some minutes before finding them a new resting place, trying several until he was satisfied that he had found the most suitable. For many years after he was gone, when we were preparing the cage for some new, temporary inmate, we would come across one of these forgotten treasures and those days would come flooding back, mingling sadness with happy memories.

Undoubtedly his favourite toy was a strip of brightly-coloured canvas tied to the roof of the cage, which he played with tirelessly. Encouraged by the success of this piece of canvas, we made the mistake of installing a second hanging plaything for him. Mike attached a piece of string to the lid of an aerosol can and suspended it in the cage. The Raven examined the new arrival with cautious interest, moving round it and inspecting it from all angles. At last he gave it a firm tap with his beak, and the lid swung rapidly back and forth. The Raven was seized with panic, and flung himself wildly at the sides of the cage in an attempt to escape the menacing object. We removed the plastic lid as quickly as we could, full of remorse for causing the Raven such distress. He soon recovered from the shock however, and continued to be fascinated by the canvas, and by the strings tying his door shut, the ends of which dangled outside the cage, and which he never tired of trying, unsuccessfully, to reach.

We could not pass the cage without stopping for a chat with the Raven. Even when we were hurrying past at great speed we always called out 'hallo'. We were completely unprepared for the day when, approaching the Raven with the usual greeting, we were met with a distinct and perky 'allo' in reply. We were quite taken aback, and tried to make the Raven speak again, but no amount of halloing on our part would elicit a repeat performance, until we began to wonder if we had imagined it. Over the next few days however the Raven used his new-found word frequently, and eventually we would have been surprised if he had not answered us. 'Allo' remained the only word in his vocabulary, but it acquired a number of subtle nuances, and his use of language seemed to bring a new dimension to the Raven's character.

Spring became summer, which in turn faded to autumn, and the Raven was still with us. He was now strong and healthy, and his feathers had a rich, blue-black sheen. As the cold, lonely days of winter drew near his cheerful presence was indescribably welcome. Returning to the house in the chill, grey light of early evening we watched the sky grow dark in the company of the Raven. The only problem was feeding him. He needed a whole rabbit each day, whatever the weather. On cold bleak days, particularly when the wind was in an easterly quarter, the rabbits knew better than to show their heads above ground. We would walk interminably without so much as a sight of a rabbit, not daring to go home without one. I remember the icy wind pressing against my head and cheeks until it seemed to penetrate right through the skin and make the bones ache. We had also grown fond of the rabbits, and Mike had a distinct distaste for shooting them. Nevertheless, it all seemed worthwhile when we returned triumphant and saw the Raven's excitement at the arrival of his meal.

The ultimate fate of the Raven was something we could not put off forever. From the day we knew he would not return to

132

the wild it was a nagging irritation at the back of our minds, but something we chose to ignore for as long as possible. The cage had been built as a temporary solution for an injured bird and, although he still seemed very happy in it, conscience dictated that we could not allow him to remain confined in it for the rest of his life. He was now as strong and healthy as he would ever be, and we had to think of his long-term future. We considered various possibilities such as sending him to a zoo, or even the Tower of London. But would anyone accept an injured bird, and might he not be miserable? I found the prospect of him ending up in one of these places intensely depressing; our cliff top bird who sang to the dawn could not go and live in a city. We could put off the decision, but it would not go away.

I don't know how or when it first began, but slowly the idea evolved between us that we might, after all, be able to keep the Raven. He was so tame now that we thought perhaps we could simply open the cage door and leave him free to come and go as he wished. There were no predators on Skomer that could harm him, we would continue to feed him, and he could use the cage as necessary for rest and shelter. The idea was too good to be true, but there was no obvious reason why it would not work.

Once the idea was fully crystallised in our minds we took the first chance to put it to the test. The day was cold but settled when, with a great deal of trepidation, we opened the cage door wide and retreated to the house. I expected him to take the first opportunity to escape from the cage after months of confinement, and we were very worried that he might take off at great speed and get lost. He would be unable to feed himself, and would die if we could not find him. We stationed ourselves behind the front door, which was just open, and peered through the gap. We had a good view of the cage, but felt sure that the Raven could not see us. We waited, but nothing happened. The Raven was well aware that the door was open. He looked frequently at the gaping hole and occasionally poked his head out to survey the world, but it seemed nothing tempted him, and he carried on about his normal business.

After about an hour he remembered the string hanging outside the cage that he had been trying for weeks to get hold of. He went to the door and leaned out, snapping at the string with his beak. He was within an inch of it but could not reach, no matter how

133

hard he stretched his neck. The struggle continued for a long time until finally, in exasperation, the Raven jumped outside, grabbed the string, and then hopped back inside clutching the end of the string in his beak. This was total contentment; he had won, and wanted nothing more. When about two hours had passed it was obvious that this was to be the extent of the Raven's adventure in the outside world. Stiff with cold and the effort of keeping still we emerged from our hiding place and went to close the cage door. I was pleased to think that the Raven was so contented in his cage that he was not desperate to make a bid for freedom, but it was frustrating to have moved no further forward with our plan to liberate him.

The following day we tried again. Huddled behind the front door we watched events unfold very much as on the previous day. The Raven showed no interest in leaving until finally his desire for the string forced him to hop outside to reach it, but he returned immediately. Then at last the breakthrough came. He left the cage twice, only for a minute or two each time, and never wandering more than a few feet from it, but he had left of his own free will. On the third occasion he walked slowly and tentatively away from the cage. We watched, transfixed, in alarm and fascination. He walked along the side of the house and disappeared in the direction of the nearby tractor track. We had no option but to follow. We dared not risk losing him, but we were concerned that our appearance might alarm him and send him scuttling for cover into the maze of undergrowth where we might never find him. We crept silently forward, pressing close against the wall of the house. As we rounded the corner we saw him standing in the middle of the dusty track and looking round for items of interest. We were edging towards him when he looked up and saw us. We froze, and the Raven froze, mesmerising us with his glittering black eyes. We dared not move until suddenly the Raven broke the deadlock by striding towards us and calling out a cheery 'Allo!'.

We joined him on the tractor track, and sat on its dry, sandy surface, keeping all our movements slow and steady, still afraid that any sudden movement might cause panic. He came to us quite readily, and bustled between us bringing stones and other exciting bits of debris. He was frightened by any movement we made towards him, and we had to wait for him to approach us.

Despite this, we felt that things were working out better than we had dared hope, and it seemed that the Raven might soon be granted the freedom of the island, provided he showed no inclination to stray. We realised that we had something of a problem when the time came to return the Raven to his cage. We walked slowly towards him trying to usher him in the right direction. He would have none of it, and dodged hastily past us. We tried several times more, but he simply grew agitated. We could have made a grab for him, but that would have risked undoing all our good work, and if the first attempt had been unsuccessful he might have fled in panic. We tried a different tack. We walked ahead of him hoping he would follow.

'Come on. Come on,' we coaxed gently.

This seemed more successful. After watching us carefully he took a few steps in the right direction. Confident of his acquiescence we moved on calling softly all the while, but when we turned back he was not behind us. He was in fact running at full speed towards the cliff, and when he reached it he launched himself over the edge. His useless wings beat the air in panic as he plunged sickeningly towards the rocks below. I wanted to turn away, but it was all over so quickly that I was still watching as he slid to a reasonably gentle halt on the far side of North Haven and disappeared into a nearby cave. Obviously his wings had broken his fall enough to give him a soft landing, but he would not survive unlesss we could retrieve him.

The narrow inlet where he had landed was only accessible from the sea, so we ran down to the beach and launched our dinghy. As we rowed quickly across the bay I felt a painful lump pressing deep inside my throat. The Raven could evade capture indefinitely among the rocks and gullies of North Haven. I had no doubt that he was now in a state of extreme agitation, and would do anything to avoid us. I despaired of ever bringing him safely home. When we reached the far side of North Haven we located him easily. He was hunched in a corner deeply shaded by the overhanging cliff, standing on a dark mound of rock completely surrounded by water. The boat slid smoothly and silently towards him until it hit the rock with a hollow sound that merged into the soft echo of the waves. The Raven's feathers were damp and bedraggled, and his head and shoulders drooped forward. He did not look up although we were now very close.

I reached out to the damp, weed-covered rock, and pulled the boat tight against it. I held my breath, not daring to make any sound or movement. Mike stretched his hand very, very slowly towards the Raven, fingers already half curled ready to grab. I tensed, waiting for the Raven to make his escape, but as Mike's hand drew closer the Raven stepped quietly on to his arm without even looking up, and allowed himself to be lifted into the boat. Then he raised his head a fraction and fixed us with his piercing eyes.

'Allo,' he said, by way of apology.

Though we were delighted to have the Raven back with us unscathed, we had sadly to conclude that it would not be safe to let him out of the cage by himself again. This time we had been lucky, but if it happened again he could easily injure himself in the fall, and if the sea was rough we would never reach him. By strange coincidence a lecturer in animal care was visiting the island. He had large aviaries in his garden where he was already caring for some injured owls, and would have loved to have offered the Raven a home, but seeing how fond we were of him had not dared ask. When we heard of this possibility of a good home we had no choice but to seize the opportunity.

A travelling cage was made for the Raven, and when the time came to leave some of his most familiar playthings were placed inside and his favourite piece of canvas was tied to the roof. I have to admit that I shed a few tears while we were preparing the Raven for his journey. He sat very forlornly in his new cage, for once not even interested in the strip of bright canvas. A slow, grey rain began to fall and so a sheet of polythene was stretched over the top of the cage, giving it the appearance of a covered wagon. Peering out from inside the Raven would have looked quite comical if it had not been such a solemn occasion.

We carried the Raven down to the beach and took him ashore in our boat. Throughout the crossing he looked as subdued as I felt. Everything was a pale, washed-out grey. The sky and sea were so uniform in colour that they merged without a horizon, and the dull drizzle continued to fall. When we reached Martin's Haven beach the Raven's cage was set down on the shiny, wet pebbles while luggage was loaded into the waiting car. Mike and I went to say a quiet goodbye before the Raven was put into the back of the car, and whisked away to a new life. He looked as dejected as on the day when we had rescued him from the beach. When we had finished talking to him he looked up and cocked his head characteristically to one side.

'Allo,' he said quietly for the last time.

TWELVE

THE PASSAGE OF TIME did nothing to endear us to the 'new' tractor. If we had felt that the old one was unsuitable for an island setting, it was still worse to have one with temperamental brakes in a place where the steep tracks swept to within feet of the cliff edge before lurching away in a hair-pin bend. Mike had wasted an inordinate amount of time pulling the tractor apart and putting it back together, and finally the West Wales Naturalists' Trust had decided that they would buy us a new tractor, but in the meantime we were still managing with the old one as best as we could. It was too essential to the smooth running of the island for us to consider abandoning it altogether, but Mike refused to let anyone else drive it.

One summer evening Mike and I were standing outside the house talking to Richard, our assistant warden, and looking out over North Haven enjoying the last of the day's sun. Into the stillness came the drone of an engine, and we were instantly curious. Looking out across the sea we could see a speck, which materialised into a small, yellow boat heading determinedly for North Haven. It did not take us long to decide that this small craft cutting a white trail through the water towards us must herald the arrival of Tim Healing. Tim visited the island for a week or so two or three times each year as part of his long-term study of the Skomer vole. After a quick cliff top discussion we decided that this arrival was definitely a mixed blessing. It was nice to see Tim again, particularly as he always brought some good food, a few bottles of wine and a selection of entertaining anecdotes, but the vast amount of luggage that travelled with him was legendary, and the subject of a great deal of leg-pulling. It was decided that Richard and I would take the direct route to the beach to help Tim land his vast array of boxes, while Mike followed behind with the tractor.

When Richard and I reached the shore all thought of carrying luggage was temporarily forgotten, and we were soon deep in conversation catching up on several months' news. After a minute or two I noticed that Tim was completely oblivious of what we were saying, and was staring past us, totally transfixed. Richard and I followed the direction of his gaze, and were startled to see the driverless tractor heading at full speed down the steep track to the beach with Mike running frantically behind it. Before I had time to take in the full horror of the situation the tractor swung in to the bank that rose steeply to the landward side of the track, and came to a stop. The three of us hurried from the beach to discover what had happened. Apparently Mike had been attempting to negotiate a sharp bend in the precipitous track when the brakes failed completely. Feeling it running out of control Mike had decided to jump free of the tractor before it plunged over the cliff. The tractor somehow remained steadfastly on the track, and continued to trundle rapidly towards the beach. Seeing the tractor was no longer in imminent danger Mike decided that he might be able to save it, and began to chase it down the rough, rutted track. It was at this point that Tim caught sight of the proceedings. The image of Mike in pursuit of the escaping tractor left us quite overcome with laughter as the story unfolded, but the serious side of the incident did not escape us, and we knew that the new tractor could not come soon enough.

This time it was a lot more straightforward bringing the tractor to the island since, in the intervening years Sea King helicopters, capable of lifting a tractor, had come to RAF Brawdy, and our friends at the air base were able to help with transportation. The appointed day was stormy, and brought with it the first rain that the island had seen for six weeks. The skies opened, and it was as though all the rain we had been spared during the height of the summer was pouring down on us. There was no possibility of the tractor being carried in that sort of weather so, to our great disappointment, its arrival was delayed until the following day. I loved our new tractor from the moment it was set down in the field with its blue paint-work gleaming in the sunshine. It was small and manoeuvrable, its engine purred gently, and above all the brakes were excellent.

139

Though we were delighted with the new tractor its arrival did not cause quite such a stir as the last one because Sea King helicopters now visited the island regularly. These helicopters had the capability of carrying heavy loads in underslung nets. The pilots that we knew well were of the opinion that there was no point in wasting their training time carrying practice loads up and down the airfield when they could be carrying useful loads of building materials out to Skomer. It was a view we wholeheartedly welcomed, and meant that it was not only when a task was impossible for us that we could call on the RAF; they were also there to help with the barely manageable. This arrangement was not quite as straightforward as it sounds. It meant that unfortunate crew members had to be persuaded to load the nets with tons of sand, cement or whatever was being carried, and that was definitely above and beyond the call of duty.

The summer was almost over by the time the tractor arrived, and as autumn came and we were alone again we were increasingly grateful for a reliable tractor. During these quiet periods Mike always managed to make sure that we had plenty of work to keep us occupied. This often left me in the unfortunate position of being an unwilling builder's mate. I was always relegated to the jobs that needed plenty of brawn and not much brain, but at least now we had the new tractor for transporting sand, cement and building blocks. There was also a perfectly good cement mixer that could be run off the tractor, and the fact that we were not using it was the cause of a certain amount of resentment.

Our current project was to build a new septic tank at the house, and Mike had decided that I should mix the mortar by hand, as this made it better quality than that produced by the cement mixer. As the septic tank was situated down a short but steep incline the mortar had to be shovelled into a bucket and carried down. When I found time I hurried down the slope with extra building blocks, while Mike laid the walls rapidly and deftly. I could not help noticing that Mike's job seemed a lot more interesting and less arduous than mine. As the days passed I grew increasingly irritated, particularly as I had yet to produce a batch of mortar that met with Mike's satisfaction. The mixes were always too wet, too dry or too sandy.

'You'll like this one. It's perfect,' I called as I slithered down the grassy bank with a bucket of mortar. Mike, rubbing a sample of the mixture between thumb and forefinger, invariably expressed his disapproval. Mike worked so quickly I found it very hard to keep him supplied with mortar and blocks. Hunched over my heap of concrete, churning it backwards and forwards with the shovel, I often felt as though I would never be able to straighten my back again. If at one of these low points I looked up to see Mike watching me, and waiting patiently for extra blocks, I felt very tempted to send the contents of my shovel flying in his direction.

At last we reached the point when only the roof of the septic tank remained to be built. Elaborate shuttering was made, and a long corrugated iron chute was constructed to carry the concrete down the slope. I was relieved when Mike decided that we would have to use the cement mixer for such a large quantity. We produced this jointly, taking turns to tip the bags into the mixer. When the first load was ready Mike examined it with the eye of a connoisseur.

'It's excellent,' he pronounced. 'You needn't have mixed the rest by hand after all.'

The autumn had started off unseasonably cold and very still. When we had been working outside building every day there had been that awful feeling of trying to force my boots on over my chilblains each morning, and the sensation that my hands were frozen in one position, clamped permanently round the shovel. However, this stillness had given way to violent storms that poured in from the Atlantic one after another, bringing with them rain and milder air. When the wind did die away, smoothing the foam from the surface of the sea and leaving behind only the deep, rounded swell waves, we were now better equipped to make a quick dash to the mainland before the weather deteriorated again. This was due to the new boat, supplied by BP after the oil spill, and a new outboard motor.

Despite this, when the storms succeeded each other with hardly a break the autumn and winter months could feel like a perpetual battle with the weather. When the full force of the wind hit the house the windows bowed alarmingly. This was particularly obvious when it was dark outside, and the reflected room was moved and distorted by the bending glass. If a gale sprang up suddenly we might not have time to put shutters up at the windows before the strength of the wind made this too dangerous. The living room always felt the most vulnerable with its huge window overlooking the isthmus which caught the winds tearing through from North Haven or South Haven. When at night the roaring grew so loud that we could hardly talk above the noise we went to bed for a greater feeling of security, because our bedroom, tucked in the inside angle of the L-shaped building, was the least exposed in the house. When it was very bad we could not sleep, and every muscle tensed in expectation when an exceptionally strong gust hit the house. At times like these I comforted myself with the thought that the house had been there for twenty years so surely it would survive one more. It was not until we had been on the island for several years that we met the builder of the house. He told us that as our wooden bungalow was nearing completion, an unexpected gale had moved it about three feet from its foundations. They had dragged it back to its original position, and held it down with dozens of wires criss-crossing the cellar. I never again felt quite as safe when the wind howled outside.

Our favourite wind was a westerly, because the house was completely sheltered from it. But roaring in, as it did, from the open ocean it had the strength to build huge, rolling waves and pile up the sea to form a powerful swell. When this happened the surging water gained such momentum it could take days to subside.

The series of early autumn gales had had little impact on us, but in mid-October the wind had picked up to storm force, and we began to feel a little anxious. It continued to blow at storm force from the west for several days, until the surface of the sea was white and the air full of foam. By nightfall of the third day the wind had reached violent storm force eleven. In the house we were completely sheltered, and not a breath of wind reached us, but in the distance we could hear its long, continuous scream, which we found almost more ominous than the storm battering at our doors and windows. The waves were now breaking half-way up the cliffs below us where previously they had only lapped at their feet. They hit the rocks with the booming note of thunder, and the noise was repeated every few seconds. The distant roar of the wind and the hollow echo of the waves left us feeling edgy; we paced the room, regularly peering out of the window and willing our eyes to penetrate the darkness.

'I think I'll go and check the boat,' Mike said at last.

142

The boat was tied with a whole network of ropes lashed backwards and forwards over it, and was next to the boat-shed, well above the beach, where it had always been secure, but in this weather nothing felt safe, especially as it was now high tide. Mike equipped himself with a powerful torch to look down from the cliff top, and was gone for ages. When he returned he looked very serious.

'The waves are hitting the boat. I think we might lose it,' he said.

I was shocked. The boat was our lifeline, and I couldn't imagine how we would manage without it.

After a period of anxious discussion we decided that we must try to save the boat. We clambered into our waterproofs fearing that we might already be too late. Mike decided to rope us together so that if I got swept away he would be able to hang on to me. I did not ask what would happen if we were both swept away. We edged our way down the track to the beach in complete darkness under a sky black with clouds. We could hear the crashing of the breakers, but could see nothing. Each time we heard the rumble of a wave hitting the rocks below we pressed close to the cliff which rose above us, and stood motionless until the noise subsided. In the darkness the sound of the sea was terrifying. The salt spray was washing over us now, and the closer we came to the bottom of the path the more I began to imagine that each approaching wave was going to break over us in a solid sheet of water and drag us into the sea. At the end of our slow descent we could make out the boat-shed in the torch beam with foam surging round it, licking at its base. The boat which lay on the seaward side of it was almost certainly beyond our reach. As the sea subsided we made a desperate dash, scrambling into the shed and slamming the door behind us. We listened, and for a moment everything was silent. Then came the rasp of the wave as it lumbered up the shingle beach. The noise grew in intensity until, with a crash which vibrated the shed, the wave hit the cliff above us, and then rained down on the roof with terrific force, the stones swept up by the water falling like hammer blows overhead. It seemed an eternity before the last of the water cascaded from the roof, and we were able to see out of the window to get a clear view of the boat. The ropes had held and, although she had been battered, the boat was still safe.

143

There was nothing we could do; we didn't even dare leave the shed. So we just watched and hoped. In time the waves became less powerful and less frequent, and we knew that the tide had receded far enough for us to venture out. We untied the rope uniting us and emerged into a waterlogged world. The boat had survived, almost unscathed, without our help. By now the strong winds had forced back the heavy cloud cover, and the scene was illuminated by a bright moon. The danger over for the night, we were in no hurry to return home and so stayed to watch the huge waves as they battered against the cliffs forming a dense foam that shone white in the moonlight.

By the next high tide the wind had dropped enough to calm our immediate fears for the boat, but the sea remained wild for several days to come. When the waves finally died down we were able to get Tim Healing across to the island again. Previously he had always confined his visits to the more hospitable times of year, when gales rarely lasted more than a day or two and a passenger boat was on hand in Martin's Haven to rescue stranded visitors. Now Tim had decided that if his research on the Skomer vole was to give a complete picture he would have to visit outside the summer season. Normally we would have been unwilling to accept the responsibility for anyone visiting the island at this time of year, but Tim had been acquainted with Skomer long enough to understand the risks of being stranded. Barely had we got Tim and all the trappings of his work on to the island when the wind started to pick up again. By daybreak a south-easterly was blowing with some force. It was a bleak, sunless day, and this was our least favourite wind. It was the only wind from a southerly quarter that broke through the island's defences, funnelling up through South Haven and clipping the eastern side of the house with all its might. South-easterlies, though relatively rare, were vicious and often very cold. Throughout the morning the wind had been increasing steadily in strength until it grew to a steady roar outside. It was an exceptionally constant wind, lacking the usual rise and fall of gusts and eddies.

It was Tim's noisy arrival at the front door that first alerted us to the problem. The door crashed open and we heard Tim calling urgently. As we realised what was happening we struggled into our coats and boots and hurried outside. We were greeted by the sight of fragments of our cedar shingle roof blowing in the air,

144

and an ominous ripping sound as more were torn loose. The hole was narrow, and only a few feet long, but we knew that if it was left unchecked the roof would soon be lost. Hurriedly Tim and I brought the ladder while Mike found tools and some old pieces of lead sheet to nail over the hole as a temporary repair. The ladder was hoisted into place, and Mike climbed carefully on to the roof and edged his way up the shingles to the apex, where the problem was. I held tight to the ladder, but the strengthening wind kept trying to wrench it from my grasp. Tim came to my aid, and it took two of us to hold the ladder still. Although we stood less than two feet apart, we had to shout to communicate above the howling wind.

Up on the roof Mike looked frighteningly vulnerable as the wind whipped round him. In only a few minutes its strength had intensified so much that I began to worry that he would not be able to move to make his way back to the ladder. The wind continued to tear at the frayed edges of the roof. Shattered pieces of shingle were hurled into the air, some of them bouncing off Mike's forehead as they passed. Although they were light they moved with enough force to cause small cuts. I watched with unease as smears of blood appeared above Mike's eyes, as though some unseen hand were dabbing him with a red paintbrush. He continued, unflinching, perhaps in the stress of the moment unaware of the splinters of wood bombarding his face.

Then, suddenly, his coat turned inside out, as though it had been seized by the hem and dragged completely over his head, despite the fact that it was a heavy, tight-fitting jacket. The situation was dangerous since Mike was both immobilised and unable to see. Despite my sickening fear, there was a momentary recognition of the humorous aspect of this strait-jacketed figure flailing on the roof. Mike fought free, and then shouted down to us, 'I can't hold on. Get me a rope.'

The words were snatched and broken by the wind the instant they left his mouth, but after several repetitions we deciphered the most important parts. The tractor was brought round to the front of the house, and a heavy rope was secured to the roll bar. The other end was passed up to Mike and he tied it round his waist. It seemed to me that it offered rather more moral than practical support, but whichever was the case it served well, and work progressed smoothly.

As Mike prepared to hammer the last sheet of lead in place, the wind whisked it out of his hand and took it off across the island. Leaving Tim holding the ladder I raced after it. The lead bowled along the ground at such a speed that I could not keep up with it, and I was surprised that the wind could carry its heavy weight so easily. It finally came to rest in a hollow, and by the time I reached it, it was rolled into a ball like a piece of crumpled paper. I made my way slowly back, trying to straighten the lead sheet as I went. By the time I returned to the house the lead was still very far from flat, and Tim turned to help me, momentarily forgetting about the ladder. No sooner had he released his grip than the ladder was toppled by the wind. Glancing up I saw it plummeting down towards Tim, who now had his back to it. I opened my mouth to speak too late. Within a fraction of a second the ladder had crashed down on to the back of Tim's head. Despite the fact that almost every sound was blotted out by the monotonous roar of the wind, I distinctly heard the thump. Tim fell forward, and the ladder landed on top of him.

Looking at Tim lying face down in the wet grass, his yellow oilskins covered with droplets of water, I felt a moment of utter despair. Judging by the sound of the crash Tim was either dead or severely injured. Mike was stuck on the roof with no possibility of my being able to lift the ladder back up by myself in the wind, and I was stranded there alone. I tried to lift the ladder off Tim. Each time I had raised it more than a few inches the wind forced it back down again. I had not been struggling long when Mike's voice drifted down to me. Despite the fact that it was barely audible in the howling air, I could hear that it was distorted with anger and the effort of competing against the wind. The words he used were quite unrepeatable, but the general meaning was, 'Where's the ladder?' I could understand his annoyance. Tim and I were close in under the house, and therefore out of sight of the roof top. From where Mike was situated it must have appeared that we had taken the ladder and gone away, leaving him stranded. Under the circumstances I considered it best to ignore these shouts, and continue trying to free Tim.

To my astonishment, Tim came round and pushed his way out from under the ladder. I was so startled I had to suppress a hysterical giggle. It was rather like seeing someone push back the coffin lid and rise from the dead. Tim however continued with the job in hand quite unaffected, and I decided that in my panic I must have overestimated the extent of his injuries. Mike's frenzied shouts brought me quickly back to reality, and between us Tim and I replaced the ladder. Once the missing piece of lead was restored to him, Mike quickly finished the work and returned to ground level.

The wind was screaming with an alarming intensity, and the eastern side of the house was being battered mercilessly. We had storm-shutters to protect the largest windows, but now even the small windows were flexing perilously. The weather was much too severe to allow us to construct any makeshift protection from the outside, so we tacked thick blankets across the inside of the most exposed windows to protect the rooms from shattering glass. With the house reasonably secure we could not resist trying to snatch a glimpse of South Haven. Although it was only a very short walk we made surprisingly slow progress. The wind put up strong resistance to every step we made, so that it felt as though we were wading up a fast-flowing stream. Tiny strands of hair whipped painfully at my face, and any loose cords on our jackets were so dangerous that they were quickly secured out of harm's way. As we came closer to the cliff edge a needle-like barrage of fine spray rained on to our faces and stung our eyes, forcing us to turn away.

The wind was so strong and steady that we were able to lean right into it and remain supported by its grip. The brink of South Haven stayed tantalisingly out of reach. The wind forced up and over the cliff was skimming the ground with such force that it formed an almost impenetrable barrier. Several times we had been forced back until finally we decided to crawl forward on our hands and knees. This was slow, but effective. The densely burrowed ground gave us good hand holds, and we were able to flatten ourselves against the earth and hang on tight when the worst gusts came. When we did reach the edge there was very little to see. The swirling, biting sea spray made it impossible to look down. Turning my face sideways and peering out through a slit between my fingers I was just able to glimpse the arching mounds of surf, their crests pluming into a haze of droplets, all colours muted to a soft grey in the shimmering, damp air. Edging back from the cliff and then rising to our feet the driving wind forced us to retreat at a run. Reaching the house we were gasping from the exertion of trying to draw breath from the wind that pressed

147

so hard against our faces we felt it was smothering us, and our cheeks were red and tingling.

Inside the house as we took our coats off I realised that I had not had the opportunity to explain to Mike where Tim and I had disappeared to, leaving him stranded.

'When you were on the roof,' I began, but suddenly the ludicrousness of the situation overwhelmed me, and I could not find words to describe the horror I felt as I remembered Tim collapsed on the ground, and Mike's angry shouts floating down from the roof. Attempting to balance on one leg while I removed my boot I fell back against the wall, helpless with laughter and unable to stand. It was the sudden relief of tension, and every time I tried to speak laughter gushed forth instead. It was some minutes before I could tell Mike the full story, and he hurried out to make sure that Tim was suffering no after effects.

Mike's most time-consuming project that winter was the work on the old farm buildings. He was completely renovating what had always been rather grandly termed 'the chalets'. These were in fact stables that had undergone a very makeshift conversion to visitor accommodation in the fifties, complete with asbestos partitioning and crumbling floors. Mike was now turning these drab rooms into bright, self-contained units. Towards the end of the summer, with whatever help that was available, he had completely gutted the interior of two of the chalets, demolishing the walls, and smashing up the old concrete floors so that only bare earth remained. He was now rebuilding the interior and re-cladding the rough, leaking walls of the existing structure. When everyone had left we continued working by ourselves, and then Tim stayed on for an extra few days to help before heading back to the mainland. By the time Tim left the rooms were still empty shells with earth floors, and we felt almost overwhelmed by the amount of work that was still to be done before the spring.

It was a dreary December day when we arrived at the old farm at first light to start laying the floors. My job, as usual, was to mix the concrete, but at least I was allowed the assistance of the cement mixer. Mike had the more skilful task of getting the floor smooth and level. I tipped the bags of sand one after the other into the cement mixer, carefully adding just enough water and cement powder. The mixer seemed to have an insatiable appetite, and devoured an enormous quantity to make one load. I was very disappointed to see that the first mix of concrete covered only one tiny corner of the floor.

By mid-morning I was exhausted. Each time I lifted a heavy, wet bag of sand and poured it into the mixer I thought I would never be able to lift another, but always I managed just one more. It was well into the afternoon when we finished the first floor. I watched with satisfaction as Mike smoothed the last finishing touches, and felt relieved that we had finished in good time to get the tools cleaned up before the light failed. Plunging my hands deep into the pockets of my boiler suit out of the cold, I was already visualising the prospect of a hot cup of coffee when Mike looked up and saw me.

'Come on! Get the next load ready for the other room,' he called.

'We can't. We'll never finish before dark,' I protested.

'Of course we will, we're getting quicker all the time,' insisted Mike.

Reluctantly I started the next load.

Darkness had descended before the second floor was three quarters completed. We continued as grey turned to black, and Mike had to finish the floor by feel rather than sight since we did not even have the benefit of a torch. Before we left I retrieved my packed lunch which I had not had time to eat. I pulled out one of the sandwiches and took a bite out of it as we walked home through the darkness. It was stale brown bread filled with peanut butter. I had thought it a very unappetising combination when I was making them, but there was not much else to choose from. It had the texture of sawdust, but I was so hungry it seemed quite pleasant.

'Where are yours?' I asked Mike.

'I've eaten them,' he replied a little self-consciously.

I didn't ask how he'd found time for lunch, but simply handed him a sandwich. I was not desperate enough to eat two anyway.

THIRTEEN

W HEN YET ANOTHER SUMMER PASSED and faded into memory there
were always compensations; what the autumn lacked in birds
and flowers it made up for in seals and solitude. The clamorous
cries of the birds diminished until, by September, the island was at
times almost silent. The cliffs echoed instead to the long, doleful
wail of the seals, more in keeping with the melancholy mood of the
season which, for all its charms, still signalled the end of summer.
Though autumn invariably brought mellow days, it could be as
bleak and as wild as the howl of the seal suggested.

At its best September was an idyllic month, when the
beauty of summer merged into the grandeur of winter, and
the best of both were captured. The dying bracken blazed
red in the low evening sun and the brilliant purple heather formed
blocks of colour that extended for acres. The lichen-covered cliffs
were at their brightest, the intense colour lingering somewhere
between yellow and orange. The sheltered, ivy-clad slopes around
North Haven attracted butterflies that came to taste the last nectar
of the year. In some years they gathered in such profusion that
their red and orange wings looked like flowers mingled with the
deep green ivy leaves. Red admirals and painted ladies came
in their hundreds to enjoy one of those early autumn days that
masquerades as high summer; unconcerned or unaware that when
the season showed its true colours their fragile links with life would
be severed. Everything was enhanced by the crisp clarity of the
light, rarely seen in the hazy heat of summer. The distant view
was so unbroken that sea met sky in a hard, curving line as far
as the eye could see in all directions.

More often than not September meant gales. These could
arrive with a ferocity that turned summer to winter over-

night. The powerful winds lifted sea-spray from the foaming water and poured it over the island. The salt-laden air blackened and withered the bracken, while the relentless charge of the wind beat it to the ground. The exotic purple-red blossoms of the fuchsias in the farmyard were hurled to the ground, and the blackberries were smashed from their bushes. It was very disappointing to see the slow, subtle changes of autumn pass in a single day, and to know that we would not see another for a whole year.

The weather we liked least was fog. Although autumn is supposedly the season of mists it could also be a period of crystal clear skies, but if the fog did arrive it could remain for days, hanging so densely around the island that even the sea seemed to have disappeared. The effect of this weather was very depressing, and when we woke to the dull drone of the foghorn echoing from the distant Skokholm lighthouse it was enough to make us roll over in bed and shut out the grey world for just a little longer.

For me autumn meant seals, and whatever the weather the numbers around the island increased steadily as the season progressed. These were grey seals, and my interest in them grew as the years passed. The seals hauled out on the beaches round the island, allowing themselves a respite from the waves. The two main haul-out sites were at Castle Bay and just below our house in North Haven, but over the years Castle Bay gradually became the most well-used site. We could watch the North Haven seals from our kitchen window, but I preferred the setting of Castle Bay. It was a beautiful picturesque little cove set into the southern tip of the Neck. Craggy forbidding cliffs swept round it in an arc, making it inaccessible from the land except with the aid of climbing equipment. On one side an arm of grass-topped rock reached out into the sea. From the end of this projection it was possible to look down on an uninterrupted view of Castle Bay, and any seals sheltering there could be watched completely undisturbed.

In the later years on Skomer we undertook an intensive study of the seals, and I visited Castle Bay and the other seal beaches without fail each day through the autumn, winter and early spring. For me those early morning walks in September, when the seal season was just starting, captured the essence of what made Skomer so special. Each day was unique and different from the last. To reach the Neck I had to cross the narrow isthmus of land that separated it from the main part of the island. On some days the wind that ripped between North Haven and South Haven made it almost impossible to stand, solid, dark sea churned below me and I had to fight for every breath. On other days the air was so calm, and the sea so clear and smooth, that the shimmering yellow of the sandy sea bed mingled with the blue water turning it to liquid turquoise. The sea was so transparent that it seemed to have little more substance than air, and the seals that drifted in it appeared to defy gravity, while deep below their shadows flickered across the rippled sand.

Leaving the isthmus I would follow the cliffs for the length of South Haven before turning east and walking along the ridge of an Iron Age fort. Skirting Castle Bay I would cross a dense area of thrift, the pink flowers now dry and papery, the fine-leaved, green cushions springing under foot. Even well into the autumn pockets of flowers burst into life in the sheltered hollows of this south-facing slope, forming little islands of spring completely out of step with their surroundings. Until September was well advanced, my route took me through lesser black-backed gull territory. Always resentful of any intrusion they screeched and dived angrily, but as summer faded they deserted the island, and their harsh calls gave way to subtler songs.

However much this walk varied from one day to the next I always hoped to find seals at the end of it. Surprisingly, good weather reduced my chances. When the sun shone and the sea was calm the seals abandoned the beach at Castle Bay in favour of the offshore rocks. As I edged out along the promontory to get a view of the bay below, the sounds that drifted up hinted at what I would see. When the cliffs resounded to long, sonorous, haunting howls echoing from the water I knew that there would be seals. On warm, tranquil September days the seals dragged themselves with difficulty on to the weed-covered rocks that littered the waters of Castle Bay at low tide. Others drifted in the sea, heads above the surface surrounded by stars of sunlight that skittered across the water, bodies trailing downwards, resting motionless. Others still played in the gentle waves that brushed against the shingle. Lying inert at the water's edge they allowed the lapping movement to tumble them back and forth. It was a scene that conveyed a contentment I found infectious.

In bad weather the picture was a very different one. Strong winds heaped the sea into opaque, grey waves that shattered into a cloud of foam as they crashed on to the shore. In search of a more peaceful resting place the seals crowded on to the tiny beach of Castle Bay. Sometimes, particularly as autumn drew into winter, there might be as many as 180 present. At low tide the beach could accommodate these numbers comfortably, but as the tide crept relentlessly up the beach the seals moved closer together, the ever diminishing patch of sand, shingle and rock almost disappearing under a carpet of seals. Forced into uncomfortably close proximity with each other, skirmishes broke out and the air filled with hissing growls. The once peaceful group moved restlessly, the pattern of smooth bodies broken as they turned incessantly to snap at a neighbour that edged too close. These encounters were often noisy and dramatic, with foreflippers flailing wildly at the opponent and teeth bared in an angry hiss, but they rarely resulted in injury. The most likely outcome was that all parties would lose interest and go back to sleep, or that a more timid seal, feeling itself intolerably harassed, would head rapidly for the sea scattering everything in its path. Inevitably as the tide moved on up the beach those closest to its onslaught would peel away from the main group and head out to sea, eventually leaving only a few of the most tenacious animals sheltering in the remaining corners of exposed shore.

The grey seal comes in every shade of that colour ranging between black and white, often warmed by tinges of brown. The females, or cows, are mostly mid-grey in colour dappled with darker patches, and paler on the underside. The bulls are usually darker, sometimes almost pure black, and more even in colour, but can occasionally be quite pale. They are all covered with thick, dense fur which looks smooth and shiny when wet, but which dries soft and matt. The bulls are larger than the cows, sometimes over seven feet long. Males and females can be easily distinguished, even when only the head is above water, as the facial characteristics are very distinctive. The bull has a heavy, Roman nose, while that of the cow is gently concave in profile and altogether more delicate. The neck and shoulders of the bull are thick and muscular, often shrouded in rolls of loose skin, whereas the cow is slimmer and sleeker.

A cow is likely to have her first pup at around six years of age. Under ideal conditions grey seals do not form pairs, but the bull will have a harem of perhaps seven cows. Under the less than perfect breeding conditions on Skomer however, they did frequently form pairs. Many of the barely accessible caves and tiny, rock-strewn beaches supported only one breeding cow at a time, and therefore any bull holding one of these territories would have only a single cow within his domain. In this situation the bull often spent a great deal of time with the cow and pup, whereas a cow who formed part of a harem usually kept the bull well away from her offspring.

The first pup was usually born in late August or early September, but I always began looking well in advance, afraid of missing this important event. During the season about seventy pups were born around Skomer, and to me each new birth was as exciting as the first. Seal pups are almost always born during the hours of darkness, and so I made a point of getting out early each morning to discover what the night had brought. Occasionally births do take place during the day, and several times I came tantalisingly close to seeing this, arriving at a breeding beach to discover a fresh, damp pup wailing its disapproval of the world, and realise that I had missed the birth by minutes.

When I did finally see the arrival of a pup it was as unspectacular as everything I had read suggested it would be. The birth was over in a minute or two, and could easily have been missed on a beach crowded with seals. I have rarely felt more pity for any living creature than for that new-born seal pup. I tried to imagine with what bewilderment it found itself transferred from warmth and darkness to the harsh world outside, without the slightest shelter to soften its arrival. Still damp, with its yellow fur clinging to its body and emphasising its bony outline, the new-born pup looked pathetically small and helpless. Its cries for attention sounded remarkably like those of a human baby. With temperatures around freezing at the time it was born, its only resting place was the cold, hard stones of the beach.

The cow seemed to want only to rest, despite the apparent ease of the birth, while the pup clamoured anxiously for attention from its first moments of existence. The mother

154

took her only chance of peace and moved a few yards from the restless pup, but the young animal followed determinedly. Its muscles weak and unco-ordinated, it scrabbled clumsily at the slippery stones gradually propelling itself forward with its flippers. Within an hour or so the warmth of its body had combined with the effect of the chill sea breezes to dry the pup's fur. The skinny animal with skull-like head was softened and rounded as the golden fur fluffed out around its body transforming it into the most endearing of creatures. The stark, protruding black eyes blended into the face like deep, dark pools, radiating new-born innocence.

The cow at last fed the pup but then slid quickly away to the sea. The pup did not settle. Perhaps it had not fed well; it seemed to be uncertain of what was expected of it and had taken the milk only erratically. When it was alone again it continued to search the beach, calling and moving aimlessly. All the time its vague movements were causing it to slip further down the shingle slope towards the sea while the tide, quite imperceptibly, was moving up the beach. Inevitably the two met and suddenly the pup was afloat. It was tossed in the foam at the edge of the stones. Sometimes it was lost and then it appeared again, its white fur almost indistinguishable from the surf. I lost all trace of the pup and was sure it was gone, then, appearing from nowhere, it was swimming, brilliant white against the smooth slatey waves further out in the bay. It flailed almost out of control, its front thrashing one way, its back the other. There was no co-ordination in its unused muscles, but somehow the pup crept towards the shore. It ducked through the foam and emerged again dragging its wet body, heavy with waterlogged fur, on to the stones. It was a scrawny new-born once more, the camouflaging fur now slicked smooth against its skin to reveal every imperfection, but it was beautiful. I felt a great wave of relief. To me every pup was an individual, and I already had a special affection for this one.

Although pups are capable of swimming from the day they are born, some knew nothing of the water until they had been abandoned by the cow and were forced to learn for themselves. The best way for a pup to be introduced to the sea was by a wise and experienced mother. Some cows led their pups down the beach when they were a few days old and offered food only at the water's edge. The cow would wait patiently with her

155

back pressed against the wash of the sea. Hunger for milk would eventually tempt even the most timid pup into the gently lapping waves and, although it probably swallowed a few mouthfuls of sea water along with its milk, it soon forgot to be wary of the sea. Such scenes were idyllic, but the sea was quick to change its moods, and could not always be considered a plaything.

Pups were most vulnerable in their first days of life, before they had gained strength and experience. Few of Skomer's beaches offered protection from the worst storms whose furious waves could reach right to the cliff edge inundating every refuge, and snatching a sheltering pup into their cold grasp. It always surprised me how few pups actually succumbed to the storms, and those that did were often already sickly or possibly had a young and inexperienced mother. A good cow seemed to be able to bring her pup through almost anything. I can remember watching the waves build throughout one particular day as a gale strengthened to storm force, and seeing the water turn to a white frenzy around the base of the cliffs. At the end of the day dusk drained away the light, until only the foam shone out of the twilight with a weak inner glow. Pale tongues of surf licked up the smooth shingle of Driftwood Bay to stroke the three pups cowering at the base of the cliff. One of the pups was only two days old, and looked frighteningly small and fragile. The tide would not start to fall for another two hours by which time the beach would be completely under water. The three cows were with them, agitated but seemingly helpless.

Darkness finally forced me to abandon the cliff top with the aching certainty that there would be no live pups left on the beach by the morning. At first light when the storm had subsided a little and the sea had ebbed away I saw the beach scoured and dragged smooth by the waves, and at the top of it the three pups, wet but alive. Their mothers had obviously taken them to sea to ride out the storm and saved them from being smashed against the rocks. I should have had more faith in the cows. I had seen others guiding their pups to safety, using their own bodies to shield them from the waves, but I knew that some cows did not have the experience to deal with such danger.

During the time I was studying the seals I saw some very unexpected incidents involving stillborn pups. I came across behaviour that I had not seen mentioned anywhere else despite searching through dozens of scientific papers on the subject. I had always thought that a stillbirth was of little significance to a grey seal cow, and had in fact been present when a cow had given birth to a dead pup without even a fleeting glance in the direction of her lifeless offspring. Two incidents in particular forced me to reconsider this idea. The first happened at Amys Reach, a very narrow, rocky inlet, so inaccessible that perhaps only two or three pups were born there each year. One morning I discovered a cow and new-born pup lying close together between the boulders on the shore of Amys Reach. The pup was lying awkwardly with its head twisted unnaturally to one side. I suspected it might be dead, but the close attendance of the cow made me doubt this. The cliffs of Amys Reach were steep and straight, and it was impossible to find a point that gave me a good, uninterrupted view of the beach without disturbing the cow. Even using binoculars I could not see whether the pup was breathing and, anxious to avoid alerting the cow to my presence, I left, uncertain as to the condition of the pup. When I returned later that day the young animal still lay with its neck strangely twisted and, despite the fact that its mother gazed at it intently, I had to conclude that it was dead.

This strangely disturbing situation continued for four days, with the cow never leaving the beach but remaining in rapt admiration of her motionless pup. The fifth day was very stormy, and I arrived to discover that the surging waves had dragged the pup from the beach and wedged it between two rocks smothered by the crashing surf. The desperation of the mother was obvious from the way in which her wildly flailing flippers sent droplets of sea water spraying into the air. She was sliding her nose under the pup and trying to lift it to the surface, but was hindered by the waves, the weight of the pup, and its awkward position between the rocks. I was so upset by the tragedy of this devoted mother trying to save her long-dead pup, and so conscious of the feeling that I was intruding in a very private grief, that I left without waiting to see the outcome of the struggle. Later in the day I found mother and pup lying side by side safe above the tide-line, the inert pup enfolded in its mother's foreflippers. They remained together for a further day, but on the morning of the following day both were missing. What became of them, and what finally

157

persuaded the cow that her pup had no further need of her I do not know.

A similarly distressing sequence of events took place the following year in Castle Bay. A stillborn pup was being closely guarded by its mother who growled threateningly if any other cows strayed too close. Both were well below the tide-line, and as the sea moved up the beach the pup was gradually lifted by the waves and began to float on the surface. The cow remained close, and when she finally grew tired of the water she ushered the pup back to the beach by swimming behind it and moving it forward with her own body. Once ashore she went slowly ahead of the pup, obviously expecting it to follow, but when she turned the pup was drifting back out to sea. This was repeated many times until the exasperated mother finally took the pup's foreflipper gently in her mouth and pulled it up on to the shingle. A similar process continued throughout the following day, with the pup being brought ashore whenever the tide took it out to sea. On the morning of the third day neither cow nor pup were anywhere to be seen. As it was such a perfect day I settled myself to watch quietly. The sea was a pale, translucent blue, and its surface barely moved. The water was so clear that the sun's rays reached right to the sea bed and reflected back off the sand. It was while I was watching these dappled patterns of light that I noticed something white shimmering through the water. I wondered if it might be the body of the dead pup lying at the bottom of the sea. I was certain that this was the case when I saw another shape draw close. It was unmistakably an adult seal, despite the fact that the outline was broken and distorted by the light refracting through the rippled water. Deep below the surface I watched the cow patrol the sea bed, inspecting her pup, then moving out to survey the surrounding area, and always quickly back to her pup. If any seal passed too close to her charge she darted towards the intruder, causing it to change course. After a minute or two the cow took the front flipper of the pup in her mouth and lifted it to the surface. After a brief struggle she changed her grip to the scruff of the pup's neck and held its head above water for a few seconds. Letting the pup drop slowly back to the bottom of the sea the cow followed close behind, and continued to guard its watery resting place.

This scene was re-enacted over and over again, with

never more than a few minutes passing without the pup being brought to the surface, and the cow always ensuring that the pup's head was held out of the water. It is something I have never encountered before or since, but I can only guess that the cow, believing her pup to be alive, was aware of the necessity to have air at regular intervals.

The pups must grow and develop extremely rapidly. After only two to three weeks all contact between mother and pup is severed. The pup gains weight so quickly that each day the change is obvious; loose folds of skin fill out and the yellow fur fades to white. By about ten days to two weeks old the pup may already be beginning to lose its characteristic white fur. Dark shadows are seen first around its face and flippers as its shorter, darker coat begins to emerge.

As weaning approached a small number of pups became so fat that movement was an unnecessary exertion. When this happened the pup would lie on the same spot, rotund and contented, any suggestion of a neck having vanished under layers of chins. These immobile pups usually moulted rapidly over the course of a day or two, since loose fur was not shed gradually by natural wear and tear, and the moulted pup was then left lying on a carpet of its own fur. Pups in this condition sometimes remained in exactly the same place for several weeks after weaning, either because the absence of hunger pangs gave them no urge to venture further afield, or because they were genuinely hampered by their enormous weight.

Only about two out of three pups survived the first three weeks of life. Those that did survive were by this age rapidly losing the white fur of babyhood, and appeared resplendent in a coat of short, velvety fur in any of the various mixtures of grey sported by the adults. During these weeks of rapid growth the increase in size had been almost entirely outwards, while the body length had changed less dramatically. This left them with the appearance of small but very fat adult seals. A well-fed pup would have enough reserves of fat to help it through the first weeks of independence from its mother's care, and over the following months would slim down to the proportions of a miniature adult.

Those early weeks were a pleasure to watch. It was a time when suddenly the natural, playful curiosity of a young animal was combined with the freedom and mobility to go out

159

and explore. For an animal as ungainly as the seal on land, whose every movement seemed to be a tedious exertion, the discovery of how easily it could move through the water must have been one of sheer exhilaration. Soon after weaning it was not unusual to see a pup drifting in the sea for hours. They often floated on the surface quite motionless, bobbing up and down on the waves, with their heads under water as though they were studying the murky depths that held the key to their survival.

At this stage learning and playing were so closely allied as to be indistinguishable. The young, moulted pups gathered in small groups, perhaps assembling round a rock pool, taking turns to splash in its shallow water. They had curiosity for everything, tugging at the vegetation that trailed down the cliff face as far as the beach in sheltered inlets, rolling under a tiny stream that cascaded from the island to feel the water droplets on their faces. I saw one take a stalk of kelp that had broken loose in the storms and, rolling on to its back, it held the kelp in its mouth and waved it overhead like a banner, watching the brown weed flutter against the sky.

Their inquisitive sense of adventure could lead the newly moulted pups into difficulty. One afternoon Mike and I were passing High Cliff, the steep rock face that towered over the southern edge of South Haven, and heard what sounded like a pup crying. We were surprised by this, not knowing of any pup in the area, and so began to investigate. We tried every vantage point, but could see nothing. The sound however was unmistakable, and carried in it such a note of distress that we decided to climb down to the rough boulder beach. A steep grassy bank just to the north gave us easy access to the base of the cliff. The closer we came, the louder the noise grew, but there was still nothing to be seen. We began to scramble over the boulders, certain now that the source of the sound must be very close at hand. Then we saw it, a moulted pup, its dappled grey coat camouflaged against the rocks, only its head visible. While making its way across the beach it had obviously slipped tail first into a gap in the rocks where it had become wedged.

We walked around it, studying the predicament from all directions to see how best to help, while the moulter continued to scream at us in angry terror. The only access to this stone prison was from above. This posed problems, since

160

it was necessary to reach past the moulter's head to get a grip on its body and pull it free. This Mike attempted to do, but the moulter snapped and snarled, causing Mike to jerk his hands clear of the bared teeth every time they drew too close. It was obvious that this approach was not going to work. The head and jaws of the animal were similar to those of a fair-sized dog, so were not a threat that could be ignored. I took off my jumper and Mike wound it round his arm, hoping that while the moulter vented its anger on the folds of wool he could slip his other hand down and pull the animal free. This too failed, since the moulter was more than capable of fending off an attack from two angles at once.

With every passing minute the struggle was gaining urgency. The tide was coming in rapidly, and had now reached the moulter's shoulders, while the regular surges as the waves moved in and out pushed the water up round the helpless animal's neck. We searched the beach desperately for anything that might give us some assistance. We found two planks of wood and attempted to lever the creature free, but to no avail; it was too firmly wedged. All the time the tide rose inexorably higher. The gap in the rocks where the moulter was trapped was like a pool filling from below, the level rising with the incoming tide. With each incoming wave the moulter's head was now submerged, its frantic cries momentarily lost in a rush of bubbles. We had only minutes left, and we were no nearer to freeing the animal than when we arrived. In a desperate last attempt Mike took off his belt and looped the end through the buckle to form a noose. He dropped this over the moulter's head and pulled hard. The fat little animal had no obvious neck around which to place the belt, but it tightened and gripped just long enough to drag the moulter free of its trap. It immediately slipped out of its tether and struggled in blind panic the last few feet to the sea. From this point of relative safety it glanced back towards its tormentors before plunging deep into the embracing security of the sea, where no-one could reach it.

As with most animals, the grey seal's fear of people grows with maturity. Some pups showed little reaction when approached, though others growled angrily. Moulters often produced a very fine display of aggression when disturbed, but frequently rolled over and went back to sleep when their snarling and hissing had no effect. To find a sheltered resting place it was

161

common for newly-moulted pups to make their way up our concrete slipway to the path above and settle themselves down to sleep outside the boat-shed, or next to our boat. When this happened we were left with the problem of how to manoeuvre boat and trailer past a small sleeping seal. Our attempts at stealth invariably failed and the startled animal, still confused from sleep, would express its irritation vociferously at such an unexpected interruption before losing interest in our slow, trundling progress. Adult seals were much more nervous. The glimpse of a silhouette on the cliff top, or a waft of human scent was enough to send them crashing down the beach to the sea. The only adult seals who might hold their ground were exceptionally tenacious mothers who refused to leave their pups, and might even lunge at a hapless intruder.

In the sea they behaved very differently. There the seals had the security of knowing that they had the speed and ingenuity to avoid danger. They were transformed from timid, apprehensive creatures and became extraordinarily inquisitive, even playful. Any seal drifting idly in the water became immediately alert at the sight of a figure on the cliff above. It would usually draw closer and watch intently, almost certainly being joined by others within a minute or two. Sometimes a dozen curious seals assembled in the water, and looking down from the cliff top we would see only twelve disembodied heads gazing up at us. If we were taking a route along the cliff edge the seals followed, still staring curiously, until eventually our path took us inland. Mike could never resist calling a greeting to hear their low, wailing replies.

When we were at sea the seals grew bolder still, often approaching within a few feet of our boat. When they appeared from behind and we were too busy to notice them the seals grew impatient and attracted our attention with a loud snort. Once we were under way they often followed behind the moving boat, playing in the trail of bubbles left by the propeller. Boldest of all were the young seals of about a year old. They occasionally came right up to us when we were standing in the shallow water launching the boat. Mike returned from a fishing trip one evening fascinated by an encounter with one of these yearlings. He told me that while he had been fishing he became aware that a young seal was watching him. It followed him wherever he went, and in its curiosity forgot all fear, until it gradually crept so close

162

to the boat that Mike could have reached out and touched it. Mike offered it one of the freshly-caught mackerel and, to his complete amazement, the seal took it from his hand. Using its long, sharp claws the young seal delicately sliced a fillet from each side of the fish which it ate, discarding the head, tail and bones. Having deftly disposed of one mackerel it was quickly back for a second. This was quite exceptional behaviour; we had never before known a seal to take fish that it had not caught live itself. But it was their unpredictability that made the seals such fascinating companions, particularly through the lonely days of winter.

FOURTEEN

AFTER NINE YEARS on Skomer I thought I understood everything there was to know about isolation. But with hindsight I don't think that anything could have prepared us for those few days in early autumn. Our troubles began on a beautiful October morning. The winds had reached storm force during the night, and now the wave tops were being lifted into streaks of foam and the air glistened with sea spray. Clouds that looked too heavy to remain suspended in the air raced each other through the sky, subtly changing shape as they went. Shafts of sunlight pierced the gaps, highlighting patches of sea beneath, so that the surf glowed white against the leaden grey. Leaving the shelter of the house to discover how the seal pups had survived this tempestuous weather I was, for once, in no hurry to be on my way. It was the first storm to sweep over the island for very many weeks, and I stood for some time enjoying its freshness and beauty. The autumn had been unusually calm and I had missed these bright, boisterous days. The mild, damp, gentle atmosphere of the preceding weeks had been kind, but characterless. Walking slowly, hardly taking my eyes from the frenzied sea, I began to cross the isthmus. The wind skimmed the narrow strip of land with such force that I had to breathe very hard to draw in any of the rapidly moving air.

I knew that there was a pup in North Haven and I moved warily to the cliff edge, with the wind gusting hard against my back, to try to find it. I saw it at last, huddled between rocks at the top of the beach where, being on the sheltered side of the island, it was in a good position to survive the ravages of the weather. I was relieved that, unless the situation had changed during the night, there were no pups on the exposed, storm-raked beach of South Haven. Reaching the far end of the isthmus I looked down into the sandy curve of South Haven. I started as if jolted by a physical blow, and my heart thudded with rapid, explosive beats. My brain raced ahead trying to deny what my eyes were seeing. There was someone on the beach, lying face down, arms outstretched.

I searched in confusion for an explanation. I looked frantically for a boat that might have brought someone to the island, but of course there were none. It was far too rough for anyone to have ventured ashore through those pounding waves. It must be a shipwreck. A ship had been dashed against the rocks during the night, and this was a survivor who had crawled ashore and collapsed exhausted on the beach. But there was no sign of wreckage. These scraps of thought were churned up and discarded in seconds. In fact I already knew the answer. The figure was clad in a purple wetsuit, and I noticed how the weight-belt bit into the flesh which bulged grotesquely on either side of it. I was looking at a corpse bloated by weeks of decay.

Although I knew what I was seeing, I still did not understand how this could be. I was already remembering the August bank holiday, almost eight weeks earlier. Switching the radio on for a routine call to the coastguard we had immediately realised that something was wrong. The normally quiet radio frequency buzzed with conversation. It took us only a few minutes to discover that two divers had been lost in the waters around Skomer. They had disappeared beneath the surface some hours earlier, and had not been seen since. Everyone on the island had joined the search, but as darkness fell nothing had been found. At first light the following morning we had begun to scour every inlet and sea cave, this time in the grim knowledge that we had little hope of finding a survivor.

As the days passed, and no trace was seen, we could only conclude that the bodies had been swept far out to sea and would never be found. The currents around Skomer are fierce and powerful, and they were particularly strong on that day of exceptionally high tides. Had the divers surfaced unseen by the waiting boat, they could have been swept many miles out to sea even before the alarm was raised. I remembered with a shudder that I had noticed, but paid little attention to, the boat waiting off the southern tip of the Neck for its two doomed passengers. I was haunted by the image of such a lonely and terrifying death.

165

But all this had happened nearly two months earlier, and I did not understand how this tragic mystery could have been so vividly re-awakened. I turned and moved slowly towards the house, but after a few steps I began to run. It was much too late for any sense of urgency, but I felt somehow that to stroll casually home would have been disrespectful. The front door burst open and my boots clattered heavily up the hallway. Hearing this uncharacteristically noisy home-coming Mike immediately knew that something was wrong. Breathlessly I began to explain what had happened. Mike continued to listen as he pulled his boots on, and punctuated my sentences with exclamations of horror.

As I took Mike back to the beach I continued to recount everything I could remember, as if to convince myself that what I had seen was real.

'Don't look,' said Mike as we stood gazing down on the body, 'or you'll never be able to forget it.'

It was too late for that. Every last detail was seared indelibly into my memory. It was an image that returned frequently over the following days, like a photograph held in front of my eyes. I remembered the brilliance of the colours; the purple wetsuit and the yellow life-jacket, which, still bright and fresh and so unremarkable in life, seemed a cruel mockery in death. Above all he seemed so alone; small and insignificant against the towering grandeur of South Haven, isolated from us by a gulf of fear which we could not bridge.

Back in the security of the kitchen Mike called the coastguard. We consoled ourselves that at least it would all be over in a few hours. I felt a definite sense of relief. The awful riddle was solved, and for everyone concerned that unique misery of not knowing what had happened would be ended. We waited while the coast-guard considered the best course of action, and in the silence Mike and I turned our thoughts to another, as yet unspoken, problem. Two divers had been lost, and it seemed likely that whatever conditions had led to one body being washed ashore in South Haven would have cast up the second somewhere on Skomer. It would be preferable if any arrangements made to recover the first body could also include the second, and it was therefore necessary to find the other as quickly as possible. As Mike was still waiting for a reply from the coastguard, I volunteered to go out and start the search.

The first and most obvious place to look was South Haven which, earlier in the morning, had received only a cursory glance. Returning to the spot which an hour before I had found exhilaratingly beautiful, but which now seemed desolate and forbidding, I scoured every hollow in the cliffs, every pile of seaweed tumbled ashore by the storm, all the time trying to keep my eyes from the point where the body lay. Finding nothing I passed on to all my favourite seal-watching bays. It was disconcerting to be following so familiar a route for such a grisly purpose. After a very thorough search I was disappointed not to have been successful. However horrible the prospect of a second body was, not finding it seemed even worse.

Home was in sight as I crossed the top of South Haven, but I was distracted by the fact that the body was now being lifted and moved by the largest waves as they rolled up the beach. I waited for a few moments to assure myself that it was not about to be swept out to sea.

'Please don't turn over,' I implored silently, terrified that I might catch a glimpse of that hidden face. Satisfied that there was little time to spare before the lifeless form was lost to the waves yet again, I hurried back to warn Mike. He in turn told the coastguard of the urgency of the situation, and between them it was agreed that as a temporary solution the body should be moved to the top of the beach.

We had the enormous good fortune of not being alone on the island. Had this happened in any other year Mike and I would have been left to our own devices, but as it was we were overwhelmingly grateful for the presence of George, our assistant warden, Paul who was studying rabbits and Tim who was paying a short visit to check on the progress of the Skomer voles. Paul was unlucky enough to be the first person Mike found, and so his help was enlisted in moving the body. While Mike and Paul put on waterproof suits, I found a blanket from the bedroom. They prepared their climbing ropes which were now necessary, the easy access to the beach having been denied to them by the incoming tide, and set off, just a little subdued and ashen-faced. I watched them disappear below the cliff, and then I was alone, with only an occasional crackle of speech from the radio for company.

It seemed a very long time before they both returned, looking somewhat shaken by their ordeal. Mike contacted the coastguard again to report that the body was now safe for the time being, and then the waiting began. We sat in the kitchen watching, through salt-frosted windows, the smooth, green, glassy waves which exploded into a wall of foam as they reached the beach. To the background of this soft, rhythmic clatter of sea on shore Mike explained to me the mystery that had troubled us frequently in the past two months, and which had intensified dramatically in the preceding hours. We had discussed endlessly the circumstances under which two people could disappear without trace, and this startling reappearance only a few hundred yards from the spot where they were last seen had confounded all our theories.

The first part of Mike's explanation was already known to me. For the sake of safety it was essential to dive with a partner and, as this pair had done, it was desirable to carry a line attached to a small buoy which would float on the surface and indicate the position of the divers below the water to those in the waiting boat. We knew from our involvement with the initial search that this buoy had disappeared below the surface almost as soon as the divers left the boat, and was not seen again.

Mike's chilling account of what he found filled me with horror and pity. The body was completely tangled with string – undoubtedly the cord that had been attached to the buoy. There were signs of a desperate struggle to escape the imprisoning line, and it took little imagination to visualise that in such circumstances the more frantic the struggle the more tightly the victim would become ensnared. The life jacket had been inflated, but by that time the diver must already have been tied fast to the kelp, the strong weed that grips the sea bed. In order to break free of the line all the diving equipment around which it was tangled had been unbuckled, but had remained firmly attached to the diver by the string. Even the air bottle with the last dregs of its precious supply had been discarded, but remained caught fast in the web. The knife had been removed from its sheath in an obvious attempt to fight free, but this too had fallen victim to the maze of tangles and become hopelessly trapped.

The body must have remained tied to the weed throughout the intervening weeks; its natural upward movement restrained by the cord, leaving it suspended above the sea bed, sufficiently close to the surface to be reached by the drag of the storm waves, and finally set free. It was a sobering story. The idea that a reel

168

of string was all that stood between life and needless death was awful.

The day was bright and wild, the sort we always found irresistible, and being the first real storm of autumn our first thought would usually have been to go out and rediscover the magic of Skomer's cliffs and offshore rocks veiled in clouds of sparkling sea-spray. Instead we waited, transfixed by the horror of the situation, and hoping every minute to hear news of how and when the body would be removed. When George and Tim were found they were told of the events of the early part of the morning, and an uneasy restlessness settled on the island as we waited to be rescued from the oppressive atmosphere. Throughout the day messages passed back and forth from the coastguard, and it seemed we had only an hour or two to wait before help was at hand, but this deadline continued to slide backwards, and remained always just out of reach. At last came some disappointing news; the RAF helicopter would not carry the body because of the risk of contamination. But we were encouraged by the prospect that the lifeboat would soon be with us.

When we were told that the sea was too rough for the lifeboat to get out we felt a sense of helpless despair. We could not leave the body on the beach over night; there was nowhere we could be certain the waves would not sweep it away. These fears were passed on to the coastguard, and after a few moments back came the hesitant reply.

'Do you think you could find somewhere safe to store it?'

We stared at each other, and for a moment Mike was speechless.

'Stand by, and I'll give you a reply,' Mike answered, and as he lifted his finger from the 'transmit' button we had a few minutes to decide what to do.

'Not in the house,' I gasped in horror, before I had had time to collect my thoughts.

There followed one of those nightmarish situations that no-one expects to encounter. As we sat discussing where we should put the body the situation felt unreal, like a scene from a terrible black comedy, and it seemed out of place in our own cheerful kitchen. The garage, being linked to the house, was dismissed, and the old farm buildings were ruled out as they were too far away. We finally decided on the boat-shed on the quay in North Haven.

169

This was a newly-constructed building which was clean and dry, and which we felt would offer a suitably dignified resting place.

Once the decision was made Mike went to break the news to the others. Unhappy, but uncomplaining, they put on protective clothing and found a stretcher, polythene sheeting and ropes. Secured to the stretcher, the awkward and heavy load was carried with difficulty up the cliff and then down the other side to the boat-shed. By the time everything was finished darkness was falling. I was reasonably resigned to spending the night with this unsettling presence on the island. Mike, having been in closer contact with it, was rather more edgy. I slept well at first, but as the night drew on I was frequently jolted awake by images of that forlorn and isolated figure on the sand. Long before dawn broke I was wide awake, straining my eyes for any sign that the blackness was growing paler, knowing that with the light I would have to leave for my early morning seal round. For the first time ever I did not want to go.

As I left the house not even the freshness of the morning air could lift my spirits. I walked very slowly towards the spot where I had made my dreadful discovery the previous day, lingered a moment, and then with a great effort of will forced myself to look. Of course there was nothing but a ridge of dark, shiny weed thrown ashore by the sea. Following my almost total composure of the previous day, I was surprised by how nervous I now felt. I started each time a seal surfaced in the water close by, and approached each new site with a dull, aching dread. Despite everything, as I retraced my steps across the isthmus, leaning hard into the wind to maintain my balance and snatching breaths from the air that tore past my face, I was sorry not to have found anything. Sorry that I would continue to dread going out, and sorry that the whole sad affair could not be drawn to a close.

The violence of the weather continued unabated, and it was obvious from the start that we were beyond help for yet another day. The time was spent in a very determined search for the second body. This at least gave us something positive to do. Equipped with climbing ropes Mike and the others gained access to the sea caves around the Neck. I could not pass South Haven without examining every scrap of flotsam. The stormy weather had driven it into the bay where it collected offshore in ever-changing pools amalgamated by a layer of floating seaweed torn adrift by the sea. From this grey-brown mass pieces of man-made debris emerged partly concealed by the weed. A yellow petrol can appeared almost indistinguishable from an inflated life-jacket, and a flaccid, pink rubber glove gave me a moment of heart-stopping panic, but no genuine trace was ever found of the missing diver. Despite this it was several weeks before I could visit my favourite seal beaches again with total ease. How exactly they both met their deaths in the silent, green twilight beneath South Haven is something that we will now never fully understand, and for me the whole incident remained disquietingly unfinished.

On Saturday we entered our third day of waiting, and the weather remained unchanged. The atmosphere on the island grew uncomfortably tense, and we were startled by every unexpected sound. That night the noise of the wind rattling against the house seemed magnified by our inability to see into the darkness outside. The weather sounded worse than ever, and we held out little hope of an improvement in time for the following day. The forecast told a different story; there was to be a brief lull as the depression passed over before the full force of the wind returned. We began to feel cautiously optimistic. The following morning, although the wind had eased considerably, the previous days of storms had built such force into the sea that the stretch of water between Skomer and St Ann's Head seemed forbiddingly uncrossable. Most boats had already been taken ashore for the winter, and the few that remained in the water were far from Skomer, on very sheltered moorings such as those at Dale, and to reach us would have to cross the notoriously turbulent area around St Ann's Head.

We need not have worried. As soon as Campbell Reynolds, who had taken over the job of running the boat to the island in the summer months, heard of our plight he was ready to leave immediately. In fact he was angry at not having been contacted sooner, insisting that, storm or no storm, he would not have left us in such a distressing situation for a moment longer than necessary. This encouraged us enormously as we knew that once Campbell had decided to come it would take a hurricane to stop him. Nevertheless, we did cast a few anxious glances in the direction of the towering waves off St Ann's Head. Now that we knew help was on its way the tension eased considerably, and I decided to make use of the intervening few hours by continuing with the seal survey work for which I had had little heart over the past three days. When I returned Mike was decidedly gloomy; all the earlier optimism had vanished. He explained that he had received a message over the radio saying that we did not have authority from the coroner to move the body, and therefore it would have to stay. To make matters worse, the coroner was on holiday and his deputy could not be contacted as it was a Sunday. Mike had already tried everything, including contacting the police over the radio telephone, but as always bureaucracy was immovable.

The real cause for our despair was not just a delay of one more day, but the knowledge that this was just a temporary respite in the weather. Already the wind was increasing, and if we lost this opportunity the wait could be indefinite. Once again there was nothing we could do but sit by the radio, but now it seemed to be without hope or purpose. It was not until early afternoon that we learned of our reprieve. The coastguard had pulled out all the stops, the matter had been dealt with at the highest level, and somehow the necessary permission had been obtained. Campbell was preparing to leave for Skomer.

We watched the *Dale Princess* as it dipped and plunged and rolled, sometimes disappearing in a cloud of spray, dwarfed by the waves which attacked it from all sides. From a distant speck, just visible under the steep cliffs of St Ann's Head, it grew larger and clearer as it approached. Finally it disappeared into Little Sound to emerge again in the calmer waters on the north side, sheltered by the island. The boat was a welcome sight as it slid smoothly into North Haven, its blue and white hull gleaming with salt water, and on board Campbell was as calm and cheerful as ever.

Mike and the others trooped solemnly down to the boat-shed. Although North Haven was sheltered, the sea was far from settled. The body on the stretcher had to be ferried in our small dinghy to the *Dale Princess*, which required very careful handling. I watched the small craft move gingerly through the water, rearing up as each wave passed, until at last it was alongside the *Dale Princess*. The stretcher was transferred to the larger boat and, with little time to lose as the gathering storm drained the light from the sky, the *Princess* moved swiftly out of the bay towards Martin's Haven, leaving me quite alone on the island. It was a damp, dark, oppressive day, which felt entirely suited to the occasion. I watched the light fade until eventually the colourless shape of the *Dale Princess* re-appeared through the gloom.

172

The disturbing prospect of this one last encounter with the dead had become magnified in the days of waiting until everyone's nerves were stretched so taut that one small tug could have made them snap. In North Haven Mike, Paul, George and Tim transferred to our dinghy to row ashore, while the *Dale Princess* sped rapidly homeward, already obliged to make most of the blustery crossing in darkness. The four seated themselves in the dinghy; Mike in the middle with the oars, Paul in the bow facing backwards, and the other two in the stern. The boat moved steadily, the oars cutting silently into the dark water and then breaking free with a trail of shimmering droplets. They had not made much headway when a violent shout arose from Paul.

'Row! Row! It's a whale! Row faster!'

Glimpsing the black shape bearing down on them Mike was fired into action, and the oars thrashed frantically through the water. The others sat grim-faced and helpless in the realisation that their pursuer was still gaining on them.

It must have been some seconds before they realised that this predatory sea-monster was none other than a large sheet of black polythene. It had been used to protect the deck of the *Dale Princess*, and as the boat rounded Rye Rocks the plastic sheeting had been lifted by the wind into the sea. Billowing in the stiff breeze it had moved rapidly across the water giving the illusion of an alarmingly solid shape. With both feet on dry land everyone was able to see the funny side, but the incident was an indication of our lingering unease.

Within a few days the others left and Mike and I were by ourselves again. It was only three weeks before Mike was due to leave the island and I would be alone. Messages came from various sources insisting that I should not remain by myself, and I was sufficiently unnerved to give them serious consideration. For the first time what I had come to think of as my island did not seem a hospitable place to spend a week or more in complete solitude. By the time Mike was due to leave, although we still did not feel completely relaxed, things had settled down, and nothing more had happened to disturb us. I decided therefore that I would stay behind by myself and continue with the seal research.

The week passed surprisingly easily. I was perhaps a little more sensitive than usual to any sudden noise or movement, but I loved the island too much not to find pleasure in being there. I was very careful, particularly during the long nights, not to let my thoughts follow any course that might be unsettling. I scanned the bookcase carefully, rejecting anything that might be even faintly frightening. I believed strongly that everything would be all right as long as I stayed in control, but I knew that the first seeds of panic might take root and grow in the dark, empty night. And in the morning there would be no cheerful sounds of reality to push away the fears, only more silent days and nights stretching ahead of me. But it did not happen; I stayed calm and relaxed. The weather had been settled, almost too settled: I liked the combination of wind and waves to complete the certainty of my isolation. However, the day before Mike was due back the wind began to rise, and by the evening there was quite a storm blowing. I sat in the bath with the radio for company babbling cheerfully in the background. Steam was billowing in the cold air and the sound of the storm was occupying my thoughts more than the radio until I heard the words, 'The next programme is not suitable for those of a nervous disposition.'

I turned and looked at the radio; it was on the other side of the room across a chasm of cold lino. I decided to leave it. Before this my mind had been wandering, but now that I did not really want to listen I took in every word. The story went on to describe an isolated house somewhere in America. A violent storm cut off the electricity, plunging the house into darkness. There was a hideously bloated body in a bath full of water, which somehow rose up and stalked the darkened house, strangling its victims. I was not impressed.

When I left the bathroom and heard the sound of rain being driven against the windows on the exposed side of the house, I realised how much the storm had increased. I took a torch together with cloths and a bucket, and went to see if rainwater was pouring into any of the rooms. I made my way by torchlight since it was easier than trying to light the gaslights in every room. The shadows moved and jumped back out of sight as I approached, cowering round corners and behind furniture, then closing in behind me as I passed. The flooding was worse than I expected. Water was bubbling through every tiny crack around the windows, pooling on the window sills and spilling over on to floors and tables. Every time I tried to move something out of the way I found another puddle of water. Mike's desk was

174

flooded, and important papers soaked. I tried to spread things out to dry, dabbing at them with a cloth. The faster I tried to clear things up the bigger the problem seemed to grow. As I worked in the little pool of light from the torch beam the darkness that pushed against my back was oppressive. Every time I moved the torch shadows danced provocatively. The roar of the wind against the blackened window enveloped me so completely that I knew it would mask every other sound. Anything could move unnoticed through the darkness behind me and I would not hear it. I cleaned up the worst of the mess and hurried from the room. As soon as I stepped into the hallway I knew that something was wrong; there was no welcoming glow of gaslight from the kitchen coming down the corridor to meet me. I hadn't turned it out; I never turned it out. It always stayed on until I went to bed, spilling light into the hallway to guide me round the house. I crept slowly into the kitchen and saw the faintest red glow coming from the mantle. The gas cylinder had run out. I would have to go outside and change it. At that moment a sharp gust of wind sent a volley of raindrops hammering against the window. No, I wouldn't go outside. I would go to bed and leave it until the morning.

As I lay beneath the security of the bedclothes surrounded by a solid, impenetrable blackness I had a disquieting thought. If anything disturbed me in the night I would not be able to put a light on to see what was happening. I was jolted into wakefulness so sharply that I had a cold, hollow feeling deep inside. The darkness seemed stark and empty, but at the same time smothering. I tried to subdue my imagination with logic; I knew that I was safe here. Gradually the dark and the fear and the sound of the wind nudging at the house seemed to flow together into a single, indefinable sensation, and then they were gone completely.

175

FIFTEEN

W HEN MIKE RETURNED the uneasiness we felt had somehow lifted. It was in the past and we began to think again of the future. We were in fact looking ahead to Christmas. This was traditionally the time of year that we went to the mainland to see family and friends and to have a brief taste of the comforts of civilisation. In the blustery autumn, as the days were growing shorter, it was possible to see the positive side of this arrangement, but inevitably as December wore on thoughts of leaving the island depressed us. In the winter months we grew increasingly isolated from the outside world, and became more dependent on the island and on each other's company. We had a strange, timeless sort of existence which made it very difficult for us to adapt back to mainland life. We had come close to spending Christmas on the island before, when storms had kept us trapped until the last moment. Despite our shortage of food I had jealously guarded a tin of ham for our Christmas dinner, but with our lack of provisions it had promised to be a very dull Christmas. We had therefore not been sorry when the wind paused to recoup its strength and we had a few settled hours in which to make our escape.

This year it was as a result of the seal research that we had finally decided to stay on the island over Christmas. It had long been believed that Skomer, in common with other British sites, had a seal breeding season that lasted for about two months in the autumn. Pembrokeshire however differed from the rest of the country in that a few pups were born in the spring. We quickly realised that this was not the case, and that breeding continued throughout the winter to form one unbroken period from early autumn to early spring. Pembrokeshire's isolated breeding beaches had been so inaccessible in the stormy winter months that such a

176

comprehensive study had not been possible before. The work had been so intensive, not just on the pups but on the adult seals as well, that we could not afford to have a gap in our knowledge at such an important time of year, and that was how we came to spend Christmas on Skomer.

Although the weather often toyed with us and tore all our carefully-made plans to shreds, we had to admit how kind December weather could be. Despite the wind it was sunny and mild. Tucking ourselves into a sheltered hollow and looking out at the sun-streaked sea there was no feeling of winter in the air. The only things that troubled us in the period leading to Christmas, and convinced us that winter really was upon us, were the short days and long, dark nights. By about four o'clock the light would be gone bringing the day to an uncomfortably premature end in what was essentially an outdoor way of life. I found it an awkward time; too soon to be evening, and yet no longer day. At this time I found the gaslights very comforting. At the touch of a lighted match the flames leapt up around the mantle and then died to a hissing glow. The light was not bright, and sometimes seemed frustratingly inadequate, but it was golden and mellow, and gave out just enough warmth to blunt the edge of the cold on a winter evening. By the time Christmas arrived we would have the consolation of knowing that the worst was over and the days were already lengthening steadily. However much we regretted being confined to the house by darkness, and however long the evening stretching ahead of us seemed to be, we always managed to fill the time easily, sometimes talking late into the night rather than leave the warmth of the wood-burning stove.

We began making preparations for Christmas early, hoarding supplies whenever the opportunity arose. Back in the summer we had been collecting bottles of wine to set aside. Cards and presents began arriving in good time as people realised that anything sent at the last minute might lie uncollected in the post office. We were amazed by the bundles of cards that had gathered by the time we made one of our infrequent trips to collect the post, and opened them as soon as we arrived home. The presents we left resolutely untouched, although we were often tempted just to peel back a corner of the paper.

I was beginning to suspect that Mike was making his own preparations for Christmas. I had become used to Mike and his secret projects, and always knew when there was an idea forming in his mind. He became restless and preoccupied, often sitting up late scribbling unfinished sketches. Eventually, amid great secrecy he would shut himself away and give me strict instructions not to enter the room. I always readily agreed to this since I loved surprises, and secretly hoped that he might be making something for me. There had been some wonderful presents over the years; a tiny writing desk, an intricately panelled chest, and beautifully carved love spoons. This time I missed these early signs of an idea taking shape because Mike was busy refitting the kitchen in the research quarters and I assumed that all his energies were being channelled in that direction, but gradually his prolonged absences and general unwillingness for me to intrude made me suspect that there might be something else in progress. One night it had grown dark, but there was still no sign of Mike. I resisted the temptation to go and find him from an instinctive feeling that my presence would not be welcome. I settled instead for the dubious pleasure of a shallow, lukewarm bath, the best I dared risk without putting too much strain on our gas supply.

I was already beginning to doubt the wisdom of my attempt to brighten a cold December evening. Scooping up handfuls of water and letting them stream down my back to rinse away the soap I shuddered at their tepid touch. Suddenly all doubts were frozen by the sound of angry hammering at the front door. In the instant before conscious thought could surface I knew that the door was locked. Our front door was never locked, except on a night like tonight when the wind refused to let the door stay shut. The gale had been beating at the house and repeatedly throwing the door open. With a final surge of power it had slammed the internal doors with a volley of splintering crashes and dashed the pictures lining the walls of the hallway to the floor. Unable to take any more of these nerve-jarring intrusions I had locked the door. Now the image of Mike waiting impatiently on the doorstep, lashed by wind and rain, sent me cascading from the bath.

I opened the front door in a rush of cold air to be greeted not by irate impatience, but more by a sort of agonised despair. In the half-light from the gas lamps I could just see that Mike was clasping one hand with the other and that from beneath the tightly closed fingers a pool of blood was oozing and dripping on to the ground. I followed Mike and the trail of blood up the hallway into the kitchen.

'What happened?' I panicked, blinking into the brightness.

'I cut my hand,' replied Mike, stating the overwhelmingly obvious.

I stood back anxiously, uncertain of what to do. As Mike ran cold tap water over his hand I peered from a distance trying to ascertain the extent of the injury without having to expose myself to the full glare of it. By the time Mike was drying his hand I felt sufficiently acclimatised to the wound to take a closer look. It was not as bad as I had at first feared. The cut was between the thumb and forefinger, about an inch long and very deep, but also very clean. I clung damply to my towel, pulling it closer to myself, and feeling ridiculously relieved that all the fingers were still there.

We both looked at the cut, Mike constantly dabbing away the blood that impaired our view. Ideally it needed a few stitches to keep it closed, but we could not contemplate calling out a helicopter on a night like this for a cut. Instead I found a bandage from the first aid cupboard and did my best to stem the flow of blood.

'It's my own fault,' Mike wailed as I wound the bandage tightly. 'It was going to be a Christmas present for you, and now it's completely ruined.'

I began to realise that Mike had been carving something that had been damaged at the time of the accident, and he was more concerned about that than the injury to his hand.

'It was getting dark,' Mike continued miserably. 'I knew I should have stopped and sharpened the chisel, but I didn't, and I slipped. . .'

He broke off, the conclusion too awful to relate. I had lost count of the number of times I had urged him not to try to work by gaslight, but this time I did not have the slightest inclination to say, 'I told you so'.

As soon as the bandaging was completed Mike rushed out through the stormy night to retrieve his carving from the laboratory where he had been working, and assess the extent of the damage. He quickly returned carrying a snail, about six inches high, perfectly carved in West African mahogany that had washed ashore as driftwood. The shell flowed in a smooth spiral, and through every curve the wood grain echoed. The snail had a bulbous head

179

surmounted by a single, large, round-tipped antenna. The place of the other antenna was taken by a rough scar in the wood, giving the creature a very lop-sided appearance. Mike explained miserably that as the chisel had grown blunt he had had to apply too much pressure and the blade had finally slipped, hacking off the antenna before gashing into his hand.

'Perhaps you could take the other antenna off to match,' I suggested comfortingly, but even as I spoke I could see that the result would be a very shapeless blob of a head, and nothing less than perfection would suit Mike.

We spent a very gloomy evening. Mike placed the snail on the table and sat staring at it dejectedly, continually lamenting his own stupidity. It was the fact that it was such an avoidable accident that so upset him. I sat close by watching the dark red stain on the bandage grow. We changed the dressing several times, but the bleeding would not stop, and it made me feel quite anxious. At times like this I always wished that we had taken the trouble to have our tetanus injections.

The following day Mike regained his composure and remodelled the snail's head. The end result was much more effective than the original design. Although the surprise was spoilt, it was still a nicer Christmas present than money could buy. I named the snail Diggory, and it remains to this day one of my most treasured possessions.

A few days later we were leaving the house late in the afternoon for a last breath of fresh air before darkness closed in when we heard the sound of a helicopter roaring overhead. Its flight was low and purposeful, so we guessed that it must be going to land in the central fields. We raced up the hill behind the house and reached the top breathless. In the distance we could see the helicopter winchman standing on the Bread Rock, a steep outcrop at the intersection of two paths. As we came into view over the brow of the hill he waved a long, black package in our direction. We renewed our efforts to run faster now we were on flat ground, and arrived just in time to see the helicopter take off with a wave from the crew. We clambered up the Bread Rock to see what was there, and one feel of the spiky shape through the black plastic was enough to tell us that it was a Christmas tree.

We hurried home with the treasured object carefully disguising our excitement. Unpacking it we found not only the tree, but holly, mistletoe, crackers, balloons, streamers and tinsel. There was also a green shoe box.

'I wonder what's in here,' Mike said, picking at the tape round the lid.

'I hope it's not fairy lights,' I laughed.

The tape peeled back and the lid opened to reveal two neat rows of brightly coloured Christmas tree lights. As we looked at each other our confusion turned to laughter. We set up the Christmas tree and decorated it straight away. The fairy lights looked lovely, despite the fact that without any electricity we could not switch them on.

With presents piled under the tree, and the living room crowded with cards, we needed only one final ingredient for a complete Christmas, and that was a turkey. We knew that this was a luxury we would probably have to manage without, but nevertheless we listened carefully to the long-term weather forecasts, trying to judge when there might be a brief spell of calm, and trying to strike a balance between crossing too early and leaving it so late that we missed our opportunity completely. However, the wind was so continuous that there was no decision to be made until three days before Christmas. Despite an atrocious forecast we woke to a grey but settled morning. A brief talk with the coastguard indicated that the approaching storm was still a few hours off. We waited for the light to improve, to ensure that no huge waves were being masked by the gloom beyond the shelter of North Haven, and when we had satisfied ourselves that the sea was calm we set off.

As we trundled back to Martin's Haven in the Land Rover I studied every leaf and blade of grass carefully to try to see how hard the wind was blowing and from what direction. I imagined what it would be like to be able to drive home, park outside and walk indoors. Instead we had to pack all our shopping in polythene bags to protect it from the elements and carry it down the steep shingle slope of Martin's Haven. By the time we had dragged the dinghy down the beach and were ready to row out to our boat on the mooring, small, white wavelets were flicking across the bay. The crossing was wet and bumpy. Shallow waves were slapping hard against the boat, while the wind caught the remnants of the spray before they could fall back into the sea and scattered them over us. The wind was strengthening by the minute and breaking up the surface of the water, but it was a superficial roughness and the boat bounced easily over the waves. By the time we reached the slipway in North Haven rolling white crests were pushing in hard behind us. As we edged slowly towards the beach a large wave washed against the stern of the boat and sent us surging forward. I jumped out of the boat and grabbed the bow to save it from being pushed on to the rocks. The wave lumbered forward, breaking round my legs and filling my boots with water. When we had managed to guide the boat through the waves on to the trailer and then haul it up the slipway we set off up the precarious cliff path loaded down with boxes. My wet feet were sliding uncomfortably in my wellingtons, but the satisfaction of arriving home was so enormous that deep down I knew I would find any other way of life dull. We had everything we needed for Christmas now; the weather could do its worst and we would not mind being cut off indefinitely.

We decided that from Christmas Eve we would make it a proper holiday, and do only the essential work necessary to keep things running smoothly. The observation of the seals of course continued, and I spent the morning checking on the seal beaches. In the afternoon we walked most of the coastline. It was a beautiful day. The light was bright and golden, the sea exceptionally rough, and the wind, though vicious in its strength, was very mild in temperature. The sea was white with foam, and this collected, tumbled by the wind, like mounds of soft, white soap suds in the inlets. On the exposed western coast great pools of froth gathered round offshore rocks. Pigstone Bay, one of the wildest places on the island, was the most spectacular. Here the force of wind and waves sent clouds of foam over a hundred feet into the air. Shattered by the wind into small fragments it rained down on us like snowflakes and covered the surrounding grass. It gave the day a wonderfully seasonable feeling, despite the warmth of the wind and the bright sun which made the sea-spray glisten.

We returned to the house exhilarated, in time to start the real work. Soon every work surface in the kitchen was covered with a light dusting of flour, and the smell of mince pies drifted tantalisingly from the oven. Several different kinds of stuffing were in preparation, sausage-meat, chestnut with lemon and of course sage and onion. As Mike lit the stove in the living room the smell of wood smoke tinged the air, mingling with the sharp, green scent of the pine needles. Under the Christmas tree the brightly coloured packages caught the gentle glow of the gaslight. In the preceding weeks we had wondered if Christmas on Skomer might be sad and lonely with only each other for company and with no outside influences to set the day apart and make it special. We should not have worried; this Christmas we felt the sort of excitement we remembered from childhood.

Christmas morning started like any other with a visit to the seal beaches to see how the seal pups had fared during the night. This morning though I set out later than usual, and Mike came with me. The wind had moderated from the previous day but it was still blustery, and dark, oppressive clouds raced across the sky temporarily obliterating the brilliant sunshine. As we crossed the isthmus we were greeted by the chuckling calls of the fulmars. They had returned to Skomer over a month before, and were among the few seabirds now on the island. They glided stiff-winged at cliff-top height only a few feet from us, turning curious glances in our direction as they passed. As we continued our unhurried tour of the area I pointed out all my favourite pups to Mike, and explained what I knew of their short lives.

We came home to a breakfast of bacon, egg and mince pies accompanied by champagne and Christmas crackers. We began opening presents, and very much later we had an empty champagne bottle and a kitchen strewn with torn wrapping paper. While the turkey was cooking we went for another long walk. The day was lovely, despite the damp, drizzly mist that now hung in the air, and the smell of gently roasting turkey that came to welcome us at the front door was almost as good as the dinner that followed.

As New Year approached we wondered again if it might not be rather dull by ourselves. After all, New Year was a time for parties. But at least we had a second bottle of champagne to celebrate with. We rummaged through our hampers sent as Christmas presents by thoughtful friends and relatives. Mike's sister had sent a really grand one which contained everything from caviar and cassoulet to sherry and sugared almonds. We chose the caviar as the most appropriate accompaniment to seeing in the New Year. At five minutes to midnight Mike took the champagne bottle which was glistening with condensation and slowly untwisted the wire. The cork eased almost imperceptibly from the neck of the bottle, then with a gentle push it exploded with a ceiling-denting crash, and the champagne cascaded into the waiting glasses. Switching on the VHF radio Mike called the coastguard at St Ann's Head to wish him a happy New Year. As we listened greeting calls came in from the distant lighthouses, and we toasted the New Year with champagne. We walked outside and listened to the silence. We had expected perhaps a celebratory hoot on the foghorn from a passing ship, but there was nothing. We were quite alone in the still night, and there was nowhere else that we would rather have been.

With the end of the old year the weather changed dramatically. The ground froze solid, and echoed with a hollow ring under our feet. On my early morning walks I left a trail of footprints through the sparkling, frosty grass. Working outside was no longer a pleasure when our fingers ached and our faces stung. Keeping warm in the house was also a problem. Our wood-burning stove was blissfully efficient, but it was in the living room, and basking in its warmth was a luxury reserved for the evenings. During the daytime we had a butane gas heater for times when desperation overwhelmed us, but we always tried to conserve our gas supplies for essentials such as cooking and lighting, as we never knew how long it would be before we could replenish our stocks. When we grew really cold the only thing we could do was to find something to keep us busy outside, and then by comparison the house always felt welcomingly warm.

This weather was not without its compensations. We listened avidly to the weather forecast several times each day, and there was no doubt that snow was heading in our direction. Day after day snow was forecast for our area, and we went to bed each night expecting to wake up on a white island. We stared enviously at the distant, snow-capped Preseli Mountains, and in time even the surrounding lowland grew white, but Skomer was spared. Our longing for snow may seem strange, but by this time we knew the island so well that snow was the only extreme of weather we had yet to experience. Our west-coast situation was so mild that after nine years we had seen no more than a light dusting of snow, and the idea of seeing Skomer transformed fascinated us.

The reality when it came was less perfect than we had imagined it would be. It was very early in the morning when Mike's voice intruded into my dream.

'It's been snowing in the night, and now we haven't got any water.'

I was freezing, and used this interruption to my sleep to edge a bit more of the duvet on to my side of the bed before rolling over and burying my head.

'I got up in the night for a drink of water, but the taps were dry. The pipe carrying the water from the spring must have frozen. I didn't want to worry you in the middle of the night, but I think we ought to do something about it now,' Mike continued.

I was wide awake now, and there was no point in pretending to be asleep any longer. I was very worried about the prospect of not having any water, but did I really have to leave my warm bed for the icy blackness outside? It seemed I did. A quick survey revealed the most likely cause of the problem; it was a small section of pipe close to the water tank on the hill above the house, the only portion not buried under ground. It was obvious that in the cold night air this had frozen. We hoped that this was our only problem. Mike took what seemed to me the rather drastic step of building a bonfire on top of the pipe, while I scuttled to and fro turning taps on and off according to vague, shouted signals drifting semi-audibly down the hill. Before long I heard promising thumping and gurgling sounds from the pipes, and soon the water trickled forth. To prevent a recurrence of this spectacular dawn ritual the protruding pipe was lagged with fibreglass loft insulation material. (The following spring the pipe had to be buried underground when the choughs discovered that glass fibre was ideal for nest lining.)

With the minor problem of the water solved, we were free for the first time to take in our surroundings. The first glimmer of day lightened the sky, and beneath it the covering of snow seemed to shine with an inner glow. As we stood in silent admiration we became aware of how uncannily still the air was; the usual drone of the wind was completely absent. Through the quietness came a distant, high-pitched clamour. Looking up we realised that the sky was darkened by thousands upon thousands of birds, all heading west. As the icy weather had swept across Britain from the east in the preceding days, the birds had been driven west by

185

its onslaught. Now, having reached the furthest point of land, their only option was to head out to sea towards Ireland. This overhead passage continued all day until it was hidden by the onset of darkness. How many tens of thousands of birds passed overhead that day I could not begin to imagine.

We put on our warmest clothes and left at once to see the island transformed under its white covering. The day had now fully dawned, and was crisp, clear, bright and quite staggeringly beautiful. Before long a haunting, half-forgotten sound reached us. There was no mistaking the plaintive wail of geese rising and falling in the still air, and as we looked up they soared overhead with a rush of wings. They looked magnificent, flying effortlessly with their elegant wings outstretched. After circling twice they executed a perfectly synchronised landing on the frozen shore of North Pond. It may be hard to imagine our excitement, but for us these barnacle geese were the most welcome of all winter visitors, coming as they did at a time when almost every other bird had deserted our bleak, windswept island. For the past three years they had arrived in mid-November, but this winter they had failed to arrive, and as it was now the middle of January we had almost been resigned to the fact that we would not see them again.

The enjoyment of our surroundings was tempered by the extreme cold. Stamp and kick my feet as I might, I could not restore any feeling to my toes. By the time we reached the farm the biting cold had overwhelmed our desire to explore any further, and we returned home. We thought that such an exceptional day called for an exceptional breakfast, and decided to open our last, carefully-hoarded tin of sausages. After breakfast I knew what was coming next, but my heart sank, as it always did, when Mike said, 'I think we'd better go ashore and get some gas.'

He was right of course. The day was unusually calm, and we could not risk running low on gas in this cold weather, but it was still my least favourite chore. We loaded the box on the back of the tractor with the empty cylinders.

'You bring the tractor, I'll go and get the boat ready. See you down there,' Mike called as he set off for the beach.

I began the slow ascent of the steep hill behind our house, my hands feeling as if they were frozen to the steering wheel. About half-way up, water flowing across the track had frozen to form a solid strip of ice. I tried repeatedly to cross it, but the wheels just slithered uselessly and sent me sliding back. I was about to abandon the attempt and go in search of Mike, but the thought of the exasperated look on his face when I told him I could not manage spurred me on to one more try. Nervously I edged the tractor on to the snow-covered bank at the side of the track and steered it round the ice, all the time imagining the still more exasperated expression if I had to confess to toppling the tractor over.

When I reached the beach Mike and the boat were ready, and it only remained for us to roll the boat, on its trailer, into the sea. Water running from the cliffs had frozen, turning the aptly-named slipway into a sheet of ice. Our normal procedure for launching the boat was to lift the front of the trailer, each holding one side, and to roll it down the slipway, across the beach and into the sea. The boat was heavy for two people to manage, and if it started to run out of control on the right-angle bend of the steeply sloping jetty we simply dropped the front of the trailer, which acted as a brake. We set off, but as soon as we reached the ice the boat took off. We dropped the trailer, but instead of slowing down the boat hurtled on at increasing speed. We had failed to take the corner before losing control, and the boat was now careering towards rocks, where it would undoubtedly smash. I could not look, and started to cover my eyes, but Mike grabbed the rope which trailed behind the boat and tugged it hard. The boat lurched sideways, and came to rest gently on the pebble beach missing the rocks by inches. We edged ourselves and the gas cylinders gingerly across the sheet of ice and, after manhandling the boat with some difficulty on the last stretch to the sea, we loaded up.

The full gas cylinders that we carried on our return journey were heavy. I found them only just manageable over the slippery stones of Martin's Haven beach, and each one felt progressively heavier until by the end I was half dragging and half carrying them. When Mike returned from parking our Land Rover in a nearby farm we heaved the cylinders into the boat and then slid out across the smooth water, which was pale and shining in the fading daylight. As the outboard hummed through the silence I could feel my cheeks burning from the exertion of carrying the gas cylinders and I felt as though I would never know what it was to be

187

cold again, but soon the icy breeze reached through my clothes to touch my skin. As we approached the deserted island, and turned into North Haven I felt momentarily that unsettling sensation of being overlooked, and half glimpsed a figure on the skyline. An uneasy tension ran through my muscles and then immediately relaxed. I knew that it was only the Harold Stone watching over us, dark against the greying sky. This was a standing stone, a rough pillar about six feet high and tapering towards the top, its origin and purpose unknown. Despite its small size its location was so extraordinary that viewed from the sea it seemed to be visible on the skyline from all angles, dominating North Haven. It had tremendous presence, and had often given us this feeling of being watched as we returned to the island, but I never felt that there was anything sinister about the lonely, vigilant stone.

After landing the cylinders in North Haven there was still just enough time left for us to bring the boat ashore in daylight. The boat could not be hauled on its uphill journey without the tractor and after surveying the sheet of ice that blocked our way with some concern, Mike decided that it would break up under the weight of the tractor, and present no problem. As soon as the tractor hit the ice on the slipway it slewed sideways, and continued this lateral progression until it came to rest with its front wheels partly overhanging a sheer drop and the carrying-box at the back wedged against rocks. There was not a fraction of an inch for manoeuvre. The only way out was the way it had arrived – sideways, and that was out of the question. The one glimmer of hope was that if the box could be removed from the back of the tractor a few feet of space would be gained to ease the tractor back to safety.

We were very cold and tired by now, but had to press on as it was almost dark and the boat was stuck on the beach with the incoming tide approaching rapidly. With a lot of cursing and hammering Mike set about freeing the wedged tractor box while I tackled the sheet of ice. I tried to thaw it by dousing it with buckets of seawater. With the tractor blocking the slipway my only route to the ice was straight up the retaining wall. I made this journey repeatedly with two full buckets of water until my arms felt wrenched from their sockets and my legs were covered in bruises where I had braced them against the wall. The whole thing seemed futile. After being saturated with gallons of seawater the surface of the ice was only slightly softened. I hacked at it

188

furiously with the boat-hook to no avail; it was two inches thick in places.

Mike had now freed the tractor and, despite my misgivings, we had no option but to take it back across the ice. It would have taken hours to clear the slipway and we needed to get the boat off the beach. To add to our problems it was now completely dark. As Mike tried to move the tractor the wheels spun uselessly, and it slid so alarmingly I was terrified that it would plunge over the edge of the slipway on to the beach below. Mike suggested I throw gravel under the wheels to improve their traction. I hurried back from the beach with buckets of gravel and threw the contents down in the path of the tractor. The spinning wheels flung this offering disdainfully to one side, but we persevered, and I continued to throw gravel under the churning wheels until at last the tractor edged forward slightly. We maintained this slow progress with me running back and forth from the beach for extra supplies of gravel. Sometimes the tractor slid back so that we lost almost all the ground we had gained, but gradually, inch by inch, it crawled off the ice.

The following day was less painfully cold, but more snowy than ever. After the brief respite of the day before the wind had returned, and blizzard conditions prevailed all day. The sky was a deep, leaden grey, and the air so full of flurrying snowflakes that the distance faded into obscurity. Even the sea had disappeared behind the heavy curtain that hung in the air. The snow was being heaped into drifts which were sculpted by the wind into smooth curves. The ponds had vanished, their frozen surfaces shrouded in snow. Our solitude freed us from the necessity of conventional behaviour, and clearing back a little of the snow from North Pond we skated, at first gingerly, then with increasing boldness, across the ice. Liberated by the exhilaration of skidding over the pond we built a huge, smiling snowman to watch over our peaceful white island.

Much as we were enjoying this weather we realised that the wildlife was not. Rabbit tracks criss-crossed the island, but not a blade of grass penetrated the white covering and the animals were forced to dig through the snow to the frozen ground below to find food. At the entrance to almost every burrow the tracks of small birds could be seen disappearing inside. They were obviously seeking warmth, but I am sure that many never again emerged from

189

their snowy prisons and died unseen underground. The birds that we had seen passing overhead and out to sea the day before were being washed back on to the beaches dead. When we returned to the house, we found it surrounded by weak, hungry birds huddled close to its sheltering walls. Some had even made their way in down the chimney. We found everything we could for them to eat, cooked batches of rice and pasta, put out tubs of margarine, and sacrificed to them our stock of apples, but still they died by the score. Beautiful as the snow had been, we were relieved for the sake of these pathetic birds when the next morning it was gone, the mild sea winds having erased every trace of its existence.

SIXTEEN

ALTHOUGH AT THE TIME we had no way of knowing, that icy January had brought us to the beginning of our final year on Skomer. I wish that I could say that the last year was the best, but it was without doubt the worst. From the start there was a nagging sense that things must one day change, that reality would eventually intervene in our lives again. We had, after all, reached ten years, that arbitrary target we had set ourselves so long ago when we were young enough to believe that ten years was a lifetime. That deadline alone we could have evaded, but adding to our sense of foreboding were the persistent rumours that a vacancy for a job that Mike very much wanted was soon to be announced. However hard we searched for an escape route that would allow us to stay on the island, we came back to the realisation that our days on Skomer were numbered. All our discussions ended in the same inevitable conclusion; if we remained on Skomer very much longer we would be completely unable to adapt back to mainland life. For myself, I believed that the point of no return had already passed, and I could not imagine myself living on the mainland ever again. I tried hard, but could think of no compensations the mainland had to offer. Any luxury or entertainment I might have once looked forward to was now so long-forgotten I preferred to be without it.

If this alone was not enough to depress our spirits, we had the more immediate problem of Mike's ill health. The years of lifting and loading and building had taken their toll, and Mike was increasingly plagued by backache. By this stage though it had become quite serious. Instead of gradually easing after a few days, the pain continued without respite for months. Spring came again and I could not bring myself to think that I might be seeing it all for the last time. Somewhere deep down was a conviction that

191

I would never be parted from the island. By April when the boat started to cross from the mainland again Mike was little improved. Things finally came to a head when we were unloading a large consignment of building blocks. When we returned to the house Mike confessed that he had twisted his back awkwardly, and was now in severe pain. We were sufficiently troubled for Mike to make the journey ashore to see a doctor. He returned with no more than a bottle of pain-killers and the feeling that doctors should not be troubled with such trivial ailments.

We were becoming very worried. Mike's back was now bent sideways, and one leg had grown numb and would not support his weight, causing him to walk with a strange, lop-sided gait. Another visit to the doctor produced only more pain-killers. Mike had been in this condition for about a month when he arranged his third visit to the doctor. When the appointed day arrived the weather was wild, and it was obvious that no boat would reach us that day. By the time the boat did arrive it was Saturday. Mike had no pain-killers left, and no doctor would be available until the following week. He was feeling very miserable indeed. Campbell, our boatman, was full of sympathy having suffered similar problems himself many years ago. Later in the afternoon Campbell was back, having contacted a local doctor and been given a small supply of pain-killers to last through the weekend. Mike eventually made his third trip to the doctor and returned with the news that he was to see an orthopaedic surgeon as soon as possible. We were torn between feeling pleased that something was being done at last, and distressed by the implications of further treatment. When a few days later Mike went to see the specialist I was down at the landing stage as usual, waiting anxiously for his return. The moment I caught sight of Mike on board the boat I knew that all was not well. He always greeted me with a wave and a smile as soon as he saw me, but today he looked lifeless and dejected. As the *Dale Princess* swung across North Haven and drew alongside the fendered rocks I pulled on the bow rope to hold the boat in close, and Mike leant over the rail to talk to me. As he spoke my eyes focussed idly on the fountain of water that sprayed rhythmically between the boat and the rocks with each incoming wave. Mike explained that they had wanted to keep him in hospital there and then, and that he had had the greatest difficulty in persuading them to allow him to come back

192

to the island for just one night. He was going to be put into traction for about ten days to allow a displaced disc to right itself. I felt very miserable, but had to agree that it sounded less alarming than surgery. I was surprised by the suddenness of it all, having assumed that whatever happened I would have had weeks, or even months, to get used to the idea.

There were lots of preparations, and only a few hours to make them in. Mike was to leave first thing in the morning. Of course I had been alone on the island very many times before, and this time I would not even be alone. It was late spring, the busiest time on Skomer, the time when research workers came to study the breeding birds. I knew everyone would help me, but there would be so much happening in the next week or two, and I wished that Mike could be there with me. We talked about everything I might need to know as we put together a collection of things for Mike to take into hospital. In the morning Mike made his way slowly and painfully down the landing steps. I walked beside him and we both felt very downcast. I watched the boat pull away, but I was quickly distracted and was mostly kept too busy to dwell very much on what was happening. The following day Campbell sent a note saying that if I came ashore on the boat that evening he would take me in to the hospital in Haverfordwest.

I can still remember how vividly I was impressed by what I saw when I reached the mainland. It was late May; the countryside was alive, and the colours vibrant. White blossom clouded the trees, and the newly-emerged leaves had that intense, translucent freshness I had completely forgotten existed. I was astonished, and could not prevent myself from saying so until I knew I must be becoming boring. By comparison Skomer was still in the bleak grip of winter. The spring had been unremittingly miserable. Just as our first summer had been one of unrelieved blue skies and hot sun, our last brought relentless wind and rain. Everywhere the bracken lay brown and dead, flattened by the winter gales, and so far nothing had received sufficient encouragement from the sun to penetrate this drab covering. The usually abundant display of bluebells and cliff top flowers had been beaten down by the weather, and really the island looked little changed from January. I concentrated on the mosaic of dappled green flickering past the car window, partly because I

193

was fascinated by it, and partly to take my mind off the hospital. When we did finally arrive I was relieved to find that the wards were bright and friendly, and Mike was very cheerful. Above all he was out of pain for the first time in many weeks, and now felt confident of being cured. The traction did not look nearly as gruesome as we had imagined. Mike's legs were covered in sticking plaster from knee to ankle, and small weights, like the ones used for old-fashioned kitchen scales, were attached to them and dangled over the end of the bed. That was all there was to it; none of the harrowing contraptions we had envisaged. Before I left I tried to ask Mike about all the things I would have to do in his absence.

'Oh don't worry about that. I'll be home in a week,' he assured me airily, and he looked so well I believed him.

I finally returned to the island at around eleven thirty that night, having made the long trip by boat around St Ann's Head from Dale. The sea at St Ann's Head was moderately rough. The boat rolled smoothly, skimming the water first with one brightly painted side and then the other. I stood at the back, leaning on the stern rail, watching the seething white furrow of water as we left it behind to fade into the darkness. It is rarely truly dark at sea, except in the foulest of weather, and I could see the horizon in all directions, but as we passed through the narrow gap of Little Sound and finally entered North Haven the towering outlines of the cliffs cast a deeper shadow and the bay was quite black. The only illumination came from the mast light, and the sea around us was a rapidly moving kaleidoscope of greys which disappeared as they left the pool of light.

I was taken ashore in the dinghy, moving cautiously across the dark sea, trying to pick out the faint outline of rocks close inshore. As they reached the slipway the wave crests tipped over in a cascade of pale foam. I jumped ashore, and the dinghy was drawn quickly out of the surf, disappearing into the dark chasm that lay between me and the flickering light on the boat which swung gently on the mooring. I was glad to be back on the island.

The pattern was established over the days that followed. As often as I could I went to the mainland to see Mike. Everyone on the island did their utmost to help, devising ingenious schemes to get me on and off the island and take me to

194

hospital. Campbell and his wife were always there with assistance, Campbell sometimes delivering me back to the island very late, at the end of a long and tiring day, but always remaining cheerful. I found it hard to maintain the optimistic impression that I had formed on my first visit to Mike. Sometimes he was very drugged, so much so that his speech was slurred, and he remembered little of what I told him. It was difficult not to feel anxious. Then one miserable evening Mike confessed to me that he did not think that the treatment was working at all. The apparent improvement was an illusion caused by a combination of the traction relieving pressure on his back, and a constant high dose of pain-killing drugs. If the weights were temporarily removed, or the drugs reduced, he was in as much pain as ever. This came as something of a shock since, even at our most pessimistic reckoning, he was due to come home in a few days, and now obviously this would not happen.

During this period I was kept very busy, and fortunately this drastically reduced the amount of time I was able to spend worrying. Not only was there a lot of extra work caused by Mike's absence, but during the summer term groups of schoolchildren visited the island, and it was my job to show them round. Skomer's wildlife was so spectacular and so accessible that we believed a visit to the island could be enough to trigger a lifelong interest in conservation, and these visits by schoolchildren were therefore arranged free of charge. This was a relatively new venture and I quickly learned, to my surprise, that it was the city children who were most excited and impressed by the island, although they also complained most about walking.

Delighted though I was by their response, I was troubled by the fact that they found the concept of a natural environment impossible to grasp. The bluebells eventually put in a late but welcome appearance, and I loved to watch the amazement on the children's faces as we waded through a scented, blue lake of flowers that stretched for acres. I was gratified by the effect this was having one day as a group of children stared in wide-eyed wonder. Imagine my disillusionment when a small boy came up to me and asked in tones of awed admiration,

'Did you plant all these, Miss?'

Flattered though I was by their faith in my creative abilities,

I could not help feeling sad that they understood so little of what Skomer really was.

'Feeding time' was another idea that was difficult to overcome. The children loved the puffins above everything else, with the possible exception of the rabbits. Very often, as we were watching the puffins performing their clumsy antics, the question would arise, 'When are you going to feed them?'

No matter how carefully I explained that the puffins did not need to be fed, and that they found their own food out at sea, I saw young eyes narrowing in barely concealed scepticism. I sometimes suspected that they thought I had invented such a far-fetched story to avoid having to wait for them to watch feeding time. Despite all my efforts, I think that some children still left with the impression that they had visited a beautiful park, deliberately cultivated and filled with exotic birds by us.

The weather was far from settled, and many of the children trudged uncomplaining through cold drizzle. I made a point of not wearing a complete set of waterproofs since the children were never suitably dressed to withstand the elements, and I worried that if I was too impervious to the weather I might not notice when the children were becoming cold and wet. On one particular day the familiar drizzle began, and I suggested that we shelter until it passed.

'No, that's quite all right,' insisted the teacher. 'Children, waterproofs on please!'

Each child took out carefully folded waterproof jackets and trousers and put them on, and we continued on our way. The drizzle turned into a cloud burst, but the teacher assured me repeatedly that the children were still quite happy and, despite the fact that they could hardly open their eyes in the wind-driven rain, they did seem remarkably enthusiastic about the distant blurred outlines of birds. By the time I delivered the children back to the boat I was saturated. My wet hair clung to my head, and a constant stream of water trickled from the ends of my fringe into my eyes. Just as the boat was leaving for the mainland Campbell called, 'Why don't you come ashore and see Mike?'

I looked doubtful. The weather was turning very nasty now; the heavy rain continued and the wind was strengthening.

'Come on!' Campbell persuaded, and on impulse I jumped aboard and joined him in the wheelhouse.

As we pulled away from the island the boat began to pitch heavily in the deep, rolling swell driving in from the west. I recognised it at once as the harbinger of severe weather coming in from the open sea. Gale warnings hissed and crackled from the ship's radio.

'I'll never get back tonight,' I gasped in alarm.

'Don't worry, you can stay with us,' grinned Campbell.

I looked down at my muddy wellingtons, and felt my damp hair plastered to my head and dripping on to my shirt collar. I did not even have a change of clothes, and one day on the mainland could stretch to two or three or more.

Although it was the height of summer it was already growing dark when I reached the hospital at about seven. Seeing the storm raging outside Mike was amazed when I walked in. He was in a sorry state, having been taken off the traction which had apparently made him worse. He lay curled up in bed, his legs thin and wasted, his speech slow and halting. He was going to have an operation to remove a disc, but it would be over a week before anyone was available even to do the necessary X-ray. In the meantime he would just have to stay where he was and wait, despite the fact that there was no treatment he could be given. Mike told me that in his frustration he had tried to discharge himself from hospital, but found he could no longer walk, which distressed him tremendously. At this point I truly began to despair of Mike ever getting back to the island. I left feeling very dejected and on the way out met Charles, an RAF helicopter pilot who was one of Mike's most frequent and welcome visitors. He looked at me and then at the weather.

'You won't be going back to the island for a day or two,' he exclaimed, and sadly I agreed.

I lay awake for most of the night listening for a change in the weather, but by morning the wind was stronger than ever. My anxiety at being away from the island was not rational, but it was something I always felt acutely. As I was having breakfast Campbell returned from Martin's Haven, and declared cheerfully that there would be no crossing that day. I tried hard not to feel too disappointed. As we were clearing away the breakfast things the phone rang, and I was surprised to be told that it was for me.

It was Charles. Having guessed that a boat crossing would be out of the question he had discovered that an RAF helicopter would be passing close to the island in the afternoon, and he could arrange for me to be on the flight if I wanted to be. I was overjoyed at the prospect of going home. As an auxiliary coastguard I was authorised to fly in RAF helicopters, but would not have dared to ask. Within the hour Charles had arrived to pick me up, and we went straight to the hospital to see Mike before going on to the air base.

I had a long wait while they discussed the afternoon's flight, and the proposed time of departure grew later and later, but I did not mind at all, just so long as I got back to Skomer. Despite the wind it was now hot and sunny, and I was still wearing my wellingtons and trying in vain to keep my legs tucked out of sight. At last we were due to leave. I was given a life-jacket and we walked out to the aircraft. I was strapped in, put my headphones on, and then we took off. As soon as we had climbed high enough I could see Skomer far in the distance, and in between nothing but an expanse of brilliant blue sea, sparkling in the sunlight and streaked with white foam. From so high the huge waves looked gentle and harmless, and Skomer appeared tiny. As we drew closer I could see the exposed cliffs of the island fringed with white, and the tides ripping through the sounds. From the air everything was so clearly defined; every wall, every path and field boundary stood out as a hard line. The old farm buildings grandly dominated the centre of the island, while the different vegetation patterns formed a random green patchwork. I was put down in one of the flat fields in the centre of the island, the whole journey having taken only a matter of minutes.

When I next went to the mainland to see Mike he was more downcast than ever. It was being suggested that he should be transferred to Cardiff for the operation, a distance of some eighty miles, and he did not want to go. In Haverfordwest he had a constant stream of visitors, whereas in Cardiff he would feel very isolated. Obviously in his drugged and depressed state he was less objective than he might otherwise have been. It took only a short discussion between us to convince him that getting the best treatment was far more important than having lots of visitors. The deciding factor was that Mike's sister and her husband were both doctors in the hospital in Cardiff. They would be in the ideal position to keep an eye on him, and there was no reason why he sould feel isolated with them there. Sadly we agreed that I would not visit him in Cardiff. We knew that we would both feel happier if I stayed to look after the island. In the meantime Mike would remain in Haverfordwest waiting for the X-ray.

Over the next few days I felt very miserable and angry. Almost a month had passed since Mike first went into hospital. At least he had been walking when he left the island; now he could not even do that. Then one evening I suddenly felt better. Just as the light was fading I noticed that the sea was exceptionally calm. It was one of those rare evenings when not a single ripple of air movement blurred the hard surface of the water. I had been too busy to notice it, but now I stopped what I was doing and watched. The stillness of the twilight was so overwhelming that I too felt calm. I told myself that the worst was over, that at least Mike was going to be cured, and that now an end, however distant, was in sight.

The following morning I turned on the VHF radio as usual. Before I had made my routine morning radio check I was startled to hear the coastguard calling me, and answered hurriedly, expecting a message about Mike. The true purpose of the call therefore came as a great surprise.

'An oil tanker went aground on the Hats and Barrels yesterday evening. There has only been a slight spillage, no more than a bloom on the surface. It's not expected to reach you anyway, so there's nothing for you to worry about,' said the reassuring voice of the coastguard. I felt a little uneasy, but the Hats and Barrels was a reef of rocks some fifteen miles to the west of us, so it did not sound like a real problem. I had been silently pondering the potential threat for only a minute or two when I realised that another message was coming through for me on the radio. This time it was the coast station with a telephone call. To my amazement it was Mike who had somehow achieved the virtually impossible task of getting a radio-telephone link from his hospital bed. Mike's information on the oil spill was much more shattering. He believed that Skomer was under threat of serious pollution, and suggested that I begin monitoring immediately with the help of the research workers and assistant warden to assess the effect on the seabirds. I was devastated. Throughout our ten years

199

on Skomer there was nothing we had dreaded more than an oil spill at the height of the bird breeding season. Every year our sadness as the young birds fledged and the adults deserted the island was tinged with relief that they had survived the inevitable disaster for yet another year. I remembered with a sense of irony the perfect calm of the previous evening. The whole thing was a carbon copy of the *Christos Bitas* disaster that had affected the seals seven years earlier; calm, clear weather and a tanker taking a short-cut through treacherous rocks. It seemed that, far from ensuring a safe passage for shipping, perfect weather conditions encouraged recklessness.

The following days passed in a miserable blur. I wished them away, and tried to push them from my mind as soon as they were over. The memory of that period is now softened by the haze of time, with only a few incidents standing out sharply, like rocks above a sea mist. I remember the first sighting of the oil; distant, shiny smudges far off towards Grassholm. Even so many miles away the oil was a threat, both to our breeding birds and to the tiny island of Grassholm, which crowded nearly thirty thousand pairs of gannets between its rocky shores. Despite the devastation it was already causing out at sea, I willed the oil not to reach Skomer.

The sea that formed a temporary barrier between Skomer and the oil was smooth and glossy, rippled only by gentle winds and tides that brought the oil inexorably closer. As the oil approached it filled St Bride's Bay with pale grey, shimmering streaks until the oily film became dominant, and within it pools of clear blue sea were visible. How this bloom of oil affected the seabirds I could not tell. Superficially they seemed little harmed by it, but this innocuous herald brought in its wake patches of thick, brown, sticky oil. This clinging, smothering substance was lethal to seabirds. The effects were either immediate, or lingering, but the end result was death.

The worst thing about the whole incident was that there was nothing we could do but watch. When the oil had been on our beach it had been cleaned up, and the seals were moved, but now the oil was out at sea, and the birds beyond our help. This feeling of powerlessness depressed me to the point of total despair, and I found both sleeping and eating difficult. The catalogue of suffering is endless, but for me two fleeting incidents recapture the mood of those bleak, interminable days. I was sitting above North Haven waiting for the boat and watching puffins swim idly across the sparkling sea as I had done so many hundreds of times before. Suddenly a heavily oiled puffin drifted into the bay. It thrashed and writhed, breaking the serene blue surface with a shower of sea spray, and sending a growing circle of ripples across the water. In a minute or two the puffin was dead, and it was a peaceful summer afternoon once more, but the blackened body of that beautiful bird remained like a scar across the tranquil scene, a reminder that it was all an illusion.

The second incident occurred as I was walking along the cliffs trying to assess the number of affected birds on the rocks below. I remembered that I was above a razorbill nest site and edged forward to take a closer look. The chick was on the ledge alone, and the small bird looked surprisingly dark. I realised that it was covered in oil, but could not understand how a chick on a ledge high above the sea could have reached the oil. With a moment's thought the explanation became clear. One or both parent birds, despite being badly oiled, had managed to get back to the ledge to feed the chick. In their struggle to prevent the chick from going hungry they had in fact contaminated it.

Early in the morning and each evening we checked round the whole island to see how things were progressing. There were no paths at all on the Neck and so walking through the dense undergrowth was difficult. Working my way back along the north coast of the Neck one morning I felt the ground give way under my feet, and I fell heavily. Looking round I saw that a shearwater burrow had collapsed under my weight. I began to dig at the loose earth with my hands to see what could be retrieved from the mess. I quickly found a shearwater and, holding its wings firmly against its body, I lifted it from the remains of its burrow.

'Are you all right? We'll soon sort your burrow out,' I whispered soothingly as I examined the bird carefully to reassure myself that it was unhurt. Holding the bird in one hand I reached into the broken tunnel to scoop out the soft earth in preparation for repairing the burrow. I had cleared out several handfuls before I felt something warm and sticky mingled with the soil. I withdrew my hand quickly and saw that my fingers were covered with a viscous yellow liquid streaked with red. Clinging to it were particles of earth and fragments of shattered white shell. It was the shearwater's egg; I had broken it in the fall.

It was a trivial incident, but coming at the culmination of days of needless death and suffering it was enough to overwhelm me with rage. I picked up a handful of earth and hurled it at the oily sea below.

'It's your fault!' I shouted furiously at the brown scum. 'I wouldn't have even been here if it wasn't for you.'

I sank back on to the damp grass and cried. They were not tears for one lost shearwater's egg, but for all the eggs that would never be, for all the chicks that waited in vain to be fed, and for all the birds that came trustingly to the sanctuary of Skomer's cliffs and found only death.

By now Skomer was set in a sea of oil, and I could not imagine how it would all end. It ebbed and flowed; sometimes the sea looked clearer with only the shiny bloom apparent, but at other times the thick black oil gushed along the base of the cliffs. The general opinion was that in the continuing calm weather the oil could be carried backwards and forwards in the tidal system around the island indefinitely, and for every day that it remained hundreds more birds would be added to the casualty list. I could not understand how this had been allowed to happen. Surely under the perfect weather conditions prevailing at the time of the spill it should have been possible to contain the oil out at sea. It seemed impossible that with all the money and technology available to the oil companies such a relatively minor spill could not have been dealt with quickly and efficiently. Now, however, it was obvious that nothing could be done. The oil was dispersed over a huge area, causing maximum impact to the seabirds, and beyond the reach of any cleaning system.

Just when the situation seemed completely hopeless, as if by a miracle the weather changed dramatically. Storms are a rarity in June, and so when I heard that southerly gales were forecast I could not believe our luck. The direction too was perfect. Most of the oil was still on the north side of the island, and so winds from the south would drive it out to sea rather than onshore. I cautiously reserved my jubilation. Predicted gales could peter out to a gentle breeze before they reached us. The following afternoon, however, I noticed a marked change in the atmosphere. From out of the stillness a strong, gusty wind arose.

It was warm and wonderfully threatening. It lifted dust from the parched surface of the island and sent it stinging into my face. It was a peculiarly welcome sensation. Heavy, black storm clouds began to pile on top of each other, and the sun grew dim. Huge but isolated drops of rain fell, forming tiny craters in the fine, dry earth.

As the evening drew on the gusts strengthened into a steady roar and the air was full of rain, driving in almost horizontally from the south. It continued unabated throughout the night and by the following morning the worst of Skomer's problems were over. Most of the oil had been swept away, taking with it the dead and dying birds. The rain-laden storm raged on for several more days. The lingering worry was now the partially oiled birds that remained around the island convalescing or trying to raise their young. Our twice-daily inspections of the island continued, battling through the blinding rain, trying to follow the progress of these birds. The weather was so uncharacteristic for June that it felt almost as though some unseen force had come to our assistance.

SEVENTEEN

THROUGHOUT THIS TIME Mike remained in hospital. The X-ray had successfully revealed the cause of the problem. While he was in traction the disc had become completely dislodged which, although potentially dangerous, at least meant that the cause was certain, and the cure therefore more likely to succeed. I made a last visit to Mike before he was transferred to Cardiff, and did not expect to see him again until he returned to Haverfordwest, but at least knew that his sister, Tina would be there. Because of a confusion in the messages the operation was over before I knew anything about it. The first I heard was a message from Tina to say that all had gone well, when I was still expecting the operation to take place the following day.

I was able to go ashore the next afternoon and phone Mike. He sounded vague and distant, and the brief call ended with him putting the phone down because he was too tired to hold it. I received only one clear message; Mike wanted me to come and visit him. Things were very hectic on the island in the aftermath of the oil spill, and I was still committed to guiding round parties of visiting schoolchildren, but I decided that given one clear day to sort things out I could leave on the following morning.

Later that day I was flicking through a newspaper that Campbell had brought when I started, as though hit by a bolt of lightning. There in front of me was the advertisement for the warden's job on the mainland that Mike had been hoping to apply for. I knew it had to happen sooner or later, but had hoped for an indefinite delay. Seeing it before me in black and white I felt a wave of despair. Of course there was no certainty that Mike would even get the job, but I knew he would be in with a good chance. That moment was one of the worst I can remember, as it marked for me very clearly the beginning of the end. I had a momentary impulse to tear up the paper and pretend I had never seen it, but I knew it would do no good.

The rest of the evening was very busy, and it was not until about half past nine that I sat down to type a request for the job application form. Before I had finished the few lines of the letter I felt an impulse to leave it and call Tina to tell her about my plans to arrive in Cardiff the day after tomorrow. When I made contact with the coast station I was told that there was already a call waiting for me, and was put through to Mike's other sister Anne. She explained calmly that Mike was in shock after the operation, and that they thought I should get there as soon as possible.

Feeling very alarmed I went to the research quarters, where we had only just finished finalising my original travel arrangements. I was too dazed to think sensibly, and fortunately Paul, one of the research workers, organised everything without accepting any protests from me. It was already growing dark, but the weather forecast for the following day was bad, and we were afraid that I might be stuck on the island if I waited. Paul insisted that I pack quickly while he and the other research students launched the boat and, although I was worried about them making the return journey in complete darkness, I finally agreed. From Martin's Haven I was driven to the village of Dale. It was well after eleven when we drew up outside Campbell's house, and I was very relieved to see a light still shining. Unruffled as ever, Campbell welcomed me without the slightest surprise, and I was soon sitting with a glass of wine in my hand. As I swallowed the first mouthful of wine I realised that I had forgotten to eat that day. Before I had time to speak Campbell's wife, Mil, was offering me a meal, but somehow the time for eating seemed to have passed. Campbell himself had had a similar operation years ago, and was so reassuring that I began to feel happier. Alone in bed all my worries crowded in again, and I began to wonder if there were serious complications which I had not been told about. The night was long, and I slept very little.

I reached Cardiff station early in the afternoon, and felt very bewildered by the crowds and bustle. I was relieved to see Tina emerge smiling from the crowd. She looked cool and elegant in a pink dress and high heels, and I felt uncomfortably hot and dowdy in my island clothes. On the way to the hospital

Tina explained that the operation had gone very well, and that Mike was already recovering. When I first saw Mike he was very depressed, but within half an hour I realised that he was better than he had been for weeks, and far more coherent now that he was taking fewer drugs. With the worst of my worries behind me, I suddenly remembered how hungry I was and became aware of a delicious smell wafting towards me. Mike's lunch sat untouched on the bedside table. I could just see a pool of gravy oozing out from under the metal cover. I lifted the lid and was hit full in the face by the tempting fragrance. I covered it up again quickly.

'What is it?' I asked.

'Beef Bourguignon,' Mike replied indifferently. I eyed it ravenously for some minutes, wondering if I might take a few surreptitious mouthfuls, until at last the problem was resolved when the tray was whisked away.

The next few days in Cardiff were very relaxing. I was able for the first time to put the oil spill to the back of my mind, and I could visit Mike regularly without all the worry of how to get on and off the island. Tina and her husband rearranged their busy schedules, doing everything they could to help. Mike was making a miraculous recovery. On the day after I arrived he was able to stand. The day following that he could take a few steps round the room and sit in a chair. He was rapidly getting back to his old self, and that meant that he had started worrying about the island again. He was growing anxious for me to return to Skomer, and to pacify him I agreed to leave on Monday, even though I knew there would be no boat crossing that day. Mike would have to remain in hospital at least until the end of the week when his stitches were due to be removed. I left rather reluctantly, taking the train back to Haverfordwest, and spent the day wandering aimlessly, knowing that there would be no possibility of getting back to Skomer until the following day. When I went into the West Wales Naturalists' Trust Office late in the afternoon I was greeted by a buzz of excitement and a message to call Mike urgently.

When I finally got through to Mike he told me that he was being discharged the next day, and that I had to come back immediately. He had made such good progress the hospital was willing to release him into Tina's care, but Tina was anxious that I should be there to look after him during the daytime. I learned to my frustration that a message had been sent to Cardiff station to stop me leaving, but had arrived minutes after the train departed.

I spent the night with Campbell and Mil and returned to Skomer the following morning. I felt strangely sad as we crossed the calm water towards the island. The cliffs were growing empty; the bustling guillemot and razorbill colonies were now silent. The kittiwake calls echoed hauntingly from the whitened rock faces, and the puffins skimmed noisily across the water, or bobbed below the surface to avoid the approaching boat. Already the vital days of spring and early summer were giving way to that dusty, sleepy period when only the bracken seemed to flourish, and Mike had missed it all. He had left just as the island was coming alive, and now the exhilarating freshness of new life was fading. This was made all the harder by the aching worry that this might be our last summer on Skomer. I leaned on the rail of the boat staring at the stark, white guillemot ledges and wondered if I would ever again see them crowded with busy, excitable birds or hear the air echo once more to their medley of tuneless growls. I shuddered, as if to physically shake these thoughts from my head, and hurried into the wheelhouse.

As I climbed the familiar steps up the side of the cliff I felt as if I had been away for weeks rather than days. In the house everything was just as I had left it on the night of my hurried departure, including that dreadful, half-written letter glaring at me from the typewriter. I finished it hastily and pushed it into my bag. There was only time to deal with the most pressing problems and find some clothes for Mike before leaving again for the mainland. I was back in Cardiff by the evening, and Mike was already at Tina's house. It was somehow odd to see him dressed and out of a hospital bed for the first time in so many weeks.

Mike's recovery was wonderful, and he was anxious to return to the island as soon as the stitches had been removed. The general opinion was that he should convalesce for at least another week or two on the mainland, but I knew exactly how he felt. If I had been in Mike's position I could have thought of no better cure than coming back to Skomer. Unfortunately, as the week progressed we realised that, fit as he was, Mike might not be able to climb the cliff from the landing point to reach the house. We

207

did not welcome the prospect of landing him back on the island only to find that he was stuck at the bottom of the cliff. Once again Charles came to the rescue. He was sure that a helicopter on routine exercise could deposit Mike next to the house. The stitches were due out on Friday, and the airlift back to Skomer was arranged for Sunday.

In the meantime we passed a peaceful few days at Tina's house, with Mike spending a little time walking and a lot of time flat on his back on the floor, since he was still unable to sit upright in a chair for more than a few minutes. It was strange to be on the mainland in the summer. We saw Wimbledon on television for the first time in ten years. I was mystified by all the new faces and dismayed to see how the familiar ones had aged. It was difficult to realise that a decade had passed us by on the mainland, and things had changed so much, while everything on the island had seemed to remain constant.

On the Sunday of our return Tina and the family drove with us down to Pembrokeshire, and waved us off on the helicopter. Mike, as the invalid, was strapped in at the back, while I was allowed to stand at the front behind the pilots and watch the world pass below us. I noticed almost with surprise how dazzlingly clear and blue the sea looked as it stretched to the horizon, and realised that the memories of the oil spill were still painfully sharp. The helicopter settled gently on to the isthmus, and we were back on Skomer once more.

The island effected a cure that nothing else could have provided, and the next day, despite my protests, Mike walked as far as the Wick. We sat on the grassy bank and watched the kittiwakes wheel below us, brilliant against the deep green of the shadowed sea. I closed my eyes against the gentle warmth of the sun and listened. The unforgettable cry of the kittiwake echoed back to me from the cliffs, but now for the first time I heard a note of melancholy in that sound of high summer. A ripple of change had touched our lives, and I knew that I could no longer take the future for granted.

Mike continued to recover steadily, and we tried to salvage what we could from the remnants of the summer. Each evening fewer and fewer puffins returned to the island until I had to search hard to glimpse even one scuttling down a burrow with its beak brimming to feed a late chick. These solitary birds were nervous now that the colony was deserted, and they passed quickly without lingering on the grassy banks. In time the kittiwakes too departed, and the cliffs fell into empty silence. Only their large and elaborate nests remained, clinging precariously to the cliff face.

As the summer drew to a close there came the news that Mike was called to an interview for the new job in the second week of September. The distance of the venue together with the unreliability of the weather meant that Mike would be away for several days, so we decided to go together and make a short holiday of it. In that respect the trip was not a success, since we were both too sad and anxious to enjoy ourselves.

It was not until October that we learnt that Mike would be offered the job. I felt numb and empty as the period of doubt was finally ended, and I knew with certainty that my years on Skomer were all but over. Of course it was wrong to be sad. This was a wonderful opportunity; exactly the sort of challenging job Mike would thrive on. Since we felt that we had to come to terms with living on the mainland this was the ideal chance. Besides, there was no time for doubt or regret. There were too many practical problems to consider, such as how we were going to transfer all our belongings to the mainland. The boat was no longer running to the island, and October could be a very stormy month. We could have asked Campbell for help, but we decided that it would probably be easier to take small, manageable loads in our own boat.

We set about packing everything into strong, waterproof boxes, and Paul, who had already finished his research work for the season, came back to help us with the transportation. Packing is a powerfully nostalgic time, when so many forgotten treasures are rediscovered. At the end of it all we had a room full of boxes clad in black polythene, exactly like those we had brought to the island ten years earlier, only now there were many more of them. In addition we had some precious and extremely heavy pieces of furniture which Mike had painstakingly made from scraps of timber and best quality driftwood.

Fate and the weather looked kindly on us over the following days, and everything went remarkably smoothly. We would have made a strange spectacle had there been anyone to watch as we crossed the calm waters of the sounds, our little open boat piled high with furniture and its three passengers perched awkwardly on top. With the Land Rover full to overflowing, and Paul squashed somehow into the back of it, we made our way to Tenby, the home of Richard our ex-assistant warden, who had volunteered to play host to our possessions. Richard, reliable and unchanging, welcomed us as always with tea and chocolate cake. We made a further three similarly uncomplicated trips, until we had pared our personal items down to the barest minimum necessary for our remaining few months on Skomer.

Throughout this period the weather was uncharacteristically settled, and so predictable that we were able to leave the boat on a mooring overnight, saving ourselves the effort and irritation of launching and beaching the boat each day. At the end of it all the house looked rather bleak and depressing without our books and pictures and favourite pieces of furniture, but it was a small price to pay for having put such a formidable task behind us. We had often said in the past that we would never be able to leave Skomer because it would be impossible to move everything we had accumulated back to the mainland, and although it was a joke, it was not without a grain of truth.

Once we were alone we settled down to enjoy our final months as well as we could. The time was slipping away so rapidly it seemed important not to waste a single day. Although the island was small we never grew bored with it, in fact the more familiar it became the stronger the attraction grew. The island is so diverse, and its coastline so rugged and inaccessible, that even after ten years there were new things to discover. As time grew short we roamed the island tirelessly, ensuring that every last landmark was revisited. I tried to store up everything that I saw, every rock and blade of grass, knowing that soon there would be nothing left but memories. It was a time of painfully mixed emotions; overwhelming appreciation and pleasure in our unique relationship with the island mingled uncomfortably with unspeakable sadness at what we were about to lose. Inevitably an imminent parting brings the past vividly to mind, and during our long, reflective walks many sentences were prefaced with the words 'do you remember'.

'Do you remember when Togs tried to climb here and fell?'

'Do you remember when we saw a parachute floating in the sea there, and you had to wade in and pull it out, terrified in case there was something awful on the other end?'

210

'Do you remember when you first built this dam, and the pond was just a little puddle?'

When I went out alone in the early morning I found my absences becoming longer and longer. I was almost afraid to come home; afraid not to remain out of doors and in contact with the island in case it should slip away from me while I was not looking. I spent many long hours on the rocky inclines above Castle Bay. It was my own place, where even Mike rarely came. I loved its changing moods. I never lost that thrill of anticipation as I caught the first glimpse of the bay below, of the seals clustered in its shelter and the tiny white pups nestling at the base of the cliffs. The view stretched right along the southern coast of the Neck past Mathews Wick and Amys Reach, to the small, green, domed island of Midland in the distance. In the pale, crisp winter sunlight the golden, lichen-covered cliffs glowed. At that season of the year the coastline was usually deeply bordered with white foam. The strength of the waves rolling in from the open sea was formidable, and I was drawn by their hypnotic rhythm, overawed by their power, and unable to pull myself away. Solitary bird calls pierced the vague roar of the waves, contrasting bleakly with the clamorous throngs of summer. There was only the sharp, melancholy wail of a lone gull, or the desolate cry of a distant raven.

If will-power alone could halt the passage of time those days would never have ended. But however bitterly I regretted the passing of each day they trickled away with alarming rapidity, until at last Christmas was looming just a few weeks away. We tried to make arrangements for a normal celebration. There was the tree with its permanently dim fairy lights, and brightly wrapped presents. The larder was stocked, and we planned the acquisition of our fresh supplies like a military operation, but this year our preparations brought with them a sense of finality. We knew that the moment Christmas was over we would have to give up all pretence of normality and begin the last stages of packing so that we would be ready to leave very early in the new year. It was therefore difficult for us to anticipate with a great deal of pleasure the day which represented such an ominous turning point.

When Christmas morning arrived we greeted each other with bright, forced smiles, which did little to relieve our obvious tension. We decided, however, to continue as usual and try to make the best of things. We set out together for my usual morning

211

check on the seals. We had gone only a few yards from the house when, looking down into South Haven, we saw a plump moulted pup. The silvery grey fur on the top half of its head and body was tinged with green. A closer look with binoculars revealed that its head and foreflippers were completely entwined in a piece of fine, green fishing net. We scrambled down the rough path and were soon standing beside the moulter on the rocky beach below. The young animal stared miserably up at us with its huge, dark eyes, snarling angrily if we took the liberty of studying it too closely. It was obvious at once that there was going to be no easy solution. The seal had clearly put up a valiant struggle to free itself, and in doing so had become hopelessly entangled. The net was wrapped several times around the moulter's neck, with some of the strands pulled so tight that they disappeared completely between the folds of fat. I hurried back to the house for a knife while Mike surveyed the situation. The seal had apparently not been in this condition for long since it was still very strong and fit, and snapped ferociously at any tentative approach.

By the time I returned Mike had taken his coat off and, as soon as he was armed with a knife, threw the coat over the seal's head. There was a tremendous wrestling match as the seal struggled to escape while Mike delved between the folds of flesh to uncover a strand of net and cut it with the knife. Only one strand had been cut before the seal emerged from under the coat and lunged furiously at Mike who deftly avoided him. The seal was becoming very aggressive now but, ignoring its protests, Mike threw the coat over its head and began again. It was a very slow process since Mike was usually able to make only one cut of the net before the young seal wriggled free and launched another attack. Throughout the proceedings I stood uselessly on the sidelines squealing with horror each time the seal surfaced for another round in the contest. Eventually Mike won, and all the net was cut away. The seal, having regained the use of its foreflippers, headed rapidly towards the sea.

When it was over we laughed with relief, and I admitted to Mike that I had not expected him to be able to get the net off. We watched the moulter swim and dive until it was out of sight, and then suddenly we realised that the atmosphere had changed. We really were smiling and laughing, not just pretending. Despite

212

everything we felt happy, and I knew we were going to have a good Christmas.

It went so well that we extended Christmas to include Boxing Day, but after that we really did have to start our packing up in earnest. We set our date of departure as the first day of the new year; an unintentionally fitting day to start a new life. We progressed without a hitch, but we were very busy and had little time to see the island. By 31st December everything was settled except the weather. There seemed little chance of a smooth crossing the following day, and I secretly hoped for no crossing at all rather than a rough one. At the first hint of dawn we were peering anxiously into the cold light trying to assess the sea conditions. I made my own decision instantly simply from the sound of pebbles swirling in the surf on the beach, and I was relieved when the improving light highlighted the white-crested waves and Mike reached the same conclusion. Nevertheless we waited for any sign of a respite, only finally giving up at the end of the morning.

Everything was done by then so we were free to go out for one last walk. The wind was a westerly, my favourite, and the day was beautifully bright and clear. After all the chaos of the last few days I was very thankful to have one quiet day to make our peace with the island. All along it had felt wrong to be leaving without a final visit to all our best-loved places. It was almost as if the island would not let us leave until we had put things right. We passed our fading footprints in the damp, silty hollows where puddles had been. Ours were the only human footprints that marked the island now, and sometimes they remained for many days as tangible reminders of where we had walked. Would we be able to follow today's tracks tomorrow, I wondered, or would the island be deserted, left to the elements until the rain battered the imprints flat, as though we had never been there at all? By the time we reached the north coast the short winter afternoon was drawing to a close. The sun was low on the horizon, shining with a cold, dazzling light. The waves that broke over the offshore rocks were a clear, icy turquoise. The chill of the atmosphere gave a sense of finality, and we headed reluctantly for home. Our once cheerful kitchen looked bleak and empty. I lit the gaslights and their golden glow spread a faint glimmer of welcome. The sky darkened until the outside was no longer visible from the lighted windows. By five o'clock the last residue of day had drained from the sky so that the evening was as black as any night. Outside a distant purr rapidly grew to a roar, and we hurried to the window, looking out to see the bright lights of a helicopter dominating the sky. Mike switched on the VHF radio.

'Hello, what are you doing there?' came the cheerful voice of Cliff, an RAF helicopter pilot. 'I thought you had left this morning, but when we saw the lights we came to see what had happened,' he continued above the drone of the rotor blades.

Mike explained that we had intended to leave, but that the weather, as always, had thwarted our plans.

'I'll see if I can arrange to pick you up in the morning,' Cliff said, and with that the helicopter lights faded rapidly into the distance.

Later in the evening a radio message confirmed that Cliff would be able to transfer us to the mainland the following morning. That made the prospect of our leaving the next day much more probable, but by no means certain. Helicopters can frequently be grounded by bad weather and mechanical faults, or called away to an emergency. We chose a meal from our meagre supplies which we ate without much enthusiasm. Our normally well-stocked larder was now empty, and I hoped that being over-confident of a rapid departure we had not been foolhardy in running our supplies so low. That night I lay in bed wide awake with my eyes open. This was borrowed time now. By rights we should no longer be here. To one side a faint patch of light showed through the curtains. To the left I could just make out the grey, shadowy shapes of the wardrobe and dressing table. They were barely distinguishable forms in the darkness, and yet were so familiar. I remembered how many times, when sleep would not come, I had gazed around at these dark outlines, and promised myself that I would never leave the island. Now I was overwhelmed by the knowledge that this might be my last night in my own room.

Despite everything I did sleep a little, and waking in the early morning darkness I could hear the wind gusting against the northern aspect of the house. I knew immediately that it was not strong enough to cause any problems. Looking out at the black sky we could tell that there was no fog, which would have been our main enemy in preventing the helicopter from flying. All the

214

signs so far being favourable we embarked on putting together the last of our things and finally shutting up the house. As the rising sun tinged the horizon with pink I set off for the farm on the tractor with a last consignment for the rubbish pit. As I drove I had time to look around me. The winter dawn grew more brilliant, but despite its golden glow the sky looked cold. Driving alongside the farmyard I passed the place where we always found Skomer voles. I remembered that first vole Mike had shown me so many years ago, and felt that I must take one last look. Pulling on the hand brake I prepared to jump to the ground, but at the last moment I stopped myself. The time for nostalgia was over, and I continued on my way. Soon the house was ready; storm shutters in place, water drained, doors locked. Our small collection of belongings was driven to the large, flat field known as Calves Park to await the helicopter, and the tractor was safely shut away in the garage. We still had a little time to spare, so I walked out on to the isthmus and looked down into North Haven. Staring back at me, damp and helpless, was a new-born seal pup, its weak, broken cries just audible above the sound of the waves. For the first time it was a sight that made me feel sad, since I would never see it again, and no-one would know or care whether it lived or died.

When everything was done we walked slowly up the hill to wait for the helicopter. The path was so familiar to me that I could not count how many thousands of times I had walked it. Every inch of the landscape around us echoed with memories. Thoughts of the past reverberated so violently in my head that I had to look away. I stared at my feet and concentrated very hard on breathing deeply, forcing everything else from my mind. I watched as each footstep on the soft grass caused a small pool of muddy water to bubble up from the soil below, and then vanish as the foot was lifted. I shut out everything but the even tread of my steps in time to my breathing. Then, at the top of the hill I made the mistake of looking back. There was my house, my home for ten years, cold and empty, its windows darkened by shutters. Below it stretched North Haven, just catching the first of the morning sun, and in that view the essence of a decade was captured. I felt a deep, painful sob rising in my chest and forcing its way up into my throat. I gulped in a breath of air to quell the second sob, and turned quickly aside. I could not afford

215

tears now; I knew that if they started I would not be able to stop them. I walked on, and did not look back again.

We did not wait long for the helicopter. I was relieved to have the chance of this quick, clean break; I knew that a long and emotional boat journey would have been almost too much to bear. After a few minutes of idle chatter about everything but what was on our minds we heard the faint hum of an engine. Scanning the horizon we eventually saw the helicopter as a yellow dot in the distant sky. It approached rapidly, and circled once before landing next to our meagre pile of possessions. Once we were airborne we were given one last tour of the island from above. It was like seeing my life spread out below me, and yet we were so high and remote I felt detached from it. It looked like a map, with only the sea moving in slow motion to show that it was real. It was all over in minutes, and I felt as though I was being jolted from a dream when the helicopter pulled away from Skomer and headed towards the mainland. We were set down in a damp, grassy field. As the noise of the helicopter died away and we were left alone I felt a sense of isolation that I had never experienced on the island. We turned to each other for reassurance. Despite the dreadful feeling of emptiness I knew that this was not quite the end. Whatever happened, some small part of Skomer would always be with me.